UNTIL THE
FINAL HOUR

UNTIL THE FINAL HOUR

Hitler's last secretary

TRAUDL JUNGE

Edited by Melissa Müller
Translated from the German by Anthea Bell

Weidenfeld & Nicolson

LONDON

First published in Germany in 2002 by Claassen Verlag,
a division of Ullstein Heyne List GmbH & Co. KG,
as *Bis zur letzten Stunde. Hitlers Sekretärin erzählt ihr Leben.*

First published in Great Britain in 2003 by Weidenfeld and Nicolson

Typeset by Selwood Systems,
Midsomer Norton

Printed by Butler & Tanner Ltd,
Frome and London

Weidenfeld and Nicolson

The Orion Publishing Group Ltd
Orion House
5 Upper Saint Martin's Lane
London, WC2H 9EA

'We cannot put our lives right in retrospect; we must go on living with the past. We can put ourselves right, however.'

Reiner Kunze: *Am Sonnenhang* [On the Sunny Slope]. *Diary of a Year*

CONTENTS

FOREWORD

by Traudl Junge

This book is neither a retrospective justification nor a self-indictment. I do not want it to be read as a confession either. Instead, it is my attempt to be reconciled not so much to the world around me as to myself. It does not ask my readers for understanding, but it will help them to understand.

I was Hitler's secretary for two and a half years. Apart from that my life has always been unspectacular. In 1947–48 I put down on paper my memories, then still very vivid, of the time I had spent close to Adolf Hitler. At this period we were all looking to the future and trying – with remarkable success, incidentally – to repress and play down our past experiences. I set about writing my memoirs objectively, trying to record the outstanding events and episodes of the immediate past before details that might later be of interest faded or were forgotten entirely.

When I read my manuscript again several decades later, I was horrified by my uncritical failure to distance myself from my subject at the time, and ashamed of it. How could I have been so naive and unthinking? But that is only one of the reasons why, until now, I have been reluctant to let the manuscript be published in my own country. Another reason is that in view of the huge amount of literature about Adolf Hitler and his 'Thousand-Year Reich', my own history and observations did not strike me as important enough for publication. I also feared avid sensationalism and approval from the wrong quarters.

I have never kept my past a secret, but the people around me made it very easy for me to repress the thought of it after the war: they said I had been too young and inexperienced to see through my boss, a man whose honourable façade hid a criminal lust for power. By 'they' I mean not just the denazification commission which exonerated me as a 'youthful fellow traveller', but all the acquaintances with whom I discussed my experiences. Some of them were people suspected of complicity with the Nazis themselves, but others were victims of persecution by the regime. I was only too ready to accept the excuses they made for me. After all, I was only twenty-five years old when Nazi Germany fell, and more than anything else I wanted to get on with my life.

Not until the middle of the 1960s did I gradually and seriously begin to confront my past and my growing sense of guilt. Over the last thirty-five years that confrontation has become an increasingly painful process: an exhausting attempt to understand myself and my motivation at the time. I have learned to admit that in 1942, when I was twenty-two and eager for adventure, I was fascinated by Adolf Hitler, thought him an agreeable employer, paternal and friendly, and deliberately ignored the warning voice inside me, although I heard it clearly enough. I have learned to admit that I enjoyed working for him almost to the bitter end. After the revelation of his crimes, I shall always live with a sense that I must share the guilt.

Two years ago I met the writer Melissa Müller. She came to see me to ask me, as an eyewitness, some questions about Adolf Hitler and his artistic predilections. Our first conversation led to many more, about my own life and the long-term effect that my association with Hitler had on me. Melissa Müller is of the second post-war generation, and her views are formed by what she knows of the crimes of the Third Reich. However, she is not the kind of self-righteous person who always knows better after the event; she does not think so simplistically. She listens to what we contemporary eyewitnesses who were once under the

Führer's spell have to say, and tries to trace the phenomenon
back to its roots.

'We cannot put our lives right in retrospect; we must go on
living with the past. We can put ourselves right, however.' This
quotation from Reiner Kunze's *Diary of a Year* has become a major
guiding principle in my life. 'But public grovelling is not always
to be expected,' he adds. 'Shame felt in silence can be more
eloquent than any speech – and sometimes more honest.' Melissa
Müller finally persuaded me to make my manuscript available
for publication after all. I thought: if I can manage to make *her*
understand how easy it was to fall for the fascination of Hitler,
and how hard it is to live with the fact that I now know I was
serving a mass murderer, it ought to be possible to make other
readers understand too. At least, I hope so.

Last year Melissa Müller introduced me to André Heller, whom
I regard not only as an extraordinarily interesting artist but also
as someone steadfastly committed to his moral and political
views. My long conversations with him were another very valuable incentive for me to confront the girl who was once Traudl
Humps, and with whom I had been at odds for so long. Many of
our conversations took place with a camera running. André
Heller and Othmar Schmiderer made their documentary film *Im
toten Winkel* [*Blind Spot. Hitler's Secretary*] from this footage. The
film appeared in the German-speaking countries at the same
time as this book.

Sometimes you will hear the 'young Junge'* speaking in this
book, sometimes the old Junge. The young Junge, as if post-
humously, has been persuaded to let her early memoirs be published by the ever-growing interest in an insider's knowledge of
the Nazi regime, and she hopes they will cast some light on the
period. The old Junge does not set out to preach morality, but
still hopes she may make a few remarks that are not as banal as

*Traudl Junge is playing on the literal sense of her surname: *jung* = young.

they may at first appear: appearances are often deceptive, and it is always worth while taking a closer look. We should listen to the voice of conscience. It does not take nearly as much courage as one might think to admit to our mistakes and learn from them. Human beings are in this world to learn, and to change themselves in learning.

Traudl Junge, January 2002
1920—2002

A CHILDHOOD AND YOUTH
IN GERMANY

by Melissa Müller

A time between times. Munich 1947. Once the 'capital of the Nazi movement', the city is now in ruins. Its people are exhausted by cold and hunger, but at the same time they are making a new beginning. Miserable destitution and an overwhelming lust for life co-exist in striking juxtaposition. Traudl Junge is twenty-seven years old, a high-spirited young woman eager to get on with her life. She has been 'exonerated' by the denazification commission on the grounds of her youthfulness. She works as a secretary, frequently changing jobs. You live from day to day now. Traudl Junge is considered a good worker. A reference written for her at the time dwells in particular on 'her quick understanding, good letter-writing style, and her typing and shorthand, which are well above average.' In the evenings she regularly goes to the cabarets and little theatres shooting up like mushrooms in the city. Money, food and cigarettes are in short supply. Friends and neighbours stick together and share what they have. Traudl Junge's life lies before her, and so – she hopes – do love and great happiness. She has no very clear idea of the future, but she believes in it.

Cut.

Munich 1947. Once the 'capital of the Nazi movement', the city is now in ruins. Traudl Junge is twenty-seven years old and has been a widow for three years. Her last employer, 'the best I've had yet,' she says, is dead, and many of her closest colleagues from the war period are missing without trace. She doesn't know if they have been taken away to Russian camps or committed suicide. She herself has survived several months in Russian prisons, a protracted attack of diphtheria and an adventurous escape from Berlin to Munich. She has returned with mixed feelings, afraid of being pilloried or shunned. She does not hide the fact that she was Hitler's private secretary for two and a half years, and is relieved to find how little interest anyone takes in her past. Even her mother doesn't want to know any more about it. She does often get sensation-seekers asking avidly, *Do tell us, is Hitler really dead?*, but no one seems to want to hear details, let alone attempts of any kind to explain or justify herself. Others make light of her vague sense of guilt for serving a genocidal murderer and thus sharing in the blame for his crimes. *You were still so young* ... In 1947, the process of forgetting is well under way, as self-protection for Nazis, their fellow-travellers and their victims alike.

One leading lady, two scenarios – both of them accurate.

Traudl Junge's life splits in two in the early post-war years. On one side of the split are the memories weighing down on her of that carefree time in Adolf Hitler's circle and its dramatic finale. She is alone with those memories. On the other side is everyday life among the ruins, with its immediate privations and pleasures. These she can share with others – friends, acquaintances, her mother and her sister.

At quite an early stage – indeed, as she remembers it, directly after the fall of the Third Reich – Traudl Junge manages to shake off the magnetic attraction of Hitler. Perhaps that was because, while she admired what she describes as the charming, friendly and paternal side of his character as she knew it at close quarters for two and a half years, she was always indifferent to the National Socialist regime itself, indeed uninterested in it, and gave no serious thought to its ideology and its inhumanities. Her past is an undigested mixture of pleasant personal memories and the dreadful knowledge she has been slowly acquiring bit by bit since the war, although she does not really let it reach her until much later. Traudl Junge entered Hitler's orbit by chance, and her view of him was extremely narrow – hard as that is to imagine today, even for Traudl herself. She was swept into the aura of Hitler, she felt flattered, and nothing that did not affect her personally touched her. Naivety? Ignorance? Vanity? Complacent gullibility? Complicity that was drilled into her? In 1947 she does not ask herself these questions. She has survived and now – with the strength of youth, as she says – she literally begins casting off her past. Not until the 1960s will these questions begin to torment her, and go on tormenting her to this day.

In 1947, through her then lover Heinz Bald, she meets a prosperous entrepreneur who is Bald's patron. He is fascinated by her past and tells her she should write down her memories of her time with 'the Führer'. His former wife is German Jewish and has been living in the USA since the divorce on which he insisted in the 1930s, but she is still in friendly contact with him and would like to offer the memoirs to an American daily paper. Traudl Junge likes the idea and soon sets to work. Looking back, she says that she herself felt an urge to record these crucial events in her life before the memories faded. Another reason is the wild speculation about Hitler's death which constantly confronts her. If anyone should happen to interrogate her again, she can point to her written record.

Over the following months she types some 170 pages of manuscript in her leisure time, at evenings and weekends. She enjoys writing. But in the end her account is not published because it was said, in 1949, that 'readers would not be interested in such stories'. All the same, Traudl Junge feels that her writing is a kind of catharsis. Admittedly she seldom stops to reflect on her experiences in any depth, but she conceals nothing and does not try to justify herself. She is simply recording events, episodes, personal impressions, and when she has finished she draws a line – for the time being – under that part of her past. For a long while her account lies unnoticed.

In fact Traudl Junge's attitude to Adolf Hitler was still ambivalent in those early post-war years – or so at least her manuscript reads. Her memoirs are therefore bound to shock the modern reader now and then. Re-reading them decades after she wrote them down, she herself feels distress and shame at the naivety and inability to see dispassionately that are evident in long passages of them. It's banal, she says; the tone is sometimes unpardonably simple-minded. She cannot recognize its historical value, and now its immediacy and lack of artifice irritate her. She fails to see how forcefully her apparently innocuous accounts of Hitler's daily round in the Wolf's Lair or at the Berghof back up Hannah Arendt's much-quoted thesis of the banality of evil. The illuminating insights she can offer those who like to regard Hitler and his accomplices as monsters without any human features are little comfort to her. She sees her memoirs, above all, as evidence of her unthinking attitude at the time, a kind of conclusion to a guileless youth spent in an environment that itself was very far from innocuous.

Gertraud Humps, known as Traudl, is born in Munich on 16 March 1920. A month before, on 24 February, Adolf Hitler and Anton Drexler, founder of the German Workers' Party (the Deutsche Arbeiterpartei, abbreviated to DAP), announce the party's xenophobic programme at the first great mass rally of the NSDAP (the National Socialist German Workers' Party) held in the Hofbräuhaus in Munich. The fact is worth mentioning because the programme was addressed to 'The impoverished people!'

Large sections of the population are indeed in a wretched situation, which leads to discord and political protest. Between December 1918 and the middle of February 1919 alone, the number of unemployed in the city rises from 8000 to about 40,000. Homes, food and fuel are all in short supply.

Traudl's father Max Humps, born in 1893, is a master brewer and a lieutenant in the Reserve. He is regarded as 'charming but flighty' and 'not exactly cut out for marriage'. Traudl's mother Hildegard, née Zottmann, is three years his junior and the daughter of a general. She is marrying beneath her. The young couple move into a small attic apartment in the Schwabing district. But immediately after Traudl's birth Max, a native of Regen in Lower Bavaria, loses his job with the Löwenbrauerei, and financial difficulties soon make the considerable differences of character between husband and wife a problem. Hildegard is a melancholic but very emotional woman with an inflexible view of the world and a strict moral code. Max is a man who muddles his way through, takes life easy and is very humorous – it is difficult to be angry with him, but no one can rely on him.

Like many unemployed men at this time Max Humps, who has no particular aim in life and anyway prefers his circle of friends and what he called sporting companions to any kind of family idyll, joins the 'Freikorps Oberland'. This is one of the right-wing 'Freikorps' units which attract men of anti-republican, nationalist and anti-Semitic opinions. It is a strictly organized volunteer formation – nationalist and populist in nature – with many members from the Bavarian Oberland, and was founded in April 1919 to campaign against the Munich Räterepublik (Councils Republic). He works hard to recruit new members, and is popular in the deeply insecure male world of that time. The military defeat of the First World War, the tug-of-war over the Treaty of Versailles, the emancipation of women encouraged by the war, their newly won franchise, economic hardship – the groups of men sheltering behind their uniforms, their weapons and their decorations aim to draw attention to all these things and provide a counterbalance. Bavaria attracts right-wing groups because the new Bavarian government, which itself is right-leaning, is very tolerant of them.

After the march into Munich in May 1919 which aims to topple the Räterepublik, the Freikorps Oberland campaigns against Communist risings in the Ruhr in April 1920, and from May to August 1921 fights against Poland in the border war in Upper Silesia. Max Humps is present at the storming of the

Annaberg in Upper Silesia, an event that wins the Freikorps great
credit in conservative circles. Max's father-in-law the general is
looking after his wife and daughter, for he himself is seldom at
home. When the Allies enforce the disbanding of all defence
associations in the summer of 1921, some sections of the Freikorps Oberland set up the 'Bund Oberland', the 'Oberland
League', with its headquarters in Munich. Its statutes promote
the idea of a 'struggle against the enemy within', and express
hostility to the Republic. The group's new leader, Friedrich
Weber, paves the way for close collaboration with the NSDAP.
On 1 May 1923 armed units of the Oberland League and the SA
(Sturmabteilung or Brownshirts) oppose a Social Democratic
and Communist demonstration on the Oberwiesenfeld in
Munich. In September the Bund Oberland becomes part of the
newly founded 'Deutscher Kampfbund' (German Combat
League), led by Adolf Hitler.

Several companies of the Bund Oberland take part in Hitler's
putsch of 8–9 November 1923. Max Humps is with them, and is
decorated with the NSDAP Blutorden (Blood Order) for his part
in the operation. The Bund is then banned, but continues in
existence as the 'Deutscher Schützen- und Wanderbund'
(German Marksmen and Hikers' League).

It is not clear whether Max Humps supports Hitler's
attempted putsch out of political conviction, or simply for lack
of any better way to spend his time, or whether he really believes
that Hitler will give the country's economy a boost. His daughter
for one regards him as a patriotically mercenary type of character
who felt it opportune to go along with his comrades – they
included Sepp Dietrich, later to be leader of the Leibstandarte
SS (Hitler's bodyguard) – and to spout nationalist slogans. He
is not arrested after the failure of the putsch; he is not important
enough. However, he still fails to find regular employment and
his wife and children are suffering real hardship – children in
the plural now, because a second daughter is born in December
1923, a month after the failed putsch. The girls' mother often
has no idea how she is going to feed them next day. In 1925

Humps goes to Turkey, now under the control of Mustafa Kemal Pasha, later known as Kemal Atatürk. As the country moves closer to Europe it needs the practical skills of Western professionals, and Max Humps finally gets back to work as a master brewer. He leaves his family behind in Munich – and now if not before, Hildegard Humps's patience with her husband is exhausted. She wants no more to do with him and goes back to her parents' home with her children – as a housewife and mother with no independent income, she can see no alternative. When Max Humps, who has done quite well in Turkey, tries on several occasions to bring his family to Smyrna (now Izmir), Hildegard refuses to go and asks for a divorce instead.

Traudl is five years old when her father leaves. Even before that he was not, admittedly, the traditional father-figure, but on the few occasions when he did come home she found him a delightful companion and an inventive playmate.

She begins school in 1926. She goes to the Simultanschule in Munich's Luisenstrasse, an establishment which admits children of all religious persuasions, probably not so much as the result of any broad-minded attitude of her mother's as because it was close to her grandparents' apartment in Sophienstrasse, near the Old Botanical Garden. Traudl was baptized an Evangelical, but has grown up without strong ties to the church and often plays truant from the Sunday children's services.

Traudl's grandfather Maximilian Zottmann, born in 1852, rules over the five-roomed apartment in Sophienstrasse, which is quite a grand place. She finds her grandfather a stern and pedantic autocrat who regulates the course of his day to the minute, thinks a great deal of discipline and order, and doesn't understand a joke. He is no substitute for her father. He regularly tells her mother, 'Kindly bring your brats up better', when Traudl and Inge laugh just a childish decibel too loud. But little Traudl's world is still all right as long as her grandmother is alive. Agathe Zottmann makes peace between everyone in the apartment, and Traudl adores her. Agathe is a native of Leipzig and met her husband when she was visiting the spa resort of Bad

Reichenhall; Traudl later describes her grandmother as a very affectionate, understanding woman. The little girl loves to hear Agathe's stories of Leipzig in her young days, and when Traudl has to write a composition at school on 'My Dream Holiday' she chooses not Hawaii or the Himalayas like her school friends, but Leipzig.

Agathe dies in 1928, and her loss hits eight-year-old Traudl hard. After his wife's death Traudl's grandfather becomes meaner with money and more of a domestic tyrant than ever. He likes his new-found bachelor freedom and plays sugar daddy to a young dancer called Thea, and although his daughter is running his household he misses no opportunity to point out that she and the children are a financial burden on him. In 1930, when Traudl begins secondary school at the Luisenlyzeum for girls, her mother applies for reduced fees because she cannot pay the full amount out of her housekeeping money – only 4.50 marks a day to feed four mouths. Traudl often has to report sick when there is a school outing because her mother can't scrape up the 2.70 marks for expenses. However, she does not feel that her childhood and early youth are unhappy. Difficult as their situation is for both mother and children, it brings the three of them closer together. Hildegard Humps is not a particularly demonstrative woman – not the kind of mother you kiss and cuddle – but her children feel that she loves them and understands them. She provides them with security. Her educational ideals are those of her time: they must grow up to be 'decent people', truthful, helpful, honourable, modest and considerate, they must make allowances and they mustn't poke their noses into what is none of their business.

The girls have ample opportunity to practise the virtue of making allowances when their mother's younger brother moves in with the family. Hans is an artistically gifted young man who has trained as an architect, but he suffers from schizophrenia. The children are usually amused but sometimes upset by his persecution mania and peculiar notions, and they feel increasingly uneasy when they realize what a trial their mother finds her brother's crazy ideas and wild accusations. In the middle of the 1930s Hans Zottmann – like at least 360,000 Germans with what are described as hereditary disorders – will be forcibly sterilized. The family do not question the operation but accept it as a necessary evil. Hans would never make a good father, they tell themselves.

As a girl Traudl enjoys life. She loves nature and animals; the household always includes a dog or some cats. And she likes going to school – not that she is particularly eager for education, but she fits easily into classroom society and likes the company of her girlfriends. Looking back, she describes herself as a herd animal, never meant to be a loner and not notable for original ideas and lateral thinking, but a girl who seeks security, safety and recognition in her own environment and wants everything to be harmonious. Her academic achievements are not much above average; her favourite subjects are art and gymnastics, but she likes German and English too. She is thought of as a lively child, and often, when her high spirits are too much for her grandfather or her mother, she puts up a fervent prayer to heaven in the evening: 'Please make me a good girl.' She is particularly anxious not to hurt her mother, whose personal misfortunes have not escaped her notice. However, she can be light-hearted. Even at the age of six, when told reproachfully, 'Oh Traudl, if only you weren't so wild!' she replies cheekily, 'Oh dear, if only God didn't want it that way.' This remark becomes a family saying. Little highlights in her young life are her rare visits to the movies with her sister – a ticket for the Bogenhausen cinema costs 70 pfennigs, and it is an hour's walk for Traudl and Inge from Schwabing to Bogenhausen and then an hour back again – and their summer holidays in the foothills of the Bavarian Alps, where Grandfather rents a game preserve, first and for a long time in Aschau, then in Seeon and finally on the Ammersee, where he shoots his last stag at the age of eighty.

In many ways 1933 marks a watershed for Traudl, who is now thirteen. First, Hitler's advent to power is celebrated as a great event at her school, and Traudl herself sees it as a sign of change and economic prosperity soon to come. Pictures of the crowds of indigent, somehow sinister men with scowling faces loafing around Sendlinger-Tor-Platz are still alarmingly present to her mind's eye. The unemployed, she was told. Well, all that's about to change ...

Second, Max Humps turns up again in 1933. As he supported the Party in its early struggles and has won the Blood Order, someone wangles him a job in the NSDAP administration. His daughter does not know exactly what job it is, nor is she interested; it is a long time since she has felt close to her father. She does visit him at his office in Barer Strasse in 1934 or 1935 – just once, because her mother is not keen for her to be in touch with him. Number 15 Barer Strasse houses the 'Reich Management Organization', the head office of the 'National Socialist Factory Cell', as well as the 'War Victims Head Office' and the 'National Health Head Office'. At this time the SA headquarters is in the Marienbad and Union hotels, both of them also in Barer Strasse.

Max Humps tries to win Traudl over with sweets and similar proofs of affection, but she keeps her distance and nurses her grudge against her father. The divorce came through in December 1932 – in his absence – and Traudl could not help noticing that her mother felt the humiliation of the case keenly. Max Humps had shown few scruples and a remarkable amount of imagination in laying the blame for their separation on his wife. General Maximilian Zottmann considered it socially intolerable for his daughter to be – in the context of the marital laws of the time – the guilty party in a divorce, so she had to agree to a shabby compromise, offering to give up any claim to maintenance if her husband would take all the blame himself. She was therefore dependent on her father's charity, and as she was represented in court by a Jewish lawyer she had worse cards to play than Max, holder of the Blood Order. It seemed likely that the judge in their case had National Socialist sympathies or anyway was in a great hurry to conform – the NSDAP had been the strongest political power in the country since the end of July 1932, at least for most of the time.

In any case, the verdict reinforces Hildegard Humps's belief that 'that man Hitler' destroyed her marriage as early as 1923. She frequently expresses this opinion after he has come to power, which annoys young Traudl. Traudl thinks her mother's views are simplistic, she stands up for 'the Führer', and has teenage day-dreams of saving his life some day. Fame through self-sacrifice! Once she actually sees him in person during these years, when he is being driven in his car to the 'Brown House' in Brienner Strasse, the Munich headquarters of the Nazi Party – she remembers what an exciting feeling that was. The girl, now around fifteen, gains the simple idea that the Führer must be a very great man from this sighting of him. She feels proud of Germany and the German people, and is impressed by the elevating idea of the 'national community' – 'One for all and all for one.' As soon as the national anthem strikes up tears of emotion come into her eyes. She is given no political education at school or at home, either now or later. The teachers at the Luisenlyzeum maintain a low profile; Traudl does not have to write school compositions full of propaganda like those required by zealous teachers at many other schools. It is true that there is discussion of the Nuremberg Laws, and concepts such as the 'Jewish question', 'racial hygiene' and 'racial disgrace' are approached as if they were facts. The pupils absorb them in the same spirit. Traudl accepts the idea of Bolshevism as the greatest enemy of the civilized world, threatening ruin to morality and culture, as a terrifying but incontrovertible fact. The nationalist writings encouraged by the Nazis do not reach her; she has popular stories for teenage girls on her bedside table, and later on novellas by Storm or Agnes Günther's bestseller *Die Heilige und ihr Narr* [*The Saint and her Fool*].

At home no one discusses either National Socialism or any other ideology. Traudl's mother still bears Hitler a personal grudge, but she is not interested in his political measures. A small picture of Prince Regent Luitpold stands on Traudl's grandfather's desk, inscribed with a personal greeting on the general's sixtieth birthday and dated 1912, a memento of the old days. Of better days? Maximilian Zottmann does not actually say so; he recognizes whatever authority is in government, and like most 'ordinary Germans' he does not consider the National Socialist system any real threat. He belongs to a magazine subscription service: the only journal he reads is *Der deutsche Jäger* [*The German Huntsman*], and books mean nothing to him. The *Münchner Neuesten Nachrichten* [*Munich Latest News*] comes into the household daily so that no one need miss an instalment of the serial story. The family listens to request concerts on the radio, and in the evening they sit round the table, with an opera libretto in front of them, wearing headphones and listening to the performance broadcast direct from the opera house over the phone lines. Grandfather loses his temper whenever a phone call for one of the girls interrupts the transmission.

But above all, 1933 is a year of great importance to Traudl Junge because she discovers her passion for dancing. Through her sister Inge she also meets the Klopfer sisters, Erika and Lore, girls of 'good family'. Their father is a lawyer and they live in a very grand apartment in Arcisstrasse, with the domestic staff proper to their station in life. The Klopfers' mother encourages her children, whom she describes as 'rather molly-coddled', to be friends with the robust Inge, and when she enrols the girls at the Lola Fasbender Children's School of Dance, principally to learn good posture and graceful movement, she also pays for Inge to take the course. Inge's outstanding talent is obvious. During these dancing lessons Traudl presses her nose flat against the glass door so as not to miss anything. When the teacher takes pity on her and invites her to join in, she feels as if the gates of Paradise are opening to her, and begins to discover the joys of rhythmic gymnastics for herself.

Traudl and Inge do not realize that Erika and Lore are Jewish until 1936, when the two sisters emigrate to New York. This may have been because their friends didn't know it themselves. Their parents had them baptized as Protestants, says Erika

Stone, née Klopfer. Religion is in the heart, their mother used to say. She is lukewarm about her children's enthusiasm 'for the pomp and circumstance of Nazi mass propaganda, the marching and the songs', but she does not tell the girls about their Jewish roots and the danger threatening Jews in Germany until just before they leave, when the sisters are sad to say goodbye.

In the three years of this friendship Traudl hardly registers the fact that the Klopfers' father is banned from practising his profession, while the family dismiss their domestic staff and move into a much smaller apartment in Tengstrasse. But she envies the Klopfer girls the adventure of their journey to America – and they envy her for her BDM uniform.

Traudl has been a member of the Bund Deutscher Mädel, the League of German Girls, since about 1935. Her mother has scraped and saved from the housekeeping money to buy the brown velour 'Alpine waistcoat' that is part of the uniform, and when Traudl can finally wear that object of desire she is hugely proud. She is leader of a group of six girls from her class – they call themselves the Six Graces. They drill on the school terrace – right turn, march – and shout the *Sieg Heil* slogan. *Sieg*, calls Traudl. *Heil*, her charges shout back. *Sieg! – Heil! – Sieg! – Heil!* Not much else of the BDM activities remains in her memory, only boring 'socials', various events when the BDM girls formed a guard of honour: the inauguration of the first workers' housing estate in Ramersdorf, at which she and her comrades performed folk dances; collecting for the Winter Aid organization; an excursion to Wolfratshausen complete with camp fire and tents – and Herta, who is leader of their unit when Traudl is sixteen or seventeen and has started attending commercial college. Herta tells the girls about the Third Reich's ideas of art and literature, makes music with them and takes them for idyllic walks. Traudl longs to emulate her. One day, when she is visiting Herta on her own, Herta gives her a goodbye hug and kisses her on the mouth. Traudl, who has not yet developed an interest in boys, although she longs for affection, is deeply impressed by Herta's warmth of heart.

But in 1938 she loses touch with her much admired leader, for suddenly something much more interesting is on offer: Traudl joins the 'Faith and Beauty' organization, a new unit within the BDM for Aryan young women of the Reich from eighteen to twenty-one years old. 'The task of our League is to bring young women up to pass on the National Socialist faith and philosophy of life. Girls whose bodies, souls and minds are in harmony, whose physical health and well-balanced natures are incarnations of that beauty which shows that mankind is created by the Almighty,' says Jutta Rüdiger, who became head of the BDM in 1937, describing its aims. 'We want to train girls who are proud to think that one day they will choose to share their lives with fighting men. We want girls who believe unreservedly in Germany and the Führer, and will instil that faith into the hearts of their children. Then National Socialism and thus Germany itself will last for ever.'

As in most of the youth groups of the Third Reich, there is hardly any discussion of politics in the Faith and Beauty organization. Its activities concentrate on doing graceful gymnastics and dancing, deliberately cultivating a 'feminine line' so as to counter any 'boyish' or 'masculine' development. In fact this gymnastic dancing is also a way of making use of young women for the purposes of the Party and the state – not, of course, that anyone explicitly tells them so, and Traudl Junge herself hears about it for the first time decades after the war. Their artistic commitment is intended to bring these young girls up to be 'part of the community', and keep them from turning prematurely to the role of wife and mother; instead, they must continue to devote themselves to 'the Führer, the nation and the fatherland'. Finally, Faith and Beauty will also qualify some of the rising generation of women for leadership; that is to say for posts in the BDM, the Nazi Women's Association or the Reich Labour Service.

Traudl is not burdened with such subjects as 'structuring your life', or 'political and intellectual education', which are also a statutory part of the Faith and Beauty curriculum, or if she is then she cannot remember it now. But she is fascinated by the Third Reich's grand cultural spectacles – as 'capital of the movement' Munich is a city of festive parades. The pomp which ushers in the Day of German Art in July 1937 and the two following years, with a procession of 'Two Thousand Years of German Culture' covering over three kilometres, fills her with enthusiasm, and so does the 'Night of the Amazons' held annually between 1936 and 1939 in Nymphenburg castle park. The Nazi concept of emotional self-presentation as a way of binding people ideologically together is working. Moreover, Traudl's sister takes part in the supporting programme for the Day of German Art, dancing the performance of the *Rape of the Sabine Women* on the stage erected by the Kleinhesseloher See in the English Garden. Traudl herself, in a minor way, participates in the cultural endeavours of the Nazis. She has a walk-on part in the 'Night of the Amazons', and at the age of fifteen models for the Swiss sculptor and marionette carver Walter Oberholzer, who has a commission to provide a statue for a fountain. The bronze girl throwing a ball to a faun whose mouth throws up jets of water has Traudl's attractively shaped body, although not her face. This sculptural ensemble is exhibited in the House of German Art in 1937.

It is impossible to describe adolescents like Traudl as being clearly for or against the Third Reich, as impossible as is probably the case with the majority of the German population of the time, and certainly the young people. Although Traudl allows the aesthetics of the lavish spectaculars to intoxicate her, and enthusiastically joins in the rejoicings over the triumphs of German athletes in the Olympic Games and Hitler's non-political successes, she finds the cruder side of party politics distasteful. The 'extreme Nazism' and the 'machinations of its big shots' strike her, so she says today, as 'proletarian' and 'narrow-minded'. However, she is as far as most of her contemporaries from questioning the government on that account. She can laugh at the Hitler jokes that go the rounds, she finds *Der Stürmer* with its anti-Semitic caricatures strange and repellent, but she does

not realize that the very lives of Jews and political opponents of
the Party are threatened. There are three Jewish pupils in her
class at the Lyzeum. During their time together at school – that
is to say, up to 1936 – these girls are treated just like the others
by both teachers and pupils. If their Jewishness is mentioned at
all it is only as their religious faith. Later she loses touch with
the three girls. One, she hears, is emigrating with her parents,
but to this day she knows nothing of the fate of the other two.
At eighteen, Traudl knows hardly anything about the November
1938 pogrom and the 'retaliation wreaked on Jewish shops, most
of which had all their windows broken', as the *Münchner Neuesten
Nachrichten* reports next day, or about the burning synagogues
and the summary arrest of hundreds of Jewish men. When she
and her friends hear later of these acts of Nazi brutality they do
not like them, but they quell their doubts by thinking that such
an event must be unique. Ultimately, it affects them as little as
all the other anti-Jewish measures: the first boycott of Jewish
shops decreed by the state on 1 April 1933; the notices in public
places with their inscription: 'Jews banned'; the total 'de-Judai-
zing' of the economy from early in 1939; the marking out of Jews
by the yellow star after September 1941. She claims that she can
remember only a single meeting with a woman wearing it – a
fleeting impression, and she thinks no more of it. That episode
shows how well repression works.

Traudl, like many young people in Germany at the time, lives
a life untroubled by politics. Or so she feels, anyway, which once
again confirms two facts that appear contradictory only on the
surface: first the regime's skilful tactics in building up a 'state
youth' that would toe the line, and second the existence of areas
in which 'uninvolved' young people like Traudl could move freely
and – as they thought – entirely unobserved.

In these years Traudl's interests focus on rhythmic gymnastics. Her dream, her ever more fervent wish, is to make
dancing her career, like her younger sister. She has no other,
more down-to-earth ambition. She has left school in 1936 after
taking only the first part of the school-leaving examinations –

she leaves unwillingly, but she has to start earning money as soon as possible to help her mother. Take a year's course at commercial college, people advise her, and then you can get a job as secretary in an office. A friend of a friend of hers is working for the Allianz, and this girl could help to find her a position with pension rights – a nightmarish idea for the lively Traudl. She certainly doesn't want to work for the Allianz, but she unenthusiastically attends commercial college, reluctantly learning to touch-type – 'Some girls may have a gift for it, Mother, but I certainly don't!' She gets on better with shorthand and book-keeping. When she has finished her course she looks for a job, with one prime requirement in mind: it must leave her enough time for dancing. Finally she gets a position as a clerk at the Munich branch of Vereinigte Deutsche Metallwerke, and soon she is running the stockroom where drills are stored and regularly doing the inventory – a challenge in itself, quite apart from the fact that the firm's chauffeur keeps following her down to the stockroom and showing her pornographic pictures. Traudl sees nothing for it but to give notice – inventing a reason, since she dares not tell her boss the real one. Next she works temporarily in old Councillor Dillman the notary's office. She moves to Rundschau Verlag in Ohmstrasse in 1939, and becomes assistant to the editor-in-chief of *Die Rundschau*, a journal for the tailoring trade. When the deputy editor-in-chief is called up into the army she assumes his responsibilities, doing the work conscientiously and sometimes even enjoying it, but she has made up her mind to leave anyway as soon as she has passed her final dance exam.

For Traudl, her office work is only the means to an end. She lives for her leisure time, which she spends with her group of friends – they go to the movies together, or to the swimming pool in summer, or for excursions into the country, and they throw cheerful parties whenever they get the chance. But between 1938 and 1941 she devotes most of her spare time to her dance training. Her teacher at the Faith and Beauty organization thinks she is talented enough to go in for gymnastic dancing more intensively, and tells her to register at her own dance school, the Herta Meisenbach School in Franz-Joseph-Strasse in Munich. Since Traudl cannot afford the fee, the teacher offers her a position as assistant. But even when she is not dancing herself, Traudl moves in artistic circles. The famous choreographer Helge Peters-Pawlinin has been living in Munich since the mid-1930s, building up a ballet company. He discovered Traudl's sister Inge at the Lola Fasbender School of Dance when she was fourteen, and is training her to be a prima ballerina. Inge becomes a member of the ensemble of his Romantic Ballet, immediately leaves school, goes on tour with the company and is already earning money even at her young age. In 1940 she gets an engagement at the German Dance Company in Berlin. Traudl now has a clear aim before her. She plans to follow her more gifted sister to the capital.

Traudl Junge describes her adaptability – or to put it in a less positive light, her malleability – as one of the outstanding characteristics of her youth. But who are the people who influence her thoughts and actions?

Her father, who so obviously profits from National Socialism? He was promoted to the post of security director of the Dornier Works in Ludwigshafen in 1936, and has married again. In the summer holidays Traudl and Inge visit him and 'Auntie' in their villa on Lake Constance, a house which goes with the job – a frustrating experience for Traudl. She wishes she had a father who could tell her what life was all about; she cannot respect the father she does have.

Her girlfriends? When she is sixteen she loses touch with Trudl Valenci, her closest friend at school, and meets her again only many years later, after the war. Ulla Kares is her best friend in the late 1930s and early 1940s. They share an enthusiasm for the film stars of the UFA studios – Renate Müller, Heinz Rühmann, Hans Albers – and they adore Gary Cooper. Ulla becomes more perceptive about the regime's intentions as early as 1938, when the blonde 'ringleader' of their group is suddenly expelled from the BDM; it appears that her mother is a quarter

Jewish. Ulla flees from her native city of Essen to Munich, but even her best friend Traudl learns only many years after the war that she is one-eighth Jewish herself. In 1943 Ulla falls in love with her half-Jewish future husband, Hans Raff. He is interned in 1944 and made to do forced labour for the German war industry. Hans Raff manages to escape in March 1945 and is hidden by Ulla until the end of the hostilities. Traudl learns of this too only after the war; when she moves to Berlin she loses touch with her friend.

A boyfriend? An early lover? Her interest in men develops late. While her younger sister was playing with boys she was still playing with dolls, she jokes later. For a long time she feels that there is something indecent, offensive about sexuality – the result of her mother's warnings – and she waits for her first sexual experience until she meets her husband.

When Traudl is about eighteen she and her sister become friendly with a group of foreign students and artists, most of them Greek. Almost all of these young people are already in relationships; only Traudl and Inge still have no partners. The attitude of their new friends to the Third Reich is even more insouciant than their own. They can be relied on to come up with the latest jokes about the Nazis, they listen to banned foreign radio stations, they even sometimes express criticism of the regime. But ultimately they are really interested only in their world of art and the theatre.

Traudl Junge herself mentions two people who have a crucial influence on her from the middle of the 1930s until her move to Berlin. One is the choreographer Pawlinin, who influences her lifestyle and concentrates her attention on the self-contained world of the theatre, remote from reality as it is. The other is Tilla Höchtl, mother of Lotte, a dancer colleague of Traudl's sister. Tilla is a single mother, like Hildegard Humps, but unlike Hildegard is an emancipated, independent, lively woman with a strong sense of humour, an ironic tongue, offbeat ideas and a definite dislike of National Socialism. The two women become close friends. Tilla tries to put more individual, independent ideas into the minds of Traudl and Inge, and their mother Hildegard too. She has nothing but contempt for those who care more about social norms than their personal needs. She will not tolerate platitudes like, 'That kind of thing just isn't done'. She successfully introduces the term 'petit bourgeois' into the vocabulary of the Humps family as something undesirable. In addition, it seems to Traudl that under her influence the family finds itself developing more casual but more self-confident attitudes.

In the summer of 1941 Traudl takes her dance exams. She is to present the theme of 'Prayer' in the free expression class. Her knees are trembling nervously, but that does not impair her dramatic performance. Traudl passes the exam. Now she intends to put her plan to go to Berlin into action at last, but she comes up against opposition from her boss. He refuses to accept her resignation, quoting the Nazi decrees on working in wartime. In her memoirs, she herself describes how after several months of indecision she manages, after all, to get summoned to Berlin 'on labour duty' in the spring of 1942, through the good offices of Beate Eberbach, a colleague of Inge and sister-in-law to Albert Bormann, head of Hitler's private chancellery office.

Pleased as she is to be going to Berlin, Traudl feels guilty about leaving her mother alone in Munich. Her grandfather died in 1941, and since then Hildegard Humps has been sub-letting a room. She now lives on the rent and on what her daughter sends home from the capital city. The relationship has gone into reverse: Traudl now feels responsible for the mother who has sacrificed so many years for her children. And her sense of responsibility mingles with a guilty conscience for leaving her mother behind. Germany, after all, has been at war for two and a half years now.

Traudl's new life begins just when the fortunes of war turn in the Allies' favour. Germany declared war on the USA in December 1941. The severe Russian winter of 1941–42 has halted the advance of the German army; the Soviets have proved to be formidable enemies, and despite their political differences with the USA and Great Britain the three powers have come to an understanding about a second front in the West. In March 1942 Lübeck is the first German city to be the target of massive British area-bombing. The Nazi propaganda machine, of course, ensures that little of this filters through to the civilian population of Germany. The number of dead in Lübeck, for instance, is reduced from the real figure of 320 to only 50.

After a phase of great insecurity when hostilities first broke out, Traudl has become accustomed to the everyday life of wartime – air raid practices, blackout regulations, food rationing. Like probably the majority of the German population, she has been duped by Hitler's claim that Germany was attacked first and the war is an act of self-defence. None the less, she has not felt triumphant about the victory announcements in the opening phase of the war. Hitler's desire for expansion means nothing to her. She hopes there will be a swift end to the conflict. In what circumstances and how closely she will eventually see that end she cannot, of course, guess in her first months in Berlin.

The following account of her experiences in 1947/48 are Traudl Junge's personal memoirs, published as she originally wrote them. The text, with Frau Junge's own co-operation, has been slightly altered only where there were simple typing errors in the spelling of proper names, occasional omissions of words, etc. The few minor cuts in the content of the memoirs are indicated by [. . .].

MY TIME WITH ADOLF HITLER —
WRITTEN IN 1947

by Traudl Junge

I

Secretaries aren't usually asked much about their former boss. But I was Hitler's secretary for three years, so everyone is always asking me, 'Do tell us, what was he really like?' And then, almost always, comes the second question: 'How did you get the job in the first place?' People are usually disappointed or at least surprised by both answers, because I can't tell them anything from first-hand experience about Hitler's famous fits of rage or his carpet-biting, and I didn't become his secretary because of any outstanding services to National Socialism or a low party membership number.* It happened more or less by chance.

I would probably never have become Hitler's secretary at all if I hadn't wanted to be a dancer. I am afraid I must explain at a little more length so that readers will understand what I mean by that. My younger sister and I both went to dance and gymnastics schools from a very young age, and I had no doubt at all that one day I would make a career in one of those two fields. But unfortunately we lived in straitened financial circumstances, and when I left school, being the elder sister, my priority had to be to earn money as quickly as possible. I thought that would be very easy and pleasant, and believed that I could earn enough

*A low party membership number indicated that the holder had joined in the early years.

working in an office to go on training as a dancer at the same time. But it turned out that it wasn't so simple to find a firm where I could first earn enough money, and second have enough time left for what I really wanted to do. I finally found a job which, to be honest, I didn't like at all, but it did meet those two conditions. Anyway, I didn't expect it to be long before I could finally turn my back on the world of the typewriter. I just had to pass my dance exams first. By now, however, the war had begun, and gradually we all found that personal restrictions and duties were imposed on us. Myself, I realized that I hadn't reckoned with the state regulations. By the time I finally passed my dance exams in 1941, and triumphantly gave notice to the firm where I was working, rules about the state control of jobs and workplaces had come into effect.[1] You couldn't just do as you liked any more, you had to do what mattered most to the state, and secretaries and shorthand-typists were needed a great deal more urgently than dancers. In fact dancers had become completely superfluous. However, I was twenty-one, and the war looked like being not a *Blitzkrieg* and over in a flash after all, but a long, long business. In a few years' time the agility I had worked so hard to gain would be getting rusty, and then my dream of dancing would finally be over. I probably wasn't entirely objective in my disappointment, because all my despair and resentment were directed against the firm and my boss. I blamed him, and accused him of spoiling my whole life out of selfishness because he wouldn't accept my resignation, which was a terrible thing to say. But if my employer had agreed, then I could have given up the job. Anyway, I couldn't stand the sight of him any more, and I wanted to leave that office at any price. So the avalanche slowly began to roll – an avalanche that was to come near to burying me in Berlin in 1945.

My sister Inge was living in Berlin then, performing at the German Dance Theatre as a ballerina. One of her colleagues was related to Albert Bormann,[2] and through him I got an invitation one day to go and work at the Führer's Chancellery in Berlin. If

I wasn't exactly thrilled about the place and the position, the idea of getting away from home, getting to know the capital and beginning a real life at last was very tempting. The working conditions sounded all right too, so I accepted and went to Berlin. The first train journey of my life in a sleeping car was exciting in itself, but when I entered the huge labyrinth of the New Reich Chancellery to introduce myself I began to feel that I had made rather a bold decision. However, I couldn't very well go back on it now – that would have been too embarrassing. I was met by Gruppenführer Albert Bormann, brother of Reichsleiter Martin Bormann.[3] He was a friendly, pleasant man. I was working in a department of the Führer's Chancellery where post addressed to 'The Führer' came in to be sorted, sent on, and some of it dealt with there in the office. My job was extremely innocuous, and I didn't have very much to do. Albert Bormann, head of the Führer's Chancellery, was also Hitler's adjutant and was seldom in Berlin. I sometimes wondered why they had engaged a secretary from Munich specially for him, even stipulating that my job was compulsory war service. I was working in the huge, magnificent building where I was always losing my way, sliding over the shiny polished marble floor of the hall, and generally waiting for the job to develop further. And soon the first upheaval in my tranquil existence did come. All of a sudden there was a rumour going round that Hitler needed new secretaries, and they were to be chosen from the staff of the Reich Chancellery.

All the secretaries, shorthand-typists, trainees and office assistants were very excited. Competitive shorthand and typing tests were held, and I was one of the secretaries who had to take part. By now I had been moved to the Führer's Personal Adjutancy Office. This department was in the same building, but in a different part of it, looking out on the park. I didn't expect to do well in the typing competition, because first I didn't really see the point of it, and second I didn't think I was a suitable candidate to be Hitler's secretary. And the last of my self-confidence drained away when I saw how the other girls' fingers raced over the keys. But probably for that very reason I was less nervous than anyone else in the final round, made fewer mistakes, and came out as one of the best typists. And one fine day I was given a railway ticket and told to take the courier train next day to Führer headquarters, where I and nine other girls were to present ourselves to the Führer.

At this time Hitler had three secretaries. The youngest of them, Frau Christian,[4] had now married and left her job with Hitler. The other two, Fräulein Wolf[5] and Fräulein Schroeder,[6] had been his secretaries and constant companions for over ten years. All the stress and strain of such an irregular life had already affected their ability to perform well, and so had their increasing age. One day Hitler wanted to dictate a document. Fräulein Wolf was unwell; Fräulein Schroeder was out at the theatre in Berlin. He was furious to find that there was no one available when he happened to need secretarial help, hauled his adjutant Bormann over the coals and told him to make sure such a thing never happened again. Younger secretaries must be recruited to take some of the burden off the shoulders of the two veterans. And so it was that at the end of November 1942 we ten girls, all of us still quite young, were summoned to the Supreme Commander.

The courier train that we boarded one evening in Berlin, bound for an unnamed destination, came into Rastenburg station in East Prussia next morning. Here a railcar was waiting in a siding for the Führer's visitors and took us on into the forest. Finally we ended up at an inconspicuous little station building without any name outside it. We had arrived. We were received by Gruppenführer Albert Bormann, the railcar went on, and the other passengers who had got out here disappeared into the snowy forest. We could see no houses or other buildings, yet we were at Führer headquarters. Bormann took us to our temporary quarters. Only now did we see that there was another train standing at the second platform, and that was where we were to stay. It was also explained that we were still outside the restricted area of Führer headquarters itself, and the Führer's special train, which was always kept waiting under steam near the Führer himself, would be our accommodation until he had seen us and made his choice.

It is worth describing this train in more detail, since it was furnished like a well-run hotel with all the comforts anyone could need. But I will come back to that later, when I describe the journeys we made in it. For the time being each of us girls had a compartment in the guest car, where we were extremely well looked after by the well-trained Mitropa staff, and there we waited for the great event of our introduction to the Führer. But several days went by and nothing happened. In the meantime we went for short walks in the forest until we came up against a barrier or some barbed wire, with armed guards who wanted to see our papers and asked us to give the password. Unfortunately we had none of the former and didn't know the latter, and we had no intention of venturing into forbidden territory; we were just going out in little 'reconnaissance groups' to see what a Führer headquarters really looked like. By now, too, we had found out that there were a great many huts and little bunkers hidden, well camouflaged, among the trees and bushes, a number of roads in good repair ran through the forest, and a lot of people, all in uniform, lived here. We began to think of our stay in the magical winter landscape, with the train staff looking after us so well, as a holiday. We were feeling at ease and almost forgot what we were there for. The little kitchen next to the dining car stocked many good bottles, and the waiters, who hadn't had female company for ages, spoiled us and often gave us a delicious liqueur in the evenings.

We didn't guess that the great moment would come when we least expected it, in the middle of the night. We had just gone to bed when two orderlies from the Führer bunker appeared to fetch us all and take us to the Führer. Panic broke out. Our curlers got tangled up, we couldn't find our shoes, our fingers were trembling so much that we could hardly do up our buttons. We all quickly cleaned our teeth, because we knew that the ideal German woman was not supposed to smoke, or at least you shouldn't be able to smell the smoke on her.

Finally we stumbled along dark paths leading into the forest. The two orderlies steered us past the checkpoints, where guards shone dark lanterns on us and gave us temporary passes to enter the restricted area. We had no idea how the two men could find their way through this darkness. A faint beam of torchlight occasionally showed between the trees, but it was a mystery to me how anyone could go in any definite direction. I suppose the two soldiers weren't as excited as we were. (None of us had ever seen Hitler at close quarters, and we knew that in Berlin, or anywhere else he went, hundreds of thousands of people always flocked to see him, if only from a distance.) All this made it an exciting experience for us. It isn't every day that you find yourself face to face with a head of state!

At last we reached a heavy iron door with bright light shining on the other side of it. I could just make out the outlines of a low-built, relatively small bunker. The armed men on guard at the entrance let us in without any further checks. They didn't search our handbags, some of them quite large, so apparently we weren't suspected of carrying guns or bombs. Perhaps our scared faces ruled out any such suspicion from the start, because I think we must have looked more as if we were being taken to execution than to a great, inspiring event.

We passed through the low entrance into a narrow concrete corridor with a great many doors, almost like something in a big steamship, and went through the first door on the left into a waiting-room. It measured about three metres by four and was used by both the domestic staff and Hitler's orderlies.

Hitler's valet explained that we would have to wait for a little while, and got us to sit down at a round table in comfortable chairs, the kind you'd expect in a country house. Hitler was just feeding his dogs, he told us. Of course we asked how we were to address the Führer. He said Hitler would speak to us first, and then we were to reply, 'Heil, my Führer'.

We also wanted to know if we were to stretch our arms out

straight or bend them, but then Albert Bormann arrived and told us to follow him: Hitler was in his study now, he said, and wanted to see us. We were to act as naturally as possible, he added.

The narrow corridor went round a couple of corners, led through a small tea-room, and then we were outside the tall double doors of the study. The valet, Heinz Linge,[7] knocked, opened the door, and said, 'The ladies from Berlin are here, my Führer.'

We entered the room, which was very large, and stood in front of the desk. Hitler came towards us, smiling, slowly raised his arm in greeting, and then shook hands with each of us one by one. His voice was very deep and full as he asked us all our names and where we came from.

I was the last, and the only girl from Munich. He asked my age again, smiled once more, turned that famous piercing gaze on all of us again, raised his arm in greeting for the second time – and we were dismissed without ever getting around to stammering out our 'Heil, my Führer.'

Outside, the spell was broken, and we relaxed at last and began chattering about the way Hitler shook hands, his fascinating gaze, his figure and all the details that seem so significant at such an important meeting.

Bormann, glad to have completed his mission at last, gave each of us a glass of champagne to celebrate the occasion, and then took us into the canteen, a little way off. The soldiers and officers were pleased to meet us. We ate some sandwiches, because excitement sharpens your appetite, and then Bormann had us escorted back to our special train.

Next morning we were playing guessing games: which of us had Hitler liked best? We thought he would choose by our appearance, and were rather upset when Bormann told us next day it wasn't as simple as that, we must wait to take a dictation test. The staff of the Führer's special train, and some men from the restricted area who sometimes came round now that they knew there were some girls worth visiting in it, did assure me that I had a good chance of becoming Hitler's secretary, first because he had a liking for Munich and Munich girls, and second because I looked like Eva Braun. But as I never do well in exams, I thought my prospects rather poor in view of the coming dictation test.

The few days we were originally supposed to stay had lengthened into several weeks, and no one could tell when Hitler would have time for the dictation tests. We had to wait until he really did have something to dictate. By now we were sometimes being called in to help the two old secretaries, who were busy making lists of Christmas presents and Christmas bonuses. We made several snowmen, which were demolished again next day by the commandant of Führer headquarters because he thought they were too frivolous for these surroundings, and we had some keenly contested snowball fights.

And guess what – the fateful summons came after one of those snowball fights, when I was sitting in my compartment in the train with my face flushed and my hair all wet.

I and a colleague – a pretty blonde girl who also came from the Führer's Adjutancy Office – were told to come and take dictation. We felt very excited again as we went over to the Führer bunker, taking the same route as before.

I was to be the first sacrificial lamb, and if I failed Fräulein Böttcher was to step in. After we had waited a few minutes Linge took me into the study again, announced me to Hitler, and this time the door closed behind me and I was alone with him.

I noticed that he wore glasses. An old-fashioned, cheap pair of glasses with a nickel-rimmed frame – or I suppose it could have been platinum, but it wasn't showy anyway.

He shook hands with me again and took me over to a desk with a typewriter on it near his own. While I took the cover off the machine and adjusted the paper, he explained in kindly tones, as if speaking to a child about to have her photograph taken: 'There's no need to be nervous, I make more mistakes in my own dictation than you possibly could!'

I assured him that I wasn't nervous, but my hands gave me away, because when he finally began on the first sentence my fingers were trembling so badly that I didn't hit a single correct key. I stared in horror at that first line, which looked like something in Chinese, and desperately tried not to lose the thread of the dictation and to calm my hands down.

At that moment there was a knock on the door and the valet announced the envoy Hewel,[8] who was liaison officer between Hitler and Ribbentrop.[9] Hewel had a short discussion with Hitler which ended in a telephone call to Ribbentrop. When I saw Hitler talking quite easily and naturally on the phone, in just the same way as Herr Müller or Herr Schulze or any other of my former bosses, I felt all right again. The rest of the dictation went ahead without any problems. Today, however, I can't remember exactly what the document was about. I think it was probably some memo or other that was never published.

When I had finished I put the sheets of paper together and handed them to the Führer. I had been told in advance that I must type with very wide spacing between the lines so that the Führer could make his corrections easily. After he had said goodbye, assuring me that I had typed very well, he sat down at the desk.

Feeling very relieved, I left the room and met Gruppenführer Bormann outside the door. He had been sitting there on a chair all this time, looking nervously at his watch and hoping I wouldn't let him down. When I told him it had all gone well he was considerably happier than I was, as if he had some great achievement to his credit. Later I found out that he had been terribly afraid of being let down, because his brother Martin, who was his bitterest enemy, wanted to choose Hitler's secretaries himself and so go one better than him.

Of course Fräulein Böttcher had been hoping to get a chance of stepping in, but she was pleased for me when she heard that my test had turned out well. As we sat in the waiting room talking about the experience I had behind me, while it was still to come for my colleague, Hitler suddenly appeared in the doorway, sat down at the round table with us, asked me some more questions about my family and my past life, and repeated that I had typed very well.

I thought to myself: but you haven't tried any of the other secretaries yet – you'll soon find out that I wasn't very brilliant. I wasn't to know that no comparisons would be drawn, and my fate was already sealed.

It turned out that Hitler didn't want to try any of the other secretaries, because he thought that I had done satisfactorily and was suitable. So nine girls went back to Berlin next day while I stayed in the 'Wolf's Lair', as this headquarters was called.

However, I exchanged my compartment in the special train for a little room in the secretaries' bunker, was given a permanent pass for the restricted area, and now I was living about a hundred metres from the Führer bunker itself.

I wasn't entirely happy with my new quarters. I'm someone who likes light and fresh air, and I just can't stand the atmosphere of a bunker. I was working in a room with small windows during the day, but I had to sleep in an uninviting, windowless little cell. It was no smaller but definitely less appealing than my pretty compartment in the special train. Air came through a ventilator in the ceiling. If you closed it you felt you were stifling, if you opened it the air wheezed noisily as it came into the little room, and you might have been sitting in an aeroplane. That was probably why the other two secretaries, Fräulein Wolf and Fräulein Schroeder, preferred to sleep on sofas in their offices, and had made themselves combined living and working quarters in the front part of the bunker, which had windows and larger, brighter rooms. I soon did the same, and with Bormann's support and permission I furnished the general office comfortably. After all, I was to stay for an indefinite length of time.

When Hitler had something to dictate he always summoned me, and I was always in a nervous state again. I still didn't know if these were more 'tests' or if I was definitely appointed to the post. On 30 January 1943 I was called in to Hitler once more. When I entered the room the other two secretaries were with him, and I realized at once that he didn't want to dictate. I thought some kind of oath or official swearing-in ceremony must be coming, and I felt a bit odd. Hitler said he was very pleased with me, and his two experienced colleagues here also thought I would make him a very suitable secretary. Would I like to stay on? I couldn't resist the temptation. I was twenty-two, I had no idea of politics, and I just thought it was wonderfully exciting to be offered such a special position, so in short I said yes.

But that was not the end of the conversation. It looked as if Hitler wanted to say something more, and he seemed to be searching for the right words. Finally he said, smiling at me and speaking almost awkwardly, that he knew I was still very young, there were so many men here, most of them seldom went home and – well, soldiers feel particularly strongly attracted to the Eternally Feminine – in short, I must be a little careful, not too forthcoming. And if I had any complaints of anyone pestering me, never mind who it was, I was to come and tell him about it, any time.

So much for the swearing-in ceremony! I hadn't expected anything like that. I'd thought I might have to provide evidence of my loyalty to National Socialism and the Party, vow to be loyal and promise to keep secrets. Instead, here was Hitler himself showing solicitude for my virtue. I was really relieved, because I could honestly tell him that he had nothing to worry about there, but I was very grateful for his protection. He smiled, entrusted me to the care of my older colleagues, and now I was Hitler's secretary.

From then on, except for a few weeks' holiday, there were very few days when I didn't see Hitler, talk to him, work with him or share meals with him.

II
IN THE 'WOLF'S LAIR'

I got used to this strange new world relatively quickly. Nature, the forest and the landscape quickly won me over to my new workplace. There were no fixed working hours here, no office atmosphere, I could go for long walks and enjoy being out in the woods. I didn't miss the big city for a moment.

Hitler himself used to say they'd chosen him the cheapest, most marshy, mosquito-ridden and climatically unpleasant place possible, but I thought it was lovely. In winter at least there was an indescribable charm about East Prussia. I shall never forget the snow-covered birch trees, the clear sky and the spreading plains with the lakes in them.

In summer, however, I had to agree that my boss had a point, because myriads of mosquitoes plagued us, sucking our blood. The air was heavy and humid and sometimes quite difficult to breathe. In such weather it was hard to persuade Hitler to take his daily walk. He stayed in his cool bunker, and it was only for the sake of his dog Blondi that he would go for a little stroll after breakfast in the small area of land next to the bunker that was specially reserved for that purpose. This was where Blondi, a German shepherd, had to do her tricks. Her master had trained her to be one of cleverest, most agile dogs I ever saw. Hitler was delighted when Blondi managed to break her jumping record by a few centimetres, or could balance on a narrow pole a couple of minutes longer than usual. He said he relaxed best in his dog's company.

The things Blondi could do were really amazing. She jumped through hoops, climbed a ladder, and would sit up and beg nicely when she reached the little platform at the top. It was a pleasure to see the satisfaction both master and dog got from these games.

Spectators often turned up outside this piece of land to watch the games, and it was the only opportunity I myself had for contact with the Führer during those first weeks. When he saw me he would greet me with a friendly handshake, and ask how I was.

He didn't summon me to take dictation. My main business in those first four weeks was to ask every morning whether I should expect any work, and I always had to tell either the valet on duty or the telephone switchboard where I could be found.

I used the time to get to know the people around Hitler better. First there were his valets Heinz Linge and Hans Junge,[10] who relieved each other on duty every other day. They had both been chosen from Hitler's personal bodyguard, the SS-Leibstandarte Adolf Hitler, and theirs was a busy and responsible position.

To say 'valet' doesn't really cover it – the post was more like that of household manager, travelling companion, butler and maid-of-all-work combined. The valet on duty had to wake Hitler in the morning, that is to say knock at his bedroom door, announce the precise time, and give him the morning news. He also had to decide on the menu for the day, fix mealtimes, pass instructions on to the kitchen, and serve the Führer when he ate. He was in charge of a whole staff of orderlies who looked after Hitler's wardrobe and had to clean the rooms and run the establishment, and he made appointments with the dentist and barber and supervised the care of the dog.

Nobody knew the Führer's personal qualities and habits, or his moods and whims, as well as Linge, who was an extraordinarily clever, able man. He also had the calm disposition he needed, never lost his temper and had a good sense of humour, which quite often came in very useful. No wonder even Hitler's most distinguished colleagues would ask Linge, out in the anteroom, whether this was a good time to give Hitler bad news, and sometimes the valet advised them to wait until the Führer had taken a refreshing afternoon nap and was in a better mood.

We secretaries were inevitably thrown together with the valets a good deal, since they were the people who always told us if we were needed or not. That way we heard many details of Hitler's habits, and got to know them personally only much later, when we were in closer contact with him.

The only fixture in the Führer bunker, besides his valets, was Hitler's chief adjutant, Gruppenführer Julius Schaub.[11] For historical research purposes it's not worth saying much about him, but even now I'm often asked how a statesman could keep such a strange character always with him and raise him to such a position of trust. So I must try to explain, even though I never really understood it myself.

Dear old Julius thought he was an amazingly important, significant person. [...] I didn't yet know him at all when I heard the following little anecdote about him, and I can't be a hundred per cent certain that it's really true, but it's so typical that I just have to tell it. Even back in the mists of time, Schaub had been a Party member. His Party number was a very low one. Someone once asked him who really decided on the policies of the National Socialist Workers' party. Julius Schaub happened to be cleaning Hitler's boots at the time, and was acting as his valet. He replied: 'Oh, that's me – and Hitler', and after a moment's hesitation he added, 'And Weber too!'[12] [...]

Both Schaub's feet had been injured in the First World War, leaving him crippled. Later he had joined the NSDAP, and Hitler noticed him as an ardent admirer who always attended Party meetings, hobbling in on his crutches wherever Hitler appeared. When Hitler discovered that Schaub had lost his job because of his Party membership he took him on as a valet. Soon his devotion, reliability and loyalty made him indispensable. He slowly worked his way up to adjutant and finally to chief adjutant, because he was the only one of the old guard who had been through the early years of the struggle himself, and he shared many experiences in common with Hitler. He knew so many of the Führer's personal secrets that Hitler just couldn't make up his mind to do without him.

In a way we secretaries regarded Herr Schaub as our boss too. We had to deal with his post, copy out the petitions sent to him that he wanted to put before Hitler – most of them were from people the Führer knew – and deal with the mail coming into and going out of the personal adjutant's office.

Obviously we could hardly write letters exactly as he dictated them to us. Most of them had to be translated from Bavarian dialect into German first. On the whole Julius Schaub was extremely kind, but very curious too. He was always collecting anecdotes so that he could entertain the Führer at breakfast. He passed on every joke told at the camp barber's to his master, usually missing the punch line.

He had long ago given up smoking for the Führer's sake, leaving drink as his only indulgence. He had an astonishing head for alcohol. The light would be on in his room until late at night, or you would hear his voice in the mess, or from another bunker where some of the gentlemen were sitting around a bottle in earnest conversation. The amazing thing was, however, that he would go to the barber's freshly washed at eight in the morning, then walk round to the camp to show everyone that he was an early riser and a lesson to anyone who slept late. Only much later did I realize that after his morning walk, when the whole camp had respectfully noticed that Herr Schaub was up and about already, he went back to bed and slept happily until noon.

In the past Hitler always used to eat lunch in the mess with his closest colleagues and his generals, but as he didn't want to be tied to fixed mealtimes, and even during a meal could never get away from discussing official business with such people around him, he had been eating alone in his bunker for months now. But if Himmler, Göring, Goebbels, or another high-ranking visitor was present, which wasn't often, he ate with his guest in the guest's room. We had a camp chef, who cooked well but didn't have a great range. He was from Berlin, and had to rely on good advice and his imagination when he was cooking Bavarian specialities. His name was really Günther, but that wasn't a name familiar to many people, and even Hitler never called him by anything but his nickname 'Krümel' – 'Crumbs'. There was a big notice up over the kitchen door saying: 'Wer Krümel nicht ehrt, ist den Kuchen nicht wert!' ('If of Crumbs no heed you take, then you don't deserve the cake!') Little Crumbs cooked for everyone inside the restricted area, feeding almost two hundred people a day from his huge pans. No wonder someone so used to catering on a large scale, a man who had done nothing but cook for soldiers for years on end, couldn't pay particular attention to the whims of vegetarians. He heartily hated, or anyway despised, those who turned down meat. But as he now had to cook for the Führer – there was no other chef for miles around, and after all Hitler was the most important person here – he did his best to devise a vegetarian menu willy-nilly. I must say Hitler put up with a good deal in that respect, as I saw later at meals in the Berghof too. He was a very undemanding and modest eater, and only occasionally complained that his diet was very boring; he got only the side dishes without the meat, so there was definitely something missing. And Crumbs thought people couldn't live without meat, so he would add at least a little meat stock or lard to all his soups and most other dishes. Usually Hitler noticed the deception, was cross, and then of course said the meal had given him a stomach-ache. In the end he wouldn't let Crumbs cook him anything but gruel, mashed potato, and dishes guaranteed to have no animal ingredients in them. Not surprisingly, that didn't make his menu any more appealing and varied.

I gradually picked up all this information in conversations with Linge, during meals in the mess, on walks through the camp, etc.

After four weeks, on 30 January 1943, I was finally summoned to take dictation from Hitler again. I have to admit I was just as nervous as the first time when an orderly came to my table – I was eating in the mess – and told me to go to the Führer. It was a most unusual time for him to give dictation, in broad daylight! I abandoned my meal and went to the Führer bunker just opposite. Hans Junge, who was on duty that day, told me the Führer wanted to dictate his proclamation for the tenth anniversary of his coming to power. I'd never have thought of that! But the anniversary was one of the regular occasions when Hitler made a speech. This time he wasn't going to address the people in person but read out his speech over the radio and have it published in the press.

I was escorted into the study only a few minutes later, and for the first time I finally had leisure to take a closer look at the room.

After walking through the other low-ceilinged, artificially lit, cramped rooms in the bunker, it was pleasant to pass through the big double doors into the annexe which was the study. The valet announced me, and I said good day to the Führer.

He was wearing his usual black trousers, double-breasted field-grey coat, white shirt and black tie. I never saw him in anything else. His jacket was always perfectly plain, with silver buttons, but no braid or decorations. He just wore the golden Party badge on the left side of his chest, the Iron Cross and the black decoration for the wounded.

While Hitler gave his valet some instructions for the forthcoming military briefing, I took a rather closer look at the room. Full daylight fell into the whole of it through five big windows with colourfully printed rustic-style curtains. Almost the whole of the window side of the room was taken up by a long, broad table on which there were several telephones, desk lamps and pencils. This was where maps were spread out for the military conferences. Several small wooden stools served as seating. Opposite the door, at the far end of the room, Hitler's desk stuck right out into the space available. It was an ordinary oak desk, the kind you get in any modern office. There was a clock on it, but Hitler never even glanced at it. He always got one of his companions to tell him the time, even when he was carrying his gold spring-lidded watch in his trouser pocket. A broad fireplace was built into the wall opposite the windows, with a big round table in front of it, and round the table there were about eight comfortable armchairs with woven seats and backs. The furnishings were completed by a cupboard for gramophone records built in at the other narrow end of the room, opposite the desk, and several more unobtrusively built-in oak wall cupboards. While I looked around I got the typewriter ready and fed in the paper. Meanwhile the valet went away.

Hitler came over to me, asking, 'Aren't you freezing, child?

It's cold in here.' I rashly said no, and soon regretted it, because I really did feel bitterly cold as the dictation went on.

Hitler began on his speech, striding up and down the study with his hands clasped behind his back and his head bent. Once again I had to listen very carefully at first, so as to catch everything. As before, Hitler dictated without stopping, almost at the same speed as he delivered a speech, and without any notes. However, he didn't have much new to say on the subject of his seizure of power. Only at the end, when he began speaking about the present hard struggle that must end with the final victory did he raise his voice, and then I didn't have any difficulty in understanding him even when he had turned his back to me and was standing at the far end of the room. He finished dictation after about an hour, and I handed him the sheets of paper and confessed that I hadn't been able to hear him very well. He gave me a friendly smile, shook hands and said that didn't matter, it would be all right.

I left him with icy feet but a flushed face. Outside I asked the valet why it was so cold in the study. Glancing quickly at the thermometer, I could see that it was only eleven degrees. Surely a head of state could afford to keep his room warm? The whole complex had central heating, and it was warm enough everywhere else. But I was told that Hitler felt most comfortable at that low temperature and never let it rise. Now I realized why the generals and staff officers always came away from the military briefings that often lasted for hours with red noses and hands blue with cold, and immediately poured a warming tot of spirits down their throats in the valets' room or the mess. General Jodl[14] even claimed to have contracted permanent rheumatism during these conferences with Hitler.

Gradually I came to know the most important people and places in the camp. One of those places was a hut fitted out as a cinema. When so many soldiers were living cut off from the outside world in a forest, they had to be provided with a bit of variety if they were not to get stupid ideas. So a film was screened at eight every evening. They almost all welcomed the entertainment, and so many people went to the cinema that the room soon had to be extended.

Only Hitler himself never went. He had the newsreels shown to him and censored them, but he never watched a feature film, not even the first showing of a German movie.[15] However, it was while watching the films that I got to know a number of gentlemen who were really nothing to do with me, but who were members of Hitler's closest circle. Above all, I met his doctors, Professor Morell[16] and Professor Brandt,[17] who wasn't there so often. The former was a specialist in internal medicine and Hitler's physician, the latter a surgeon and the Führer's attendant doctor. Later he was Reich Health Commissioner.

These two men were about as unlike each other as you can imagine, and I shall have to keep a special chapter to describe them. Besides them, it was mostly the journalists who came to see the films: Reich Press Chief Dietrich,[18] who had a very mousy look and made a totally innocuous, insignificant, colourless impression, and his colleague Heinz Lorenz,[19] a born newspaperman, witty, charming, clever – and usually in civilian clothing. You weren't so likely to see the generals, because military briefings usually took place at this time of day, but sometimes you heard Martin Bormann's loud, booming laughter. His name was on all the orders and directives about the organization and management of the camp, but we seldom saw him personally. A thick-set, bull-necked man, he was one of the best-known and most feared figures in the Reich, although he spent almost all his time at his desk in the bunker, working hard from morning to night to carry out his Führer's orders.

The liaison officer Walther Hewel was really very nice. I first noticed him at a visit to the cinema because he had such a hearty, happy laugh and his cheerfulness infected the whole audience. I later met him in the Führer's company quite often, and I shall have a chance to describe him in more detail later.

Once we were watching that very touching German film called *Mutterliebe* [Motherly Love]. It was so moving that it affected our tear ducts more than our laughing muscles. But I was very surprised to see two older men in floods of tears at the end of the film. They looked so tough that I wouldn't have expected them to be easily affected. I asked my neighbour, Heinz Linge, who these tender-hearted officers were, and was told that they were the head of the security service, SS-Oberführer Rattenhuber,[20] and Detective Superintendent Högl.[21] They were in charge of the security of the Führer and the camp, but I felt it wouldn't be very hard to make them believe any sob-story. Anyway, my visits to the cinema brought me into contact with a great many new people, and after that I always had company at mealtimes and afternoon coffee in the mess. The remarkable thing about conversations with all these people was that they never discussed politics and all the stirring events affecting Germany and the rest of the world, and if they did mention the war, all you heard was words of confidence, expressing their certainty of victory and their absolute belief in the Führer. And behind all these conversations was something that everyone thought was his own personal conviction – but most likely it was really Hitler's influence.

I had come into these surroundings with so few preconceived ideas and prejudices that I soaked up the positive mood of this atmosphere like a baby taking in its mother's milk. Since the end of the war I've often wondered how I could possibly have felt no reservations at all at the time, in the company of these people. And then, when I remember that the barrier and the barbed wire also cut us off from all doubts, rumours and differences of political opinion outside, I realize that I had no standards of comparison and could not have felt any conflict. When I began working for the Führer, in fact right after that first dictation, Julius Schaub had told me I was not to discuss my work with anyone, and I knew that such orders were incumbent on everyone else too, from an orderly to a field marshal.

By now two months had passed. I'd settled in well and had made some friends. The time passed at a peaceful, regular pace, until one day I noticed unusual agitation in the morning.

Orderlies were hurrying in and out of the Führer bunker, cars drove through the camp, and finally the orderly on duty in the Führer bunker summoned me to Julius Schaub. He acted in a very mysterious way when I entered his office.

He gave me the manuscript of an itinerary and explained that the Führer had to fly to the Eastern Front, and it was very, very secret. He probably wished I could type out the pages without reading them. I hurried away to type this important document. It contained the orders for the column of motor vehicles and the pilots, as well as all the other people who were going.

That was how I found out that Hitler was planning to fly to Winniza on the Eastern Front to visit the Army Group there. Only a small company was to accompany him: one valet, two orderlies, his physician, the adjutants of the various Wehrmacht departments, and several other people that I can't remember now. My own name was not on the list.

In the afternoon the Führer bunker was empty. It was strange the way peace and quiet suddenly fell over the whole camp. As if the engine of the entire power plant had suddenly been switched off. I realized for the first time [. . .] how Hitler's personality was the driving force behind all these people. The puppet-master who held the strings of the marionettes in his hands had suddenly let them drop.

Today I know that it was only by a mysterious dispensation of Providence that he was ever able to pick those strings up again – because there was an explosive device in the plane bringing Hitler back from the Eastern Front, and if it had gone off it would have blown it into thousands of fragments.

As it was, when I woke up in the morning three days later the whole team was back, and Hitler never knew that his life had been hanging by the thinnest of threads during that flight.

Life in the Wolf's Lair went on as usual, but only for a few days. Then I had to type out another itinerary, and this time not only was my name on the list, but so were those of the other secretaries. The whole staff was moving to Berchtesgaden on the Obersalzberg, where Hitler was planning to relax for a while at his house, the Berghof, and also hold important state receptions.

So at the end of March 1943 I was present as the vast apparatus set off to move house. We were to stay at the Berghof for several weeks, and it was amazing how calmly and easily all the preparations were made within a very short time.

We secretaries packed our cases with our personal possessions, but we also had to take our travelling office with us. The Führer might easily decide to write something during the journey, and we must have the proper equipment on the train. So we packed two Silenta typewriters, two that typed nothing but capital letters, and one typewriter for speeches, with characters almost a centimetre high that made it easier for Hitler to read the manuscript of a speech aloud. They travelled in cases specially made for them, because there was no typewriter at the Berghof. A big case like a wardrobe with lots of little drawers and compartments contained the stationery and other office material we would need.

We had to make sure we packed some of all the different kinds of notepaper, because we could be sure that if we had forgotten any sort it would be just the one that was wanted. For instance, there was the stationery that Hitler used in his capacity as head of state for all personal letters. The paper was white with the national emblem of the eagle and swastika on the top left-hand corner, and the words 'Der Führer' printed under it in gold. For his private correspondence, he used paper which looked very much the same except that his name, 'Adolf Hitler', stood under the national emblem. And we also had to take the embossed stationery for Party business, just in case, and some sheets of paper for military matters with ordinary black letterheads. It's true that we never had to take down letters for those last two areas of work, because for Party business or military affairs Hitler passed on his instructions and orders through Bormann or Keitel[23] or one of the other military commanders. But even on the journey someone might need our supplies of stationery, and each of us had to make sure she had the working equipment she needed all packed up and travelling with her.

The people who had most work to do were the young SS adjutants Fritz Darges[24] and Otto Günsche.[25] They had to organize the journey, getting the vehicles ready, telling everyone what to do, fixing the train's itinerary and time of departure, giving instructions to those who were staying behind. Everything had to be done as fast and in as much secrecy as possible. The telephones were in constant use: the administrators at the Berghof had to be told when we were arriving, the Führer's apartment in Munich had to be prepared for him, and not least the special train, even though it was always kept near Hitler and ready to leave, had to be prepared for a long journey carrying many passengers.

We were to leave at 21.30 hours. The whole company was ready on time. Each of us had been told our carriage and compartment number in advance, then Hitler's car with his valet, his escort and the dog drove up, the Führer boarded the train, and it immediately started moving. It was a clear, mild winter night as we quietly steamed away in secret. We were soon out of the snowbound forest that looked so festive. I stood at the dark window of my compartment, looking out at the wide, peaceful landscape. I almost felt sorry to leave, and I was rather apprehensive about the new experiences ahead. Yet again I faced something that was strange to me.

I went out into the corridor. The train was moving so gently and peacefully that you hardly noticed it. I didn't feel as if I were on a journey at all. Headquarters had simply moved, taking its atmosphere with it.

When I was staying in my little compartment in the guest car while I waited to be introduced to Hitler, I had never forgotten that I was in a stationary train. Now the little cabin had suddenly become a small room like any other. In fact it was more luxurious than many other rooms!

The bed could be turned into a modern couch with lovely comfortable cushions during the day. The bedspread was made of silk, a different colour for each compartment – mine had brightly coloured flowers on a pale beige background. The walls were panelled with beautiful polished wood, and there was hot and cold water on tap in the washbasin at any time of day. There was a brass lamp on the little table at the window, a wall telephone hung over the head of the bed, so that you could get in touch with the other compartments, and there was a convenient reading lamp too. The floors of all the carriages had velour carpets.

The two guest carriages were next to the dining car that did duty as the officers' mess. Then there were carriages for the Führer's staff, his escort, the radio and teleprinter operators, the guards and the orderlies. Finally you reached the saloon car, which was furnished like a conference room. This was where the military conferences took place at the big table made of valuable wood. The chairs had red leather upholstery, and you could switch on sophisticated lighting everywhere. In the past receptions were often held in this car, and it was shown to state visitors as a sight especially worth seeing. There were a gramophone and a radio here too, but they were never in use while I worked for Hitler.

Hitler's private compartments were in the next carriage. Even here he didn't have to do without his own bathroom, although the train had a special carriage with showers and hipbaths in it. I never went into Hitler's two compartments, nor even took a look inside.

On those explorations of the train which had helped me to amuse myself while I waited after my first arrival, I had never been further than up to these private compartments of Hitler's, which ended in a dining and sitting room. But I think I remember that there were only a few other carriages between his and the engine, for the railway staff and above all the anti-aircraft crew. The train also carried several light anti-aircraft guns to protect us from low-flying fighters. As far as I know, they never fired a shot except in practice.

So now we were rolling through the night all the way across Germany, with every comfort you can possibly hope for on a train journey. I couldn't help thinking what other trains now travelling through the German landscape at the same time might be like: cold and unlit, full of people who didn't have enough to eat or anywhere comfortable to sit — and I suddenly had quite an uneasy feeling.[26] It was all right fighting a war if you didn't feel any of the ill effects yourself. Personally I had never known or seen such luxury before, even in peacetime. And when I saw the men of the government, the general staff and Hitler's entourage sitting or standing about smoking and drinking, in a good mood and pleased with life, I could only hope that their hard work and all their efforts would really help to bring the war to an end as quickly as possible. It occurred to me that those strenuous efforts might be the only way they could reconcile it with their consciences to live such a life of luxury, when ordinary people were suffering. These thoughts were still occupying my mind when there was a knock on the door of my compartment. One of the orderlies from the Führer bunker put his head round the door and told me that the Führer wanted me to dine with him.

I had had a healthy appetite before, but now I didn't feel at all hungry. I jumped up and hurried, first, to Fräulein Wolf in the next compartment, to ask if she was invited too. She said she was, and added that when the Führer was travelling he usually took his meals with a few ladies and gentlemen. Of course I was worried about my wardrobe, and asked what you wore on such an occasion. Almost everything I had was casual wear, sweaters and suits. She soothed my fears and said I didn't have to change and there was nothing for me to worry about, it was all quite innocuous.

I went back into my compartment, washed my hands, hastily powdered my nose, even put on a little rouge so that no one would see how pale my nervousness had made me, and trotted off with my two colleagues Fräulein Wolf and Fräulein Schroeder to the Führer's carriage. [. . .] It was only natural, naive and self-conscious as I was at the time, for me to feel rather weak at the knees as I made my way along the corridor of the special train to eat my first state meal.

A small table had been laid for about six people in the Führer's saloon car. Hitler himself wasn't there yet. I looked at the table settings and was relieved to find nothing unusual. There was no item of cutlery that I couldn't identify. I knew that Hitler was a vegetarian, and wondered whether everyone else had to go without meat too. I was about to ask Fräulein Schroeder when more of the guests came in. Professor Morell, who had just appeared in the doorway, must have found that quite difficult. The doors of any train, even the Führer's special train, were meant for people of an ordinary build, but the circumference of the man now trying to get through the door was so vast that I was afraid the frame would burst apart. I had already seen Hitler's physician quite often from a distance, but I hadn't realized that he was quite so fat.

The liaison officer Walther Hewel, who followed him, wasn't exactly slim either, but he was so tall and well proportioned that he looked good. Hewel's easy manner helped me to stop feeling self-conscious. He told a couple of Rhineland stories, switched on more lights so that, as he said, we could see what we were eating, and finally joked that if Hitler didn't turn up soon and begin the meal he was going to eat the sandwiches he'd brought.

We were all standing in what little space the table left free. It was quite cramped, and the staff had to push their way past behind the chairs. I was about to ask Fräulein Schroeder where I was to sit when Hitler appeared with Schaub and Reichsleiter Bormann. As he had already been talking to the gentlemen he shook hands only with us ladies, and asked us to sit down. He sat at the narrow end of the table, with Fräulein Wolf on his right and Fräulein Schroeder on his left, then came Hewel and Bormann with me between them, and finally Morell was seated — with some difficulty — at the other end of the table opposite Schaub.

It was all simple and casual. The orderlies and Linge immediately brought in trays of dishes and platters. Linge served the Führer creamed potatoes and fried eggs, and put a glass of

Fachinger mineral water by his plate. Hitler ate crispbread with this meal.

I don't now remember what the orderlies gave the rest of us. I was fully occupied watching and paying attention. I didn't eat much anyway. Professor Morell, however, had an appetite to match his girth, and expressed his relish audibly as well as visibly.

During the meal there was general small talk; I dared not join in unless someone asked me a direct question. Hitler was a very friendly, agreeable host to his female guests. He told us to help ourselves, asked if we would like anything else, and talked cheerfully and with a certain humour about earlier journeys in this train, and his dog, and he cracked jokes about his colleagues.

I was very surprised by the free and easy nature of the conversation. Bormann in particular was quiet and friendly and didn't by any means give the impression of being such a mighty and terrifying figure as I had gathered from hearsay. The Führer talked in a quiet, low voice, and after we had finished eating asked for the ceiling lights to be switched off. He preferred a dim light because of his sensitive eyes. Now there was only a table lamp on, the train was swaying with a regular, rocking rhythm, and Professor Morell drowsed quietly off without anyone noticing. I couldn't get over my amazement. Coffee and biscuits were served, quite late. Hitler drank caraway tea, and said it was delicious. He kindly urged Fräulein Schroeder to try it, but she wasn't to be persuaded. We sat together quite a while longer. I listened to every word Hitler said, but today I can't remember what he talked about. Later I shared many meals with Hitler and heard countless conversations, so I can't recollect the details of this one. That first evening was quite an experience for me because it was all so new. It wasn't what Hitler said that was important to me, but the way he said it and how he expressed his essential nature.

Sometimes the train stopped briefly at a station. Then the news officers were hard at work on the phone lines, making important connections. Now and then the valet or one of the

Wehrmacht adjutants came in with a message. The Führer never forgot that Blondi would need to go out, and would tell Linge to take the dog out of the train next time it stopped. Hitler called everyone simply by his surname, without any title. He would say, for instance: 'Linge, take Blondi out.' And then, after a while, he asked: 'What's the time, Bormann?' It was about one-thirty in the morning. He asked Schaub again what time we would reach Munich next day, and rang for his valet. The conversation was over, and it looked as if we were to disperse. Linge had to go and find out if there were any reports of air raids, and when he came back to say there weren't Hitler rose, shook hands with everyone and withdrew.

Suddenly I wasn't tired any more. The coffee had woken me up. We all went back to our compartments, but stopped in the dining car to smoke a quick cigarette, and I sat for a while with Hewel and Lorenz. Then I went to bed and slept until the sound of footsteps hurrying up and down the corridor woke me. When I raised the blackout blinds I saw the sun shining on snow-covered trees. We were going to reach Munich about twelve noon.

It was nine o'clock now. I quickly dressed and went to have breakfast. People were talking about the Berghof and Eva Braun. She was to join the train in Munich and travel on to the Berghof with us. Of course I was tremendously interested in her and her relationship with Hitler. Junge, with whom I was getting on very well – I liked his company – told me she was mistress of the Berghof, and tacitly accepted as such by all the guests there. I should be prepared, he said, for the fact that the Berghof was the Führer's private house, and we must all consider ourselves his guests and would be eating with him. However, 'all' meant quite a small circle; the rest of the staff would be staying in the buildings near and around the Berghof, and the Reich Chancellery and Wehrmacht leadership departments were quartered in Berchtesgaden.

First, however, we were to spend a day in Munich. I could hardly bear to sit still any more. We were approaching our journey's end, and I was looking forward so much to seeing my family again. I hadn't been home for six months. At last we steamed into Munich Central station, and the train came to a halt without a jolt, as smoothly as it had brought us all this way. The train carrying the rest of the staff that had left headquarters in East Prussia about half an hour before us was standing empty and deserted at the next platform. When the passengers got out of the guest carriages and went through the barrier there was no sign of the Führer. He had left the train first, got straight into his car and was driven away.

There was no other barrier, and no soldiers on guard or crowds of people either. Hitler had gone to his private rooms on Prinzregentplatz, and I hurried to see my mother so that at last I could tell her in person everything that had happened to me. She wasn't at all enthusiastic, and I think she would much rather I'd stayed in a modest little job in Munich and known none of this excitement and magnificence. Her maternal instincts saw all kinds of dangers lying in wait for me, some of them moral but some life-threatening. However, I had plunged headlong into the whirl of events without a thought, happy to have escaped the boring life of an office worker and hungry for experience.

The day passed quickly, and I had to go back to the station that evening. We set off again quietly when darkness had fallen. I didn't catch sight of the Führer again until we reached Liefering, a little place near Salzburg. There I was just in time to see the lights of the black Mercedes driving away fast towards the Obersalzberg, a long column of cars behind it, with the other secretaries and me in them too. We were driving towards the silhouettes of the mountain peaks, and soon the road, which was deep in snow, began winding uphill. A long line of headlights made its way forward at a thousand metres above sea level. At last the Berghof came in sight. The big building lay in darkness, with only the window of the Great Hall shining faintly in the light reflected from the snow.

III

FIRST IMPRESSIONS OF THE BERGHOF

Hitler had arrived just before us and had already disappeared into his rooms. His coat and cap were hanging on one of the hooks in the hall. We were welcomed by Frau Mittlstrasser,[27] housekeeper of the Berghof. She was a pretty, determined little woman, a native of Munich, and I had heard that she was very capable. She took the new arrivals to their rooms, and led us secretaries too along a broad, spacious corridor to a small flight of steps, leading to the rooms where Fräulein Schroeder and I were staying. We were right up under the roof in two little rooms of the old Haus Wachenfeld, which had belonged to Hitler's sister[28] and later became the Berghof. Everything had been modernized and improved. Mine was a delightful, feminine little bedroom decorated in pale blue and white, with a toilet mirror, a little desk and a lovely bed. Fräulein Schroeder was next door in a rather larger room, decorated in red. We shared a bathroom opposite our rooms, and one of the chambermaids had a bedroom next to it. Those were the parts of the Berghof that I saw that evening.

I had really been looking forward to seeing the mountains at close quarters. I came from Munich myself, but I'd never before had an opportunity to go up into the mountains. But when I woke next morning and made haste to draw back the curtains and admire the famous landscape, I was disappointed to see nothing but a dense wall of mist and clouds, no trace of any mountain peaks. Sad to say, I discovered that these natural phenomena were among the principal features of the area, at least most of the time we were staying there.

But for the moment I was kept busy finding my way round the interior of the Berghof. Surely there must be breakfast somewhere? No one had told me where or how you got it here. So I stole down the stairs up which I had climbed so heedlessly the previous evening. Halfway down I found the door of another room, and behind it I heard the voice of General Schmundt, the chief Wehrmacht adjutant.[29] The last bend in the stairs brought me to a forecourt on the ground floor. On the left there was a door with glass panes in it, on the right a side door out into the courtyard. The glazed door led to a farmhouse-style living room with a big green tiled stove. I shut it again on seeing nothing that looked like breakfast. There was no one in sight, and I felt a little uncomfortable. I didn't know if I might not suddenly land in Hitler's study or somewhere. The forecourt narrowed and became a wide corridor with light falling in through the windows. I turned the corner and was in the big entrance hall again. On my left I noticed a very large semi-circular double door. Judging by its position, it must lead into the famous Great Hall that I knew from picture postcards. The broad corridor led past the flight of marble steps and straight to another double door. Here I finally heard voices. No one had remembered that this was my first time here, so I would have to find the way to the dining room on my own. Well, at last I'd succeeded.

The long room lay to the left of the front entrance. It occupied a large part of the left wing that had been built on when the whole Berghof was extended to make it an official residence. The broad side of the room had windows going almost up to the ceiling, with a fine view of the Salzburger Land. The long table surrounded by armchairs stood in the middle of the room. It could seat about twenty-four people. At its far end the room broadened out into a semi-circular bay. Here stood another big table, a round one, laid for breakfast. The only decoration of the dining room was the beautiful grain of the arolla pine of which the wall panelling, the furniture, even the wooden chandeliers over the table and the wall lamps were made. The wall opposite the windows contained a built-in sideboard with glass doors. Some valuable vases added a touch of colour to the golden yellow of the wood.

We were a small party at breakfast. My colleague Fräulein Schroeder was already in her place, and told me a little severely that she had finished breakfast. Apparently I'd got up late. But no one had woken me and told me the customs of the house. The other people at breakfast were General Schmundt, Captain von Puttkamer[30] the naval adjutant, and Walter Frentz[31] the photoreporter from Führer headquarters. No one else was present. There was tea, coffee and cocoa, and if you wanted it fruit juice. A choice of different breads such as crispbread, wholemeal bread and ordinary black bread was available, but white bread was only for people with delicate stomachs. Everyone had a little piece of butter weighing ten grams, already put out on the plates. And there was jam. Since you mustn't smoke in the Führer's rooms, the company left the breakfast table very quickly to go and enjoy their usual breakfast cigar or cigarette. After that I went for a walk with Fräulein Schroeder and Otto Günsche, to get to know the Berghof and my new surroundings.

We began by climbing the broad flight of steps to the first floor. I wanted to know where the Führer lived. A very broad corridor was almost like a great hall itself – not only because of the big windows, but especially on account of the valuable pictures on the walls. Precious old masters, fine sculptures, exotic vases and presents from foreign statesmen made you feel you were in a museum. It was all beautiful, but strange and impersonal. If it hadn't been for the thick carpets that muted our footsteps we would have gone on tiptoe of our own accord. All was perfectly quiet, for Hitler was still asleep.

The first door to the left of the stairs led to a small two-roomed apartment with a bathroom where the valet on duty and the chauffeur had their quarters, and opposite, on the right-hand side of the corridor, Eva Braun's maids had a little ironing room. Outside the next door, looking as if they were cast in bronze, sat two black Scotch terriers, one on the right and one on the left. The mistress of the house's doorkeepers. They sat motionless in their place until she woke and Stasi and Negus could say good morning to her. The next room was Hitler's bedroom. There was a large bathroom between their two rooms, with no other way into it from outside. This took up the whole length of the corridor. The double door at the far end led to Hitler's study. I did not go in on that occasion, but tiptoed past.

Opposite Eva Braun's room a few steps [. . .] led to the passage from the original Haus Wachenfeld to the great Berghof building. At the end of this passage we went downstairs again and entered the living room that I had already seen briefly that morning.

There was no one about apart from a few orderlies who had some task or other to carry out. The whole house might have been uninhabited. I learned that I was now in what had once been Hitler's living room. It was well but not grandly furnished and no different from any ordinary middle-class sitting room. In fact it was the only room that had a certain feeling of comfort about it. The green tiled stove with the bench running round it looked an inviting place to sit. There was a rectangular table by the broad window, with a wooden bench at the corner. The tablecloth was made of the same brightly patterned rustic linen as the curtains and the cushion covers on the bench. On the other side of the window stood a large bookcase. Here again there were no startling books. An encyclopaedia in many volumes, some classics of world literature which didn't look as if they had been read, the comic verse of Wilhelm Busch, a series of travel writings, and of course *Mein Kampf* bound in leather. Anyone could borrow a book from this library; none of them were banned. To the right, opposite the window, a heavy velvet curtain separated the living room from the Great Hall. I just took a fleeting glance in and got the same impression as I'd already had from the coloured picture postcards: it was very big and very grand, monumental, like everything the Führer built, but cold, in spite of the thick carpets, the magnificent tapestries and all the precious things adorning the walls and the furnishings. Even later, when I spent many evenings sitting beside the great hearth of the hall by candlelight, that feeling never entirely left me. I think the room was too large and the people in it too small to fill it entirely.

But the winter garden you had to cross to reach the terrace from the living room was very much to my taste. Best of all, there were a great many flowers in it, as well as pale, deep, softly upholstered armchairs and sofas with small round tables. The whole room was at most three by three metres in size, and two of the walls were all glass.

The best thing about the whole Berghof, however, was the terrace. It was a large, square space paved with slabs of Solnhofer stone, and it had a stone balustrade. When the mist lifted you could see Salzburg castle in the distance on the gentle rise of its hill, with the sun shining on it, and down below on the other side lay Berchtesgaden surrounded by the peaks of the Watzmann, the Hoher Göll and the Steinernes Meer. Directly opposite rose the Untersberg. In clear weather you could see the cross on top of it with the naked eye. The terrace ran all round the winter garden up to the living-room window, and then turned into a small paved courtyard going all along the back of the building. The rising rock of the mountainside made a natural wall for it.

I could reach the adjutants' office through the back door of the Berghof or over the terrace. A little cottage with two storeys nestled against the rock wall right beside the west side of the main building. Its ground floor was a small room for Hewel the liaison officer and for use as a press office, and the upper floor was used by whichever chief adjutant was on duty – either Gruppenführer Bormann or Obergruppenführer Schaub – and was a charming apartment in the rustic style consisting of a living room, bedroom and bathroom. An old wooden outside staircase led up to it. This staircase looked very picturesque, but it could be dangerous in rainy weather or snow. A long, low wooden building stood next to the cottage, and contained various functional rooms. The first of these was our office. It was a plain, ugly room, only sparsely furnished.

I never did find out just why this room had been given such perfunctory treatment. Perhaps because Hitler himself had never set foot in it. In addition, it was rather dark inside, because an open gallery covered by a wooden roof ran all the way along the building. It was a pretty sight, with its columns and brightly coloured flower containers, but it didn't let a single ray of sunlight into the rooms. Next to the office was the dental surgery. When necessary, Professor Blaschke[32] from Berlin practised his trade here with his assistants and a dental nurse. The little room was equipped with the most modern dental tools and equipment, because while he was staying in the mountains Hitler generally took the chance to get his teeth seen to. The barber had a room in this building too, but he had to put up with very makeshift equipment. Finally, there was a fairly large dormitory for the soldiers of the guard, and then came the garden wall with the gate up to the guesthouse. A guard was posted here, and he insisted on seeing your pass whenever you wanted to come in or go out.

A broad paved road passed right at the foot of the Berghof, winding up out of the valley in sinuous curves and going on to the Türken,[33] the Platterhof,[34] Bormann's house and the barracks. On the other side of the road a magical landscape extended, its hills softly rolling. No gardener could have created a more beautiful design than Nature herself had done here. Meadows, woods and mountain streams made it into a natural park. Only the well-tended footpaths and a small paved road running through it showed that mankind had any hand in the design. This was the Führer's 'exercise run', as his entourage called the area. Hidden behind trees, and invisible from the Berghof, was a little tea-house that Hitler visited almost daily. [. . .]

In spite of these beauties, which I appreciated so much, I didn't feel comfortable in the atmosphere of the Berghof. We were treated like guests but we weren't there of our own free will, we were still employees. Only the men who could bring their families with them, or at least put their wives up in Berchtesgaden or the country around it, were pleased when headquarters moved to this southern part of Germany. But even their happiness wasn't complete, because although they knew their families were within reach they could very seldom take time off for their private lives. Only those who had set periods of duty and were not indissolubly bound to the Führer's daily life really enjoyed the Berghof. Everyone else was stuck with Hitler's irregular, strenuous yet very monotonous daily timetable.

In the morning the building was quiet, as if abandoned. There was a certain amount of life only in the domestic premises and the adjutancy building. Activity really began only at noon. Then cars came roaring up the road, bringing generals and military officers for the conference. The peaceful terrace was full of men in uniform who were dying for a cigar or cigarette and so preferred to stay out in the open air. The aides-de-camp would be waiting in the little winter garden with maps and briefcases, by now the phones were ringing all the time, and only when the Führer appeared did people go back inside the house. The Great Hall with its gigantic windows, a room that really seemed to be meant for peaceful, sociable gatherings and witty conversations, became the scene of violent arguments, sober calculations, and life-and-death decisions.

By now those who had nothing to do with the military briefing and were hoping for lunch were gradually turning up. Dr Dietrich and Lorenz came down from the guesthouse, Drs Morell and Brandt and the second of the Führer's attendant doctors, Dr von Hasselbach,[35] also appeared. After a few days the company was enlivened by the arrival of several ladies. The regular guests included Frau Brandt, Frau von Below the wife of the Luftwaffe adjutant, Frau Schneider,[36] who was a friend of Eva Braun, and Gretl Braun, Eva's sister.

During the conference, however, no one could enter the Hall, so you had to hang around outside somewhere or stay in your room until you were summoned. Unfortunately, Hitler himself never seemed to feel hungry, and he sometimes entirely forgot that he had a crowd of guests waiting for lunch, drinking vermouth after vermouth to soothe their rebellious stomachs. So it was sometimes three or four in the afternoon before the last uniformed officers had finally left his side and the last car had driven away again.

Then Hitler came down the few steps from the Great Hall and entered the living room, where a hungry company was assembled. It was usually at this moment that Eva Braun appeared, announced by the yapping of her two black companions. Hitler would go up to her, kiss her hand, and shake hands with everyone he had not already seen at the conference. It was at an occasion of this kind that I first saw Eva Braun and was introduced to her. She was very well dressed and groomed, and I noticed her natural, unaffected manner. She wasn't at all the kind of ideal German girl you saw on recruiting posters for the BDM or in women's magazines. Her carefully done hair was bleached, and her pretty face was made up – quite heavily but in very good taste. Eva Braun wasn't tall but she had a very pretty figure and a distinguished appearance. She knew just how to dress in a style that suited her, and never looked as if she had overdone it – she always seemed appropriately and tastefully dressed, although she wore valuable jewellery.

When I first saw her she was wearing a Nile-green dress of heavy woollen fabric. Its top fitted closely, and it had a bell-shaped skirt with a broad leopardskin edging at the hem. The pretty way she walked made the skirt swing gracefully. The dress had close-fitting sleeves, with two gold-coloured clips at its sweetheart neckline – I don't know if they were real gold. She was addressed as 'gnädiges Fräulein', and the ladies called her Fräulein Braun. Frau Brandt and Frau von Below seemed to be very friendly with her, and she immediately began a very feminine, natural conversation with them about their children, the latest fashions, dogs and anecdotes of personal experiences.

Frau Schneider, whom Eva called Herta, was an old school-friend of hers and almost always in her company in Munich too. It was her two little girls who were so often photographed with Eva Braun that many people thought they were hers.

The waiting time before lunch passed in easy conversation. Hitler talked to Eva, teased her about her dogs, which he said were nothing but a couple of dusting brushes, whereupon she replied that Blondi wasn't a dog at all but a calf. I was surprised to find that the man who had just come from a military briefing had left all his serious, official thoughts behind the heavy curtain that separated the Great Hall from the living room. His expression was that of any ordinary genial host welcoming company to his country house.

At last Linge came in, went up to Frau Brandt and said, 'Gnädige Frau, the Führer will escort you to the table.' An orderly told the other guests what the seating plan was, and then Linge stepped up to the Führer and announced: 'My Führer, lunch is ready.'

Hitler, who had also been told ahead of time whom he would be taking in, went ahead with Frau Brandt, Eva Braun took Reichsleiter Bormann's arm — this seating plan never varied — and then the other couples followed, going along a wide corridor, round the corner and into the dining room.

The Führer sat in the middle of the broad side of the table facing the window, with Eva Braun on his left, and then Reichs- leiter Bormann. Opposite Hitler and Eva Braun sat either the guest of honour or the highest-ranking officer present with his lady.

I had the head of the Reich press office as my neighbour at table. He was in civilian clothes, and his dark blue suit made him look even more inconspicuous than his uniform. I was bracing myself, expecting him to start a highly intellectual conversation, but he asked, 'Have you ever been on the Obersalzberg before?' When I said that although I came from Munich I didn't know the mountains at all well, he seemed to be as much struck by this information as if I had told him I came from the moon. Then he described the beauty of the area to me at length, and told me about any number of good walks, but unfortunately they remained a mystery to me because I didn't know a single one of the places or paths he mentioned. But at least during this unexciting conversation I had a chance to observe the lunch ceremony.

There was a beautiful flower arrangement in the middle of the long table. The Führer never had flowers, branches of foliage or anything like that in his rooms at his headquarters. But here at the Berghof there was a woman in charge of the household, and you could feel her feminine touch. The table was laid with Rosenthal china, with a hand-painted flower pattern on a white background. A cruet set with oil, vinegar, salt and pepper — and toothpicks! – stood at the top of the table and another at the bottom. Beside each place there was a napkin in a paper bag with the guest's name on it.

As soon as the party had sat down at the table and unfolded their napkins the door to the domestic wing opened and a row of orderlies came in. Two were carrying stacks of plates. The others took away the plates already in front of us on the table and replaced them with the new, warm plates. Soon the meal was served. Junge brought in a tray with the Führer's lunch, two orderlies brought large dishes of various salads for each side of the table and began serving down both sides from the middle. Two others asked what we would like to drink. The salad seemed to be a kind of starter, because everyone began eating it at once. But then the next course appeared too: braised beef marinated in vinegar and herbs, with creamed potatoes and young beans. This first menu I ate at the Berghof has stuck in my mind because I was greatly relieved to find that we didn't all have to follow the Führer's diet. I'd have had to be very ill, I'm sure, to subsist on gruel, linseed mush, muesli and vegetable juice of my own free will. During meals Hitler himself often mentioned his difficulty in getting decent vegetarian dishes. He had a delicate stomach, although later I came to believe that much of his illness was nervous or imaginary. Here on the Obersalzberg Hitler ate the diet food of the Zabel sanatorium, quite a well-known nursing home in Berchtesgaden where Professor Zabel provided the same kind of diet as Professor Bircher-Benner of Switzerland. When Hitler was at the Berghof a cook came in from the sanatorium to cook for him. He had a peculiar passion for unrefined linseed oil. For instance, he loved to eat baked potatoes with curd cheese and would pour unrefined linseed oil over them.

Eva Braun had only contemptuous pity for this diet. I should think nothing would have persuaded her to try the Führer's food. However, she too claimed to have a weak stomach and ate very little, nothing but easily digestible dishes and not much fat. Sometimes she drank bitters after the meal. But when I came to know her better I thought that she ate sparingly mainly to keep her slim figure. She hated fat women, and was very proud of being slim and dainty. The Führer teased her about it. 'When I first met you, you were so nice and plump, and now you're positively skinny. All the ladies say they want to be beautiful for their menfolk, and then they do everything they can to be the opposite of what a man likes. They claim that they'd make any sacrifice to please him, but they're sacrificing themselves entirely to fashion. Fashion is the one and only power – the strongest of all. And other women are the only judges. All women just want to be the envy of their female friends.' Eva might protest vigorously, but she admitted that she most certainly didn't want to be any fatter.

Conversations at table were usually trivial and cheerful. Hitler talked about the pranks he had played at school and reminisced about the early struggles of the Party. He often teased his colleagues. Walther Hewel, the liaison officer from the Foreign Office, was a favourite butt. Hewel was still relatively young for his high rank, and unmarried. He was about forty years old. His pleasing charm, typical of a Rhinelander, made him popular. He had lived in India for years and had many amusing tales to tell of his time there. Hitler asked him, 'So when are you finally going to write your book *From Machete to Diplomatic Dagger*? But then you're no diplomat! More of a giant diplomatic cowboy!' The tall, dignified Hewel responded to this sally only with hearty laughter. 'If I weren't a diplomat I couldn't stand between you and Ribbentrop, my Führer,' he replied. Hitler had to acknowledge the truth of this, for he knew what a difficult character the Foreign Minister was. But the fact that Hewel was still unmarried made him the object of daily teasing. 'I expect you're looking for one of those Indian tree monkeys,' said Hitler. But seriously, the Führer really was looking out for a suitable wife for his favourite liaison officer. For a while those around him thought he wanted Hewel to marry Eva's sister Gretl Braun. But Hewel himself didn't fancy the idea. Later he was discreetly pointed in the direction of Ilsebill Todt, daughter of the late architect.[37] Hitler described Ilsebill as 'a beautiful girl', and was disappointed that this comment wasn't enough to convince Hewel.

The Führer also tried to put meat-eaters off their food at mealtimes. He didn't actually want to convert anyone to vegetarianism, but he would suddenly begin to talk about the horrors of an abattoir. 'One day, when headquarters was stationed in Ukraine, my men were to be shown the biggest, most modern of the local abattoirs. It was a fully modernized factory seeing the job right through from pig to sausage, including processing the bones, bristles and skin. Everything was so clean and neat, with pretty girls in high gumboots standing up to their calves in fresh blood. All the same, the meat-eating men felt unwell, and many of them left without seeing everything. I run no such risks. I can happily watch carrots and potatoes being pulled up, eggs collected from the henhouse and cows milked.'

It is true that most of these remarks were so familiar by now that they no longer spoiled anyone's appetite, but Hitler could always find a victim. The sensitive Reich press chief put down his knife and fork, turned pale, and claimed quietly, in muted tones, that he wasn't hungry any more. Sometimes this conversation was followed by a little philosophical discussion of human cowardice. There were so many things, said Hitler, that people couldn't do themselves, or couldn't even watch, but all the same they would happily reap the benefit.

Lunch usually lasted about an hour. Then the Führer brought the meal to a close to get ready for his walk. He liked the little tea-house in the grounds better than the actual walk there, which took him only twenty minutes, but if the weather was bad he often preferred to drive in the Volkswagen. The servants and orderlies asked all the guests if they were going for the walk. You didn't have to, and then you could use the time as you liked. But ladies were always in demand – there weren't so many female guests when we first arrived, and then for form's sake there must be enough gentlemen to make up a well-balanced party. Reichsleiter Bormann almost always pleaded pressure of work. For a compulsive worker like him these hours of private relaxation, when he couldn't talk business, were a waste of time.

Eva Braun, however, loved athletic pursuits and walking. She would get her outdoor clothes on immediately after lunch, take her two dogs and her friend Herta, and go a long way round on foot all through the grounds, joining the company at the coffee table later.

The Führer would put on his soft peaked cap – the only item of headgear that he didn't place upright on his head like a saucepan – with either a long black rain cape or a trench-coat over his uniform. Then he took his walking-stick and the dog's leash and set off along the path with one of the men. The rest of the party followed informally. Usually the Führer walked so slowly that some of those following caught up with him. Poor Blondi had to stay on her leash, because the grounds here were a paradise for game. The deer, rabbits and squirrels were very tame. They grazed in the meadows and took hardly any notice of passers-by. It seemed they had discovered that no shot would disturb their peace here, and that humans protected them and would put out food for them in winter. Eva Braun's black terriers sometimes raced through the tall grass on the hillsides yapping, and the deer grazing there would look at them pityingly and leap aside only when the dogs chasing them came very close.

The tea-house lay on a little plateau of rock falling steeply away on the north side. It was a natural look-out tower. Deep below, the river Ach flowed in many winding curves, and the houses on its banks looked like little matchboxes. There was also a view from here between the mountains all the way to Salzburg, blocked only on the left-hand side by the Steinernes Meer, the 'Stone Sea'. But that mighty colossus of rock was worth seeing for its own sake. In fine weather those to arrive first waited outside on a wooden bench until the whole party had assembled.

Usually Eva Braun brought her camera or cine-camera and tried to get the Führer in front of her lens. Admittedly she was the only person who could photograph him whenever she liked, but it was very difficult to get a good snapshot of him. He liked photos to be taken without any fuss or bother. But in fine weather, when the sun was shining, he always had his cap on, so that his face was in shadow, and he couldn't be induced to take it off because bright light dazzled him. He might even be wearing sunglasses. However, Eva put so much cunning and patience into her passion for photography that she often got good shots – better photos, in fact, than those taken by her former teacher and employer Heinrich Hoffmann.[38]

The tea-house was a round, stone building and looked ugly from the outside, rather like a silo or an electricity station. Inside, apart from the kitchen, a guardroom and the necessary anteroom and adjoining small offices, there was just one large, round room that you could enter either direct from outside or through a pretty entrance hall leading there from the kitchen quarters. There were some comfortable armchairs with flowered upholstery in this entrance hall, and little tables. A telephone stood here too.

This big, round room was an architectural masterpiece. The ceiling was slightly vaulted, the walls were made of marble picked out in gilt contrasts. Half of the wall had six large windows with a view of the beautiful landscape. On the western side of the room lay the big, open hearth and the entrance door. A huge, low, round table filled the middle of the room. Around it were about twenty deep armchairs, upholstered in alternating beige and terracotta. On the hearth side of the room were four very large chairs with high backs for the Führer and his guests of honour. The staff would have been told in advance of the Führer's arrival, and the aroma of coffee already filled the house. The table was laid, and coffee was served as soon as we came in. Hitler would seat himself in his armchair right in front of the hearth, with Eva Braun to his left. There was no strict seating plan here either, and Hitler might invite Frau Schneider to sit on his right. The others spread out as they liked around the table. Usually there were several empty places.

Most of us enjoyed a cup of coffee after our walk. Some people drank black tea. Hitler himself would have apple-peel tea or sometimes caraway tea, never anything else. He ate freshly baked apple cake with it, and perhaps a couple of biscuits. The rest of us were given pastries bought in Berchtesgaden, and some of them could be stale and hard to chew.

It was difficult to get a general conversation going here. Every discussion had to be either conducted loud enough for everyone to hear it, or be between groups or couples, leaving silence on the other side of the table.

Eva Braun would try to strike up some interesting, relaxing subject. She talked about the cinema and the theatre, and sometimes tried to persuade Hitler to watch some particularly good movie. 'You see, you can have it screened in the hall so easily, and this film is art too, it's not light, it's a very serious film. I mean, you listen to gramophone records, and I'm sure the German people would have no objection if their Führer saw a movie for once. In fact I'm sure the people would like your colleagues to go to the movies more instead of driving around in big, important-looking cars getting drunk.' Hitler would always reply, 'I can't watch films while the war is on, when the people have to make so many sacrifices and I must make such grave decisions. And I must save my sensitive eyes for reading maps and reports from the front.'

Resigned, Eva would drop the subject, suddenly saying that she had seen some lovely rugs here in the entrance hall, beautiful Scottish tartan, you could make a wonderful lady's coat out of them, and her dressmaker had a particularly nice pattern for a coat like that. 'The rugs belong to Bormann, they're not mine to dispose of,' was Hitler's evasive answer. Bormann was all-powerful here on the Obersalzberg, like a version of Rübezahl the wicked mountain spirit. He was administrator of the Platterhof and all the grounds around the Berghof, and was responsible for all technical arrangements, for the construction work now going on and the air-raid shelters. He had a model farm near the Berghof, where he bred pigs and horses, with a huge nursery garden and an apple-juice factory. But although he could be very jovial and good-humoured he wasn't popular here either. People feared him. Eva Braun never got the rugs for her coat.

Hitler used to say he slept very badly, and if everything wasn't perfectly quiet he couldn't sleep at all. But no sooner had the last piece of cake been eaten and the last cup of tea drunk than he would become monosyllabic, close his eyes — he said the reflections from the window panes dazzled him — and usually he soon dropped gently off to sleep.

No one bothered about that. The conversation went on, in muted tones. Eva turned to the company at large or whichever gentleman was sitting on her left. The young adjutants, pretending they had urgent phone calls to make, hurried out to inflict damage on their fit, strong bodies with nicotine, and by now Admiral von Puttkamer the naval adjutant, who was almost never seen without a cigar, would have been sitting for some time out in the kitchen with the guards on duty, wreathed in thick clouds of smoke.

Then Hitler would wake up, unnoticed, open his eyes and immediately join in whatever conversation was going on, as if he had merely closed his eyes while he was plunged in deep thought. No one disillusioned him. Then he asked, 'What's the time, Schaub?' Schaub didn't even have to look at his watch, for he was just counting the minutes until it was time to set out. 'Six o'clock exactly, my Führer, shall I have the car brought round?' And then he would limp out to order it faster than you would have thought possible on his crippled feet.

Hitler drove around the country near the Berghof in a Volkswagen. It was a specially made cabriolet, with black paint and leather upholstery. Apart from the Führer and his chauffeur, only his valet and Blondi ever travelled in it. Cars were available for the other guests, but most of them walked back. The last days of March 1943 were wonderfully fine, and exercise in the fresh air did us good after all that sitting about.

When the walkers got back to the Berghof Hitler would have retired to sleep until the evening military briefing. So all the guests were left to their own devices for a few hours. I usually went to my own room, wrote letters, or did my own private chores like sewing or washing clothes. Sometimes I went to

Berchtesgaden to visit friends who were stationed down there and couldn't come up to the Berghof.

Eva Braun used the hours while Hitler was asleep either to show the films she had taken with her cine-camera, screening them in her own room and inviting all the ladies and gentlemen from Hitler's entourage – I wasn't invited myself at first. Or she would often have professional feature films shown down in the basement in what was really a bowling alley. All the staff could watch these films. Some of them were foreign movies that couldn't be publicly shown. The department responsible at Führer headquarters got the rolls of film direct from the Ministry of Propaganda, and they included a number of German films that we saw before the censor did and were never passed for public screening.

The guests were then told individually, by phone, what time dinner would be. You could usually expect it to be about eight in the evening. Then the same ceremony as at lunchtime began again. The living room slowly filled up. The gentlemen were generally in civilian clothing, the ladies wore their best dresses. It was very difficult for me to compete in this fashion show. No one wore long evening dresses, but all the same Eva Braun was showing off a parade of elegant clothes.

I'd had so little chance to enjoy parties and elegance before the war that all my wardrobe was casual. Now I felt right out of place. Eva almost never wore the same dress twice, even when we spent weeks on the Obersalzberg, and she certainly never wore the same outfit at dinner as at lunch or in the tea-house. I couldn't help admiring her good taste again, and the clever way she made the most of her best points. She usually preferred dark colours, and liked to wear black best of all. Hitler's favourite dress was a heavy black silk one with a wide bell-shaped skirt, very close-fitting at the waist, sleeveless, with just two broad, straight shoulder straps in old rose, and two roses of the same colour in the deep square neckline. A short bolero jacket with long, close-fitting sleeves was part of this ensemble.

That reminds me that Hitler had a peculiar attitude to

women's fashions. Eva was devoted to her wardrobe and her appearance. She couldn't have borne not to have new, different clothes hanging in her wardrobe all the time. Hitler allowed her that pleasure, but he said, 'I don't know why you women have to keep changing your clothes. When I think a dress is particularly pretty then I'd like to see its owner wearing it all the time. She ought to have all her dresses made of the same material and to the same pattern. But no sooner have I got used to something pretty, and I'm feeling I haven't seen enough of it yet, than along comes something new.'

In the same way, Eva wasn't allowed to change her hairstyle. Once she appeared with her hair tinted slightly darker, and on one occasion she piled it up on top of her head. Hitler was horrified. 'You look totally strange, quite changed. You're an entirely different woman!' He wasn't at all happy with the change, and Eva Braun made haste to revert to the way she had looked before. He noticed changes in the appearance of all the other ladies too, and either admired or criticized them. Frau Schneider, who also appeared one day with her hair worn on top of her head, won Hitler's full approval. In this case he thought the change was a new look that pleased his eye.

Supper followed the same course as lunch. Usually there were platters of cold meats and salads, 'Hoppelpoppel', which was fried potatoes with eggs and meat, or noodles with tomato sauce and cheese. Hitler often had two fried eggs with creamed potatoes and tomato salad. The glasshouses in Martin Bormann's model nursery garden provided fresh fruit and vegetables all the year round, as well as garden produce for Führer headquarters, which went all the way from Bavaria back to East Prussia by air. Hitler thought he could digest only very fresh fruit and vegetables, but didn't want them to come from a market garden that he didn't know. Of course these consignments from the Obersalzberg were only for Hitler's personal consumption, but here on the Berghof in March the whole party was enjoying young cucumbers, radishes, mushrooms, tomatoes, and fresh green lettuce.

Hitler ate fast, and quite a lot. One day when I was sitting opposite him I noticed him watching me while the food was being served. 'You don't eat nearly enough, child, you're so thin anyway.' Eva Braun cast me a scornful glance, for compared to her I was the image of a buxom Bavarian rustic maiden. Hitler took this chance to launch into another conversation about the fashion for being slim. 'I don't know what's supposed to be so beautiful about women looking as thin as boys. It's just because they're differently built that we love them, after all. Things used to be quite different in the old days. In my time it was still a pleasure to go to the ballet because you saw lovely, well-rounded curves, but now you just get bones and ribs hopping about on stage. Goebbels was always trying to drag me off to dance events, but I went only a couple of times, and I was very disappointed. Since I've been Führer at least I don't have to pay for it any more. I get free tickets.' Of course he was exaggerating and caricaturing things in such conversations, but it was still a fact that he preferred definitely womanly figures to the boyish sort.

In light conversation over meals in an intimate circle, Hitler usually preferred trivial and totally non-political subjects. He could tell very charming, witty stories about his own youth, and most of all he liked a little mocking banter with the ladies. When he noticed the red imprint of Eva's lipstick on her napkin, he began telling us about the ingredients of that item of cosmetics. 'Do you know what lipstick is made of?' We thought it might be aphids – Frau Speer[39] said she had once heard something of that sort. And Eva Braun said she used a French lipstick, which she was sure was made of nothing but the finest ingredients. Hitler just gave us a pitying smile. 'If you only knew that in Paris, of all places, lipsticks are made of the fat skimmed off sewage, I'm sure no woman would paint her lips any more!' But we only laughed a little awkwardly. We knew his tactics from the 'meat-eater' conversations. He wanted to put us off something that he couldn't actually forbid us. Apart from Martin Bormann's wife, all the women met their Führer with carefully painted lips.

As the meal came to its end, the adjutants would rise to

receive the officers who had come for the briefing. Slowly, conversation died down. Cars drove up outside, soldiers' boots clattered over the stone flags in the entrance hall. Finally Günsche appeared and reported to the Führer that everything was ready for the conference. Hitler rose and said, 'Stay where you all are, it won't take long.' Then he would go out, stooping slightly, head bent but walking with a firm step. He didn't want his guests, particularly the ladies, to come into contact with the officers. Here on the Berghof he lived more of a double life than ever. On the one hand he was the genial host and master of the house visiting his country estate for rest and relaxation, on the other, even here, he was still the statesman and military supreme commander waging war on all fronts. Purely from the spatial point of view it was often difficult to reconcile these two opposites. The house wasn't divided into a private part and an official part, and Hitler's study was on the same corridor as Eva Braun's bedroom. So the guests had to be told when to go to bed in case they burst in on an important discussion.

We were left to amuse ourselves for an unspecified length of time after dinner. Sometimes Hitler did say, as he left the dining room, 'Wait for me here, the briefing won't take long today.' From that we deduced that neither the Reich Marshal nor any other high-up military commander was present to hear the reports, and we took that as a sign that the war was going relatively well for Germany. Fräulein Schroeder and I, as the two secretaries on duty, would go off to the adjutancy office to deal with any outstanding office work. It consisted mostly of air reports from all over Germany that had arrived by teleprinter and had to be typed out to be easy for the Führer to read. At the end of March the first good wishes and presents were also arriving for the Führer's birthday. Most of them went to Berlin, but some found their way to the Berghof or were sent on from the Berlin adjutancy office.

When there hadn't been enough time for a film between the visit to the tea-house and dinner, Eva Braun had the list of movies available brought to her after we had eaten and, with the other ladies and the gentlemen who weren't at the briefing, she chose a film to be screened in the bowling alley. 'Please tell me when the conference is over,' she would ask the orderlies, and then a small party of about eight to ten people would go down to the basement to watch a movie. We were a very critical, choosy audience. The kitchen staff, chambermaids and soldiers joined us, and if we were lucky we could watch the film through to the end. But sometimes the shrill sound of the telephone ringing would break into it. 'The conference is over and the Führer expects his guests in the Great Hall,' the servant said. Then, although regretfully, we cut the screening short, Eva Braun hurried briefly into her room to freshen her make-up, her sister Gretl swiftly looked for a corner where she could smoke a cigarette in peace and then popped a peppermint into her mouth, and finally everyone assembled in the living room again. The rather old-fashioned but cosy lamp hanging low over the corner table was on, and the Speer, Bormann and Brandt ladies would be sitting on the bench that ran around the corner talking about how their children were doing. The curtain to the Great Hall was still drawn, for Hitler was always detained after the official end of the briefing by one or other of the men who had been present and who wanted to put in a quick request, or discuss a problem for which there was no official opportunity.

By the time Hitler finally entered the living room it was usually midnight. Now we would just be waiting for the Braun sisters, then the Führer led the company down into the Hall for a nocturnal chat around the hearth. By now the fire in it had been lit. Broad sofas and deep armchairs had been drawn up in a large semi-circle, grouped around a big circular table, generally with some other, smaller tables off to the sides. Far to the back of the room, in the corner, a single standard lamp was switched on, and several candles flickered on the mantelpiece and in the middle of the table. You could see the shapes of the people sitting round it only indistinctly.

Hitler himself sat on the right, in deep shadow, and to the right of him, very close to the fire, Eva Braun nestled into her deep armchair with her legs folded under her. Everyone else chose anywhere they liked to sit. Somewhere under the table or in front of the fire lay Eva's two Scotties, Negus and Stasi, looking like tangled black balls of wool. Blondi wasn't admitted to this company; the mistress of the house's dogs took precedence. But sometimes Hitler would ask, quite humbly, 'Can I let Blondi in for a minute?' Then Eva Braun took her pets out, and Blondi could make an appearance.

This was where Hitler drank his tea. The rest of the company could have anything to drink that they fancied. There was no ban on alcohol here; you could drink sparkling or still wine, cognac or strong spirits. Cakes and pastries were served with the drinks, and Hitler had his favourite apple cake again. Sometimes Eva Braun managed to persuade the Führer that at this late hour a few sandwiches would be much more welcome than sweet things. She was expressing the wish of the whole company, and Hitler would go along with her.

In this large company it was difficult to get a general conversation going. The dim light, the thick carpets that swallowed up any loud footsteps, and the gentle crackling of the logs on the hearth tempted you to stay silent. But Hitler didn't care to be left to his own thoughts. He wanted distraction. He would talk quietly to the woman next to him, perhaps Frau Bormann. But what could she tell him? She mustn't let the Führer know about the anxieties and problems she had with her husband. And anything she had to say about the ten children she had brought into the world one by one during her marriage to the Reichsleiter was quickly over. She was a silent woman, and every year in spring, when we moved to the Obersalzberg, she was pregnant with another child. Pale and inconspicuous, with thick braids of hair wound round her head, she would sit in her armchair beside the Führer counting the hours until she could finally leave this circle of elegant, carefree women. Professor Blaschke, a gentleman in his sixties, was the scholarly type. His hair was greying at the temples, while his thick eyebrows and carefully tended moustache were like black bars marking his pale, thin face. In himself he was a reserved, quiet man. But during these sessions round the hearth Hitler sometimes drew him into a conversation in which he was one of the few to defend his own point of view firmly, even when it was not in line with the Führer's. Professor Blaschke was a vegetarian too, but for other reasons. He claimed that human dentition was intended for plant food, and that such food was more easily digested by the human body. In this he agreed with Hitler to a great extent, although he often 'abused his own body' by eating meat, and he didn't count poultry as meat at all. But when Hitler wanted Professor Blaschke to agree with him that smoking was one of the most harmful abuses of all and had a particularly bad effect on the teeth, he met with firm opposition. Blaschke himself was a heavy smoker, and perhaps therefore more tolerant than he should have been from a medical point of view. He claimed that smoking was positively good for you, because it disinfected the oral cavity and stimulated the blood supply. In a normal context, he said, smoking wasn't at all harmful. But Hitler wouldn't hear of it. 'Smoking is and always will be one of the most dangerous of habits, and quite apart from the fact that I personally find the smell of cigar or cigarette smoke disgusting, I wouldn't offer anyone I value or love a cigarette or cigar, because I'd be doing him no service. It has been shown for certain that non-smokers live longer than smokers, and are much more resistant to illness.'

Gretl Braun said she didn't want to live into old age if she couldn't smoke, life would be only half as much fun, and anyway she was very healthy although she'd been smoking for years. 'Yes, Gretl, but if you didn't smoke you'd be even healthier, and just wait and see, once you're married you won't be able to have children. And the smell of tobacco isn't a flattering perfume for women. I was once at an artists' reception in Vienna. Maria Holst (a Viennese actress) was sitting beside me – a really beautiful woman. She had wonderful chestnut-brown hair, but when I leaned over to her great clouds of nicotine wafted out of it. I said to her: "Why do you do it? You ought to stop smoking and preserve your beauty."' And when Hitler actually claimed that alcohol was less harmful than nicotine, all the smokers – and there were quite a few around him – banded together to oppose the idea. I said, 'My Führer, alcohol breaks up marriages and causes traffic accidents and crimes. At the worst nicotine just damages the smoker's own health a little.' But he was not to be convinced by our arguments, and in fact he decided that the Christmas parcels distributed in his name to the Leibstandarte troops would contain chocolate and schnapps but no cigarettes. We tried to tell Hitler that the soldiers would probably take the first opportunity of swapping their chocolate for cigarettes or tobacco, but it was no good. Himmler handed out parcels containing tobacco products to the soldiers on his own initiative, and if he hadn't I'm sure the combat strength of the SS would have suffered.

Hitler always looked forward to his little tea-party every night like a child. 'I never take a holiday, I can't go just anywhere to relax. So I divide up my holidays into the hours I spend here by the fire with my guests,' he said.

He loved his Great Hall with its fine pictures. 'Isn't Nanna wonderful? I keep looking at her. She's in just the right place here above the hearth. Her hand is as radiant as if she were alive,' he said, looking appreciatively at Feuerbach's picture. 'After my death I want the pictures to go to the new gallery in Linz. I shall make Linz a fine city and give it a gallery that people will flock to see. I regard the pictures hanging here in my house as only on loan, something that brightens my life. After my death they will belong to the whole German nation.' He was speaking to himself rather than the rest of us. No one would have known what to say in any case.

Professor Morell got very sleepy after a glass of port. He would be fighting off his drowsiness with his fat, hairy hands clasped over his huge paunch. He had the curious ability to close his eyes upwards, from below. It looked horrible behind the thick lenses of his glasses. So he wasn't much fun to talk to. Sometimes Colonel von Below[40] nudged him gently, and then he would briefly wake up and smile, thinking that the Führer had cracked a joke. 'Are you tired, Morell?' Hitler asked. 'No, my Führer, I was only thinking,' Morell would quickly assure him, and then he would tell a story of his experiences as a ship's doctor in Africa, one that we all knew already. [. . .]

Eva Braun took a lot of trouble to amuse the Führer. Once she tried to draw the photographer Walter Frentz and her friend Herta into a conversation about new films. Hitler began quietly whistling a tune. Eva Braun said, 'You're not whistling that properly, it goes like this.' And she whistled the real tune. 'No, no, I'm right,' said the Führer. 'I bet you I'm right,' she replied. 'You know I never bet against you because I'll have to pay in any case,' said Hitler. 'If I win I must be magnanimous and refuse to take my winnings, and if she wins I have to pay her,' he explained to the rest of us. 'Then let's play the record and you'll see,' suggested Eva Braun. Albert Bormann was the adjutant on duty. He rose and put the record in question – I forget what it was – on the gramophone. We all listened hard and intently, and Eva Braun turned out to be right. She was triumphant. 'Yes,' said Hitler. 'So you were right, but the composer composed it wrong. If he'd been as musical as me then he'd have composed *my* tune.' We all laughed, but I do believe Hitler meant it seriously.

He was genuinely convinced that he had an infallible musical ear. Heinz Lorenz suggested, 'My Führer, you ought to give a concert in the Great Hall. After all, you could afford to invite the best German musicians, Gieseking, Kempff, Furtwängler and so on. You don't go to the opera or the theatre any more, but you could listen to music. It wouldn't strain your eyes either.' Hitler rejected the idea. 'No, I don't want to trouble such artists just for me personally, but we could play a few records.' A thick book listed all the records that the Führer owned. There must have been hundreds of them. The wooden panelling of the wall turned out to be a cupboard holding records, with a built-in gramophone that was invisible till the cupboard doors were opened. The black discs stood in long rows, labelled with numbers. Bormann operated the gramophone.

Hitler nearly always had the same repertory played: Lehár's

operettas, songs by Richard Strauss, Hugo Wolf and Richard Wagner. The only pop music he would let us play was the 'Donkey Serenade'. It usually formed the conclusion of the concert.

Hitler's colleagues enjoyed the musical evenings with the records even less than those conversations round the hearth. One after another they would leave the Hall. You could hear them laughing and giggling and talking in the living room, where the deserters assembled to amuse themselves in their own way, leaving their boss alone with the sleeping Morell and the faithful Eva, the duty adjutant and the von Below and Brandt ladies. I must admit that I sometimes slipped quietly away myself, until the valet came in to say, 'The Führer misses his company, and back there in the Hall he can hear your noise.' Then the 'faithful' reluctantly went back on duty again.

'No, my entourage isn't very musical,' Hitler said, resigned. 'When I was still going to official festival performances of opera I usually had to keep an eye on the men with me to see they didn't go to sleep. Hoffmann (he meant the press photographer Heinrich Hoffmann) once almost fell over the balustrade of the box during *Tristan und Isolde*, and I had to rouse Schaub and tell him to go over and shake Hoffmann awake. Brückner[41] was sitting behind me snoring, it was terrible. But no one went to sleep during *The Merry Widow* because there was a ballet in it.'

I asked Hitler why he only ever went to hear *Die Meistersinger* or other Wagnerian operas. 'It's just my luck that I can never say I like something without finding that I'm stuck listening exclusively to one piece of music or hearing one particular opera. I once said that *Meistersinger* is really one of Richard Wagner's finest operas, so since then it's supposed to be my favourite opera and I don't get to hear anything else. The same thing happened with the *Badenweiler March*. And I was once invited to visit Frau Ley.[42] She had a Scotch terrier bitch with seven puppies and was very proud of them. Just to be polite I said: "Those are really delightful little creatures" – although I think they're horrible, like rats. Next day she sent me one as a present. Frau Braun,

Eva's mother, has the dog now. I'd never have let myself be photographed with a dog like that, but it's really touching to see how fond of me the little fellow still is.'

The hours passed by, and it would be four or five in the morning by the time Hitler rang for his valet to find out whether any air raids had been reported. He asked this question every evening before going to bed, and never retired for the night before he was told that the Reich was clear of all enemies. Sometimes the presence of a few aircraft or attacking enemy formations was kept from him, or the day would never have come to an end. Finally he would rise, say good night, shake hands with everyone and go upstairs.

Within a short time thick tobacco smoke would fill his living room, and everyone had woken up. Suddenly there was a cheerful atmosphere that would have delighted Hitler if he had been there.

The strong coffee we had been drinking to keep us awake all this time wouldn't let us drop straight off to sleep now. But gradually the guests and the Führer's colleagues withdrew, and finally the Berghof lay in deep peace until next morning.

This was the usual way we spent our days and nights for the first few days or weeks. Gradually more and more guests arrived. Minister of State Esser[43] and his wife were invited for a few days. Frequent guests included Frau Morell, Frau Dietrich, Baldur von Schirach[44] and his wife, Heinrich Hoffmann and Frau Marion Schönmann,[45] a friend of Eva Braun. Hitler's permanent colleagues and staff were glad of any guest who would entertain the Führer. Then they didn't have to be present themselves on his walks and at tea every day.

Hitler envied his guests their civilian clothing. 'It's all very well for you,' he told Brandt, who turned up in lederhosen one day when the sun was shining brightly. 'Once I always went around like that myself.' 'You could now, my Führer, you're in private here.' 'No, as long as we're at war I shall not be out of uniform, and anyway my knees are so white. That looks terrible with shorts.' Then he continued, 'But after the war I'll hang up my uniform, retire here to the Berghof, and someone else can look after the business of government. And when I'm an old man I'll write my memoirs, surround myself with clever, intellectual people and never see any more officers. They're all stubborn and thick-headed, prejudiced and set in their ways. My two old secretaries will be with me, typing. The young ones will all be married and leave, and when I'm old the older secretaries will still be able to keep up with my speed.' I couldn't help it: I asked, 'My Führer, when *will* the war be over, then?' 'I don't know,' he replied, 'but when we've won it, anyway.' And his kindly, friendly, smiling face once again assumed the hard, fanatical expression that I knew so well from the bronze busts of the Führer.

Usually Hitler didn't talk much about the war, and said little about politics. 'We shall win this war because we're fighting for an ideal and not for Jewish capitalism, which is what spurs on our enemies' soldiers. Russia is dangerous, and only Russia, because Russia fights for its own idea of the world as fanatically as we do. But good will always be victorious, there are no two ways about that.' No one in the whole company contradicted him. There were no military men present, and the rest of us believed what we heard because we wanted to believe it. Hitler radiated a power that neither men nor women could entirely escape feeling. Personally modest and kindly, but as Führer a harsh megalomaniac, he lived for his 'mission'. He sometimes said that it demanded endless sacrifices of him. 'If you only knew how much I'd sometimes like to walk the streets incognito, without companions! I'd like to go into a department store and buy Christmas presents myself, sit in a coffee-house and watch people go by. But I can't.' We said, 'But kings and emperors used to mingle incognito with their people in the old days. A pair of dark glasses, a civilian suit, and you'd never be recognized.' He replied, 'I don't want any masquerade, and anyway I'd be recognized all the same. I'm too well known, and my voice would give me away.' For although he had said, 'I've never feared assassination when driving through the crowds in my car – at the worst I've been afraid it might knock down a child,' he still wouldn't risk recognition if he was alone. He thought that the acclamations of the people would spoil all his fun.

It was some time since Hitler had appeared in public to receive the plaudits of the population. His headquarters, of course, were officially unknown for reasons of military secrecy. But when the Führer was staying in Berlin his presence was kept strictly secret too. Once the swastika flag used to be flown above the Reich Chancellery, and the inhabitants of Berlin knew, from the busy coming and going of cars, that 'the Führer' was in town. For some years, however, only those in the know had been aware that a double guard on the entrances to the Chancellery meant Hitler was in residence. Even on his journeys by special train, everything was done to avoid drawing attention to him. The windows of his carriage were blacked out even in broad daylight and bright sunshine, and he lived in there by artificial light just as he did in his bunker. At the Berghof, where crowds once used to gather outside the last gates before the road up to the house, there was no one waiting now.

Before the war, the gates had been opened once a day when Hitler went for his walk, and people used to flock in and line his path. Hysterical women took away stones on which his foot had trodden, and even the most sensible people went crazy. Once a truck taking bricks up to the Berghof was actually plundered by a couple of madwomen, and the bricks, which hadn't been so much as touched by the Führer's hands and feet, ended up as precious souvenirs in people's living-room windows.

And then there were the love letters sent by such ladies. They made up a large part of the post arriving at the Führer's Chancellery.

In 1943, however, Hitler spent his time at the Berghof entirely with his friends and colleagues. He had a special fondness for Albert Speer.[46] 'He's an artist, and a kindred spirit,' he said. 'I have the warmest human feelings for him because I understand him so well. He is an architect like me, intelligent, modest, not a stubborn military hothead. I never thought he would master his great task so well. But he also has great organizational talents and he's perfectly capable of his task.' Speer was certainly a very pleasant, likeable character: not by any means a Party functionary, not an upstart, but someone of real ability who didn't lower himself to be a mere yes-man. Remarkably, he seemed to be one of the few people from whom Hitler would take contradiction. He himself once said, 'When I work a plan out with Speer and ask him to do something, he thinks it over and then, after a while, he says, "Yes, my Führer, I think that can be done." Or perhaps he may say, "No, it can't be done, not like that." And then he gives me convincing arguments why not.'

Speer did wear uniform, for he held an official position, and what is an official position without a uniform? However, his uniform was always slightly incorrect, and he never looked military in it. His hair usually needed cutting, although he noticed that only when his wife pointed it out. I never saw him intoxicated, and he didn't join in any of the parties thrown by people who knew Hitler. I didn't notice him being especially friendly with any of the Party or Wehrmacht people either.

Heinrich Hoffmann, however, was different. He too was a frequent and important guest of the Führer. A veteran of the days when the Party was struggling for power, he always used to be around with his camera when Hitler made an appearance anywhere. 'Oh yes, Hoffmann used to be a splendid fellow, he was still slim and supple then, and worked tirelessly away with his elaborate old camera. Back then he still had to slip under the black cloth and do all kinds of hair-raising things with his heavy equipment to get a good shot. He's a very loyal comrade.' So in the end, out of gratitude for his faithful services, the little photographer Heinrich Hoffmann was appointed 'professor'. Professor of what, I always wondered – business acumen, maybe? Or was it an award for his keen instinct? For out of thirty different political parties, he had chosen to photograph the National Socialists. And he really did take excellent shots and was also a gifted graphic artist, very entertaining and sometimes even witty – but not likeable. At least, we called him the 'Reich Drunk', and in the years when I knew him that description certainly fitted.

Hitler showed Hoffmann great affection and forbearance, as he did with other old comrades from the early days of the Party. While he would dismiss or demote members of his staff or generals without a qualm if they opposed him, or if someone slandered them, he would excuse many failings in his old companions – personal defects or flaws of character that had a far worse effect on the Party cause and Nazi ideology than honest, down-to-earth disagreement openly expressed.

It certainly upset him a lot to see that Hoffmann was so devoted to the bottle and had a reputation as a womanizer, but he knew nothing about the Professor's orgies in Vienna and Munich, and on his estate at Altötting, and the indignation they aroused among the people. Well, who was going to tell him? Who would have dared speak out against a friend of Hitler? The only person who did try to intervene was Eva Braun. She told Hitler: 'You really must do something; Hoffmann's behaviour is terrible. He's drunk the whole time, always eating and drinking massively, and at a time when most people don't have enough to eat at all.' So then Hitler did get angry and told Hoffmann off, but it didn't work for long. 'His first wife's death hit Hoffmann so hard,' Hitler explained, by way of excuse. 'He just couldn't get over it, and that's when he began drinking. He used to be a good husband.' But apparently even in his prime Hitler's comrade in the Party struggle hadn't despised a good drop of something, for Hitler himself told many anecdotes showing that Hoffmann had never been known for his abstinence. For instance, Hitler once amused the company at table by describing a drive with Hoffmann in the 1920s. 'Hoffmann had bought a new car, a Ford, and he insisted that I must try the car out with him. I said, "No, Hoffmann, I'm not going for any drive with you." But he kept pestering me, so finally I gave in, and we set out from Schellingstrasse. It was already evening, it had been raining too, and Hoffmann went tearing round the corners like an idiot, almost ran into the corner of a building, ignored street junctions. "Hoffmann," I said, "watch out, you're driving like a madman! This is terribly dangerous." "No, no, my Führer, it just seems that way to you because you haven't had a drink. If you'd put back a good glass or so of red wine like me you wouldn't notice a thing." At that I got out, and I never went for a drive with him again.'

Since the beginning of the war Hoffmann had had few opportunities to see the Führer. He had no business at headquarters, so the Berghof was the only place where Hitler could meet him. At first the Führer was always glad to see his faithful supporter again after an interval of many months, but soon Hoffmann began getting on his nerves. 'Hoffmann, your nose looks like a rotten pumpkin. I think if we struck a match under your nostrils your breath would catch fire and you'd explode. Soon there'll be red wine flowing in your veins instead of blood,' he once told Hoffmann, when he turned up at a meal and even the Führer couldn't help noticing that he'd had too much already. At least Hoffmann never used to arrive drunk in Hitler's presence, and the Führer was sorry to see his old friend and comrade letting himself go so badly.

Finally Hitler told his adjutants Schaub and Bormann, 'Please make sure that Professor Hoffmann is sober when he comes to see me. I've invited him because I want to talk to him, not so that he can drink himself into a stupor.' So poor Hoffmann had some difficulty finding drinking companions. All of a sudden none of Hitler's entourage seemed able to find Hoffmann a nice bottle of something, and no one had time to drink with him. Our guest later took to bringing his own supplies, but that annoyed Hitler so much that Hoffmann was hardly ever invited again.

For the time being he could still amuse the Führer and the rest of the company at table with his jokes and reminiscences. For instance, he once told the following joke. 'Here's a riddle, my Führer: you, Himmler and Göring are all standing under an umbrella in the middle of the road. Which of you gets wet?' No one could guess, so Hoffmann told us the answer. 'None of you, my Führer, because it isn't raining.' Hitler shook his head. 'Dear me, Hoffmann, you're getting old!' Everyone laughed. 'And just think, my Führer, the man who told me that joke is in Dachau now!' 'I don't believe you, Hoffmann, that's a really stupid joke,' said the Führer. 'Oh, but he really is in Dachau, my Führer – he lives there,' said Hoffmann triumphantly, which made Hitler laugh a lot. 'You're worse than Count Bobby,' he said.

Then there were long conversations by the hearth in the evening about art galleries and their curators, and the exhibitions in the House of German Art, organized by Hoffmann. These conversations bored everyone else terribly, but Hitler loved painting, and Hoffmann knew his taste – and above all he knew the financial value of the old masters.

Once Hoffmann's daughter, the wife of Baldur von Schirach,[47] came too. She was a nice, natural Viennese woman,[48] with a delightful flow of talk, but she had to leave suddenly when she raised a very unwelcome subject in tea-time conversation. I wasn't present myself, but Hans Junge told me about it. As Hitler was sitting by the hearth with his guests, she suddenly said, 'My Führer, I saw a train full of deported Jews in Amsterdam the other day. Those poor people – they look terrible. I'm sure they're being very badly treated. Do you know about it? Do you allow it?' There was a painful silence. Soon afterwards Hitler rose to his feet, said goodnight and withdrew. Next day Frau von Schirach went back to Vienna, and not a word was said about the incident. Apparently she had exceeded her rights as a guest and failed to carry out her duty of entertaining Hitler.

In early April – Hitler was now feeling well rested and relaxed – preparations began for the big state receptions. Ribbentrop came for talks with Hitler almost daily, and had lunch with us. Hewel really had his hands full. Almost all the leaders of our allied states were to be received. The guesthouse of the German Reich was near Salzburg. It was an enchanting little Baroque castle built by Fischer von Erlach and splendidly fitted out by Hitler.

He held his 'great state receptions' here at Schloss Klessheim; the Berghof wasn't so suitable for them.

The first and most important foreign guest was Mussolini. Hitler was in a particularly good mood on the day before his visit. 'The Duce is an outstanding statesman. He knows the way his people's minds work, and considering how lazy the Italians are it's amazing what he's made of the country in this short time. But he's not in an easy position, standing between the Church and the royal family. The King may be a fool, but he has many supporters. Victor Emanuel is the smallest king I know. When I went to Rome in 1938 in my special train I warned my companions just before we came into the station. I told them we were now arriving, and if they saw a man with a lot of gold braid on his uniform apparently kneeling down on the platform they mustn't laugh, because he was the King of Italy and had never grown any taller. Of course that really amused my own tall fellows, and I oughtn't to have said anything about it in advance. It was a funny sight to see the King at table sitting next to the Queen, who was two heads taller. As long as they were seated they looked much the same height, but as soon as they got up the King seemed to slip down lower and the Queen grew even taller. It was wonderful in Rome, though. Italy is an enchanting country, but its people are very idle.'

Then Hitler spoke enthusiastically of the great events and magnificent occasions the Duce had organized in honour of his guest. The Fascist population had given the statesman who was their ally endless ovations with unheard-of enthusiasm. Later Hitler described all this enthusiasm as nothing but a flash in the pan, and said the Italians had no strength of character. On that occasion he had been to a grand opera with Mussolini and was horrified by the audience's lack of attention to the performance. 'People were sitting in the boxes and the stalls dressed in fine clothes, gossiping on about their personal concerns, while the singers were doing their best. We didn't arrive until the middle of the second act, and I couldn't believe my ears when suddenly the opera broke off to play the Italian national anthem, the

German national anthem and the Horst Wessel song. I felt very awkward and embarrassed for the singers and musicians.'

Apparently Hitler was good friends with the Duce personally too, for I had a feeling he was really looking forward to Mussolini's visit. But it may be that he was expecting material support and aid from his friend, and that was why he was in such a good mood. At any rate, he really knew how to play on human feelings. Mussolini was to be received at the Berghof too, and eat with Hitler. The kitchen was kept very busy trying to satisfy the guest's pampered palate.

The great day of the reception was lucky enough to have real 'propaganda weather' again, as so often both before and afterwards. The sun, the snow and the clear blue sky looked so festive that they made a wonderful setting for the magnificence of Schloss Klessheim. I can't say anything about Mussolini's visit itself, because I stayed behind at the deserted Berghof with several other people and was in the office, catching up with my work without feeling rushed for once. Another big batch of air reports from the Rhineland and North Germany had arrived. Eva Braun had set out before lunch to walk to the Königsee with Herta Schneider, Frau Brandt and Frau von Below, and wouldn't be back until late in the afternoon. She was making the most of a free day to stretch her legs properly at last. Usually she had to be back for lunch, and after those late evenings by the hearth she had to sleep in late next day.

Fräulein Schroeder was not feeling well and had gone to bed, and I was on duty alone. When I had finished my work in the office I felt very bored. The fine weather made me want to go for a walk too, but I couldn't leave the telephone unattended. I felt as if I were in a golden cage when I went to sit on the terrace with a book and looked at the mountains. At this time I felt curiously restless when I was alone; it was a sense of discomfort that I couldn't explain to myself. It wasn't the mountains that oppressed my spirits but the whole weight of the machinery into which I had found my way, and which was now holding me tightly in its thousand arms.

At last a phone call came. 'The Führer has just left Klessheim. He wants to take his guests to the tea-house.' I changed my clothes. The Berghof began coming to life again. The yapping of the Scotties announced that the mistress of the house was home. Twenty minutes later cars came roaring up the road, the whole house was soon full of uniforms, and a little later the Führer set out with a small company to walk to the tea-house.

I had assumed that on days like this, when there were demanding, important talks to be held, the Führer would be tired and go to bed earlier. Exactly the opposite was the case. The Führer was excited and talkative, and the tea-party went on for ever.

Other visitors were Marshal Antonescu of Romania, Reich Regent Horthy of Hungary, President Tiso of Slovakia, and King Boris of Bulgaria. For days on end we didn't set eyes on Hitler until the evening. Only Boris of Bulgaria was asked to the Berghof too. As I was wandering around the kitchen I happened to see the King drive up to the main entrance. Planning to reach my room unseen, I quickly ran across the yard behind the house so as to use the back door. I burst right into the ceremonious procession in which the Führer was leading the King through the living room to the Great Hall. I was holding an apple I'd just bitten into in my right hand, and two ping-pong bats in my other hand. My mouth was full too, so there was nothing I could say or do. Hitler and his guest looked at me in some surprise, but not unkindly, and I hurried off to my room feeling embarrassed. When the Führer greeted me before dinner that evening, I apologized and he said, in very friendly tones, 'Don't worry, child, kings are only human too.'

The state receptions were over, but another great day was coming closer: 20 April, the Führer's birthday. Whole laundry baskets full of birthday cards and presents had been arriving at the Berghof for weeks beforehand. Boxes, parcels and packages were stacked up in Bormann's office and the adjutancy office. And this was only a small fraction of the presents. Most of them went to Berlin. Business firms and companies, local Party offices, organizations, children's homes, schools, societies and private persons all sent good wishes and presents. The gifts included all sorts of things, from toothbrushes and complete children's outfits to the finest ladies' underwear and valuable porcelain or museum pieces. Most of them were meant not for Hitler's personal use, but to be given to whatever needy recipients he thought fit. Some of the presents were from simple folk, which was very moving. An old woman had made a pair of slippers and tastelessly but laboriously embroidered the swastika against the setting sun on each slipper. Another lady sent a hand-made handkerchief with a head embroidered in each corner, showing Hitler, Hindenburg, Bismarck and Frederick the Great, all united to help you blow your nose! Cakes, tarts, biscuits, sweetmeats and fruit from all over Germany arrived, carefully and lovingly packaged. The adjutancy office looked like a department store these days. Presents and letters from Hitler's personal acquaintances were taken to his study unopened.

On the evening of 19 April we were sitting by the hearth. For once everyone was there. It was all the same as usual. Hitler talked at length about his beloved Blondi. She was allowed to join the company, and as a dog-lover myself I was really delighted to see how clever she was. Hitler played all kinds of little games with her. He got her to beg, and 'be a schoolgirl', which meant getting up on her hind legs and putting both front paws on the arm of Hitler's chair, like a good little school pupil. Her best turn was singing. Hitler would tell her, in his kindest, most coaxing voice, 'Sing, Blondi!' and then he struck up a long-drawn-out howl himself. She joined in the high notes, and the more Hitler praised her the louder she sang. Sometimes her voice rose too high, and then Hitler said, 'Sing lower, Blondi, sing like Zara Leander!' Then she gave a long, low howl like the wolf who was certainly among her ancestors. She was given three little pieces of cake every evening, and when Hitler raised three fingers of his hand she knew at once that she was about to get her evening treat.

We talked about the dog almost all that evening, as if it were going to be *her* birthday. 'She really is the cleverest dog I know. I sometimes play ball with her over there in my study,' Hitler told us. 'Now and then she knocks her toy under the cupboard, and then I have to go to the hearth for the poker and fish the ball out with it. The other day she was with me while I was sitting at my desk. She was very restless, walking up and down. Finally she stopped by the hearth and whined until I got up. Then she went to the cupboard and back to the hearth until I picked up the poker and fetched her ball out from under the cupboard. I'd forgotten about this game, but she still remembered just how I had helped her. But I'm afraid she might break her leg on the smooth parquet floor, so I've stopped playing with her in there.'

At last the big hand of the clock came round to twelve. At twelve precisely the doors opened and a row of servants and orderlies marched in with trays full of glasses and champagne. Everyone had a glass of bubbly except Hitler, who had some very sweet white wine poured into his glass. On the last stroke of twelve we clinked glasses. Everyone said, 'All the best, my Führer,' or, 'Happy birthday, my Führer.' Some made a rather longer speech, hoping that the Führer would remain in good health so that his powers would long remain at their height to help the German people, and so on.

That brought the official part of the birthday to a close as far as I was concerned. The company sat down again, the conversation continued, and later many other people came in with birthday wishes: all the servants, the guards, chauffeurs, the entire kitchen and domestic staff, all the children of the Führer's set of friends and acquaintances. Hitler's birthday was celebrated everywhere, in the kitchen, the garages, the guardrooms, the press office, the orderlies' room. Today as much alcohol as anyone wanted flowed at the Berghof. I took advantage of the general celebrations to go to bed earlier than usual for once. There were plenty of people around to entertain Hitler, and I wasn't needed any more for work.

On the morning of 20 April Hitler came down earlier than

usual. Smiling, half shaking his head, he looked at the presents on the table and piled up in the office. He kept a few small things: a very pretty sculpture of a young girl, a handsome wooden bowl that a fourteen-year-old boy had made himself, and some children's drawings that he wanted to show Eva. Everything else would go to hospitals, children's homes, old folk's homes and welfare organizations. Presents of food were really supposed to be disposed of because of the risk that they might be poisoned. But I did my bit in helping to dispose of these delicacies by using them for their proper purpose.

At lunch Himmler and Sepp Dietrich,[49] Goebbels and Esser, Ribbentrop and Chief of Staff Werlin[50] were the guests of honour. There were so many people that there wasn't an empty seat left even at the round table in the bay window. I sat next to Himmler. It was the first time I had seen this powerful, much feared man at close quarters. I didn't like him at all, not for any sense of brutality about him but because he seemed so ordinary and insincere, rather like a civil servant. That was the surprising thing about his character: he would greet you by kissing your hand, he spoke in a quiet voice with a slight Bavarian accent, always had a smile around the corners of his eyes and mouth, and seemed friendly and polite, almost cordial! When you heard him telling innocuous stories, chatting away pleasantly, who would associate him with mass shootings, concentration camps and so on? I think he was very subtle. He told us how splendidly the concentration camps were organized. 'I give people their work to do individually, and by using that method I've achieved not only total security but also efficiency, peace and quiet, and good order in the camps. For instance, we made an incorrigible arsonist fire-watcher in one camp. He's responsible for seeing that no fire breaks out, and I made sure he knew that he would be the prime suspect the moment there was any fire at all. You should just see how reliable and conscientious that man is now, my Führer.' So saying, he smiled happily, and we were bound to get the impression that as a humanitarian psychologist he didn't just imprison the inmates of the camps, he trained and educated them too. Hitler nodded his approval of Himmler's remarks, and no one had anything else to add to the subject.

Ribbentrop was a very odd man. The impression he made on me was of someone absent-minded and slightly dreamy, and if I hadn't known that he was Foreign Minister I'd have said he was a cranky eccentric leading a strange life of his own. In the middle of the conversation he suddenly asked, abruptly, why the Führer didn't drink sparkling wine. 'It's extremely refreshing, my Führer, and very digestible too.' Hitler looked at him in some surprise and told him firmly that he hated champagne. 'It's much too acid for me, and if I want something sparkling to drink I prefer Fachinger or Apollinaris water. I'm sure they're healthier.' Probably the Foreign Minister had temporarily forgotten that he was no longer a champagne manufacturer but a diplomat now. He always cut a good figure, but I like him a lot less when I remember how, on visiting London for the Coronation, he greeted the King of England by raising his arm and announcing, 'Heil Hitler!'

Goebbels brought verve and wit into the conversation. He wasn't at all handsome, but I could see why the girls in the Reich Chancellery ran to the windows to see the Propaganda Minister leave his Ministry, but took hardly any notice of Hitler. 'Oh, if you only knew what eyes Goebbels has, and what an enchanting smile!' they gushed, as I looked blankly at them. The ladies at the Berghof positively flirted with Hitler's Minister too. He really did have a delightfully entertaining manner, and his shafts of wit were well aimed, although mostly at other people's expense. No one around the Führer's table could stand up to his sharp tongue, least of all the Reich press chief, who made the slightly improper remark that he got his best ideas in the bathtub, to which Goebbels, of course, promptly replied, 'You should take a bath more often, Dr Dietrich!' The press chief went pale and said no more.

So the chatter round the table went on, and Goebbels aimed his sallies, which hit their mark and were not returned. Curiously enough, Himmler and Goebbels entirely ignored each other. It wasn't too obvious, but still you couldn't help noticing that their relationship was a superficial veneer of civility. The two of them met relatively seldom; they didn't have much to do with each other, and were not, like the warring Bormann brothers, kept on the same leash by their master. The hostility between the Bormanns was so habitual and firmly established that they could stand side by side and ignore each other entirely. And when Hitler gave a letter or request to the younger Bormann to be passed on to the Reichsleiter, Albert Bormann would go out, find an orderly, and the orderly would pass instructions on to his big brother even if they were both in the same room. The same thing happened in reverse, and if one Bormann told a funny story at table all the rest of the company would roar with laughter, while his brother just sat there ignoring them and looking deadly serious. I was surprised to find how used Hitler had become to this state of affairs. He took no notice of it at all. Unfortunately I never managed to find out the reason for their enmity. I think there was a woman behind it. Or perhaps those two fighting cocks had long ago forgotten the reason themselves?

Afternoon tea was taken in the Great Hall on Hitler's birthday. The important military men, Jodl, Keitel, Schmundt and so on, were there too. Göring came only for the conference, and took the opportunity of offering his congratulations then. In the afternoon, however, his wife 'the Queen Mother'[51] arrived in a huge, cornflower-blue cape, bringing little Edda to offer birthday wishes. We could see them only through the window as Hitler greeted them on the terrace, and Eva ran up to the first floor to fetch her camera and take a picture of little Edda reciting her birthday poem to Uncle Hitler. For once, Hitler had gone out on the terrace without his cap, and Eva didn't want to miss such a good opportunity.

Later, Hitler paid his traditional visit to the field hospital at the Platterhof. He always visited wounded soldiers on his birthday.

I made an interesting new acquaintance myself that day. I met my predecessor, of whom Hitler had always spoken with real enthusiasm. She had been Fräulein Daranowski, but now she had married Colonel Christian, head of the Luftwaffe operations department, and reluctantly she had given up her job with the Führer. Eva Braun didn't mind that, because the Führer sometimes spoke a little too warmly of his secretary. She really was a very pleasant, charming person, well groomed, a brunette, spirited and youthful, the embodiment of life itself. Her glance was irresistible, and her laughter sounded like little silver bells. And while the Führer liked her sex appeal, she was also an extremely good secretary. I seldom saw such nimble fingers on the typewriter keys. Her hands were so supple they might have been made of rubber. Later we worked together.[52]

By now it was no secret in our close-knit circle that I was on particularly friendly terms with Hans Junge. If I excused myself from a meal it was usually when Linge was on duty, so that Hans Junge and I could take long walks in the mountains together, or go on expeditions to Berchtesgaden or Salzburg. But not only was Julius Schaub as naturally nosy as a washerwoman, he was always on the look-out for subjects of conversation to serve up to the Führer at breakfast. However, while gossip about little love affairs might be very interesting, that wasn't really what the Supreme Commander wanted. If he heard about such things he recognized only serious, long-term relationships.

Hans Junge was a particular favourite of the Führer's, serving him devotedly and with a strong sense of duty. All the same, he was anxious to get further away from Hitler. He was one of the few people to realize that in the long run Hitler's ideas would have such an effect on you that in the end you wouldn't know what you had thought of yourself, and what was due to outside influence. Junge wanted his sense of objectivity back. He had applied several times to go to the front, which was the only way he could give up his job with Hitler. Every time his request was turned down on the grounds that he was indispensable; there were plenty of good soldiers but few trustworthy valets and adjutants. Finally Junge saw his chance in getting engaged to me. He knew very well that Hitler was as unwilling to lose me as his secretary as he was to lose Hans as his valet. And an engagement wasn't too firm a tie, but would give us the chance to spend time together and get to know each other. So we both decided to tell the Führer we were engaged, and at the same time Junge would ask for a transfer to the front again.

Schaub was delighted when we asked him to tell the Führer about our intentions. Soon after Hitler's birthday, he took his master this world-shattering news. I found the whole thing terribly embarrassing. I could feel Hitler's eyes resting on me with a surreptitious smile at table, I thought I saw faces full of sly glee around me, and I felt like getting up and running away. I remembered, with a rather guilty conscience, saying with heartfelt conviction only three months earlier that I took no interest in men.

That evening by the fireside Hitler suddenly said, 'Well, I certainly do have bad luck with my staff. First Christian marries Dara and takes my best secretary away, then I finally get a really good replacement, and now Traudl Humps is leaving me too and taking my best valet with her into the bargain.' Then he turned to me. 'But you'll be staying with me for the time being. Junge insists that he wants to go to the front, and while you're on your own you can carry on working for me.' So now I was suddenly engaged, although I didn't really feel quite up to this new dignity. However, I thought confidently, who knows what may happen between engagement and marriage?

On the First of May, National Labour Day, Hitler at last dictated a document to me again, quite a long one. In the old days he had spoken at mass meetings and personally attended celebrations and huge rallies. During the last years of the war, however, Hitler nearly always recorded his speeches, and then they were broadcast on the radio. Often his proclamations were just read out by someone else or published in the press. And he had made no unscripted public speeches since the beginning of the war. 'I prefer to improvise,' he said, 'and I speak best off the cuff, but now that we're at war I have to weigh up every word, because the world will be listening attentively. If some spontaneous impulse leads me into making a remark that doesn't go down well there could be unfortunate complications.' It was only on internal occasions, for instance addressing Gauleiters, officers or industrialists, that Hitler spoke without notes. Although I had been reminding him of the forthcoming speech for days beforehand, it wasn't until the night of 30 April that he felt in the mood to dictate it to me and could find time to do so. I spent all night typing it out. I finished in the early hours of the morning, Hitler recorded the speech at ten, and at twelve noon it was broadcast on all the German radio stations.

Soon afterwards Hitler and a small entourage went to Munich. He didn't want to miss the opportunity of seeing the exhibition at the House of German Art. It was to open in July,[53] but he intended to be back in East Prussia well before then, so he got Heinrich Hoffmann and Frau Professor Troost[54] to show him the pictures and sculptures that had been selected.

I was the only woman to go with him. Fräulein Schroeder had gone to Berchtesgaden for a course of treatment at the Sanatorium Zabel, and on the way back we were to pick up Fräulein Wolf to return to the Berghof with us as Hitler's second secretary. While Hitler went straight to his apartment on Prinzregentenplatz, I paid a surprise visit to my mother. Our happy reunion didn't last long, for Schaub summoned me to Hitler's apartment a few hours later. I knew the building, but I had never been in his private rooms. I was particularly surprised to find that Hitler occupied only one floor. The ground floor contained a porter's lodge and offices for the police and guards, and there were some guestrooms available to Hitler on the first floor. His private rooms were on the second floor, which he shared with his housekeepers Herr and Frau Winter. All the other floors of the building were occupied by private tenants. Hitler's apartment was no different from the home of any respectable, well-to-do citizen. There were basket chairs in the roomy entrance hall, and the windows had curtains with a brightly coloured flower pattern. A cloakroom was tastefully furnished with big mirrors and wall-lights. You trod on soft carpets everywhere. The broad corridor ended on the left in a door leading to the Winters' rooms. This was where the housekeeper had her kitchen, bathroom, living room and bedroom. The living room was also used by Hitler's employees as a sitting room when the government was staying in Munich. Hitler's big study and the library were directly opposite the front door. Originally they had probably been two rooms, now turned into one very large one by the removal of a wall. Hitler had a great liking for spacious rooms, and I was sometimes surprised that he could bear to be in his little cage-like bunker, with its low ceiling and tiny windows. The room next to the library was always kept locked. This was where Hitler's niece, of whom he was very fond, had apparently killed herself for his sake. The Führer sometimes mentioned his niece in conversation, and an oil painting of her had a place of honour in the Great Hall of the Berghof. Much later Erich Kempka[55] the chauffeur, who was already in Hitler's employment at the time – I think it happened in 1935[56] – told me the whole story. Hitler was Geli's guardian – his niece was called Geli – and she lived very close to him. She was in love with a man whom Hitler didn't like. When he went to Nuremberg to the Party rally, she shot herself in her room in his apartment.[57] It wasn't entirely clear whether or not her death was the result of an unfortunate accident while she was cleaning her pistol, but anyway Hitler was very upset, and no one had been allowed to use Geli's room since her death.

Eva Braun had a room in Hitler's apartment too, but she seldom used it, and never while Hitler was in Munich. There was another guestroom in the right-hand part of the apartment, which I used as an office when I had some typing to do, and Hitler's bedroom must have been somewhere as well. I never entered it.

I had been summoned because Hitler had something to dictate. Unfortunately I can't remember for the life of me what it was. But anyway it wasn't anything long and difficult. When

I'd finished my work I took it into Hitler's study. He was sitting at his desk when I came in, and I waited standing beside him while he read through what I had typed and corrected it. Suddenly, without looking up, he said, 'You're engaged to Junge, wouldn't you like to get married straight away before he goes to join the troops?'

Now I was in a fix! For a moment I looked at him dumbfounded, because I'd had absolutely no intention of committing myself so firmly to the relationship when Hans and I had known each other for such a short time. I tried desperately to find some good argument against the idea, but nothing much occurred to me. Finally I said, 'Oh, my Führer, why should we marry now? It won't make any difference. My husband to be is going to the front and I'll go on working for you just the same anyway, and we don't need to get married for that.' I was wondering why the Führer should take any interest in my marriage. Love isn't an affair of state, this was my own private business, and I was quite annoyed to have such a VIP meddling with it. All the same, I was surprised to hear Hitler say, 'But you two are in love, so it's best to get married at once! And you know, once you're married I can protect you any time if someone tries pestering you. But not if you're only engaged. And you'll still be working for me even if you're married.' I almost laughed out loud. How very respectable! But I'm afraid I also felt very uncomfortable, because how could I explain to him that love on its own isn't always reason enough to get married straight away? I said no more, and told myself this wasn't important and he would soon probably forget all about it again. I told Hans Junge what the Führer had said to me, and he too laughed out loud. 'That's typical of him – when he scents the faintest possibility of a marriage he'll do his best to encourage it. But never mind, he won't have taken it as seriously as all that.' I decided that one day I'd have my revenge and ask Hitler why he hadn't been happily married himself long ago. After all, he said he loved Eva Braun. But at the time I was still too shy and too young to say such things.

At lunchtime Hitler drove to a small café where he had often eaten in the past, the Osteria Bavaria in Schellingstrasse. The proprietor, a man with the very Bavarian name of Deutelmoser, had been informed just before our arrival and had his best suit on when we entered the place. The main lunch hour was over by now, and there were only a few guests sitting at some of the tables in the café. Of course I looked to see if they were police officers, wondering what precautions were taken for Hitler's security in such cases. But either they were particularly intelligent officers or genuine customers, because they acted entirely normally, looked with interest at the distinguished guest, and some of them left quite soon.

The least comfortable table, right at the back in the corner, was the one Hitler regularly occupied. We were only a small party of six, Hitler with two adjutants and Professor Morell, Professor Troost and me. Professor Troost was the widow of the late architect who had built the House of German Art. Hitler had thought very highly of him, and Professor Troost, who herself was an interior designer, was carrying on some of her husband's work. She designed and produced tapestries, interiors, mosaics and so on for the Führer. For instance, she had designed and worked on the document appointing Göring to the post of Reich Marshal, and on the design of his marshal's baton too. She was a very lively, natural, witty woman, and took the lead in conversation during lunch. She talked so fast and vivaciously that Hitler could hardly get a word in. She laughed at him and his diet, and claimed he wouldn't live long if he nourished himself on such wishy-washy stuff and didn't eat a decent piece of meat for once.

The meal didn't last long, and then Hitler left, got into the cars with the other men and drove back to his apartment. That afternoon he had talks with political leaders and Gauleiters in the Führer Building on Königsplatz, where I wasn't needed. I walked home and stayed on in Munich for another day, while my boss and his staff drove back to Berchtesgaden that evening, taking Fräulein Wolf with them.

When I turned up at the Berghof again two days later, Hans Junge too had been told that we should get married at once. He couldn't think of any particularly good reason against Hitler's persuasions either, and anyway I believe at heart he rather liked the idea. Finally I came to terms with it too, and the wedding was fixed for the middle of June 1943. I rebelled only once, when I saw the mountain of forms and questionnaires I must fill in because I was going to marry an SS man. I lost my temper and told my future husband that I'd throw the whole lot in the wastepaper basket if my marriage depended on this kind of thing.

Hitler laughed heartily when I read him out some of the questions on the forms. For instance, they asked, 'Is the bride positively addicted to housework?' He himself said that of course all this was nonsense, and he'd have a word with Himmler about it. Anyway, I was spared having to fight a battle on paper, and before I knew it June came and I was Frau Junge. My married bliss lasted four weeks, while we went on honeymoon to Lake Constance, and then my husband joined the army and I moved back to headquarters.

IV★

Meanwhile the Supreme Commander had moved back to the Wolf's Lair in East Prussia. The forest [. . .] had been cleared around it to make room for several more huts and bunkers. What we called 'hut disease' had broken out and proved very infectious among the upper ranks. Everyone wanted his own hut to live in, and the bunkers were used only for sleeping. Speer built himself a whole housing estate, Göring's hut was nothing short of a palace, and the doctors and adjutants erected summer residences of their own. Morell – but no one else – was even allowed a bathroom. Once again he was the butt of many jokes in the camp when it turned out that a normal bathtub was too small for him.

★This and the following chapter divisions were added later by Traudl Junge.

He could just about get in, but he couldn't get out again without help.

When I came back to the camp as a newly-wed wife, of course I too was the target of much male jocularity. I reported to Hitler that morning when he was about to go for his walk. 'Why, you're all pale and thin,' he said, in a friendly and well-meaning tone, but Linge, Bormann, Hewel and Schaub grinned broadly, making me blush with embarrassment. From now on Hitler generally addressed me as 'young woman'.

We secretaries were far from overworked. Fräulein Wolf and Fräulein Schroeder, the old guard, were working for Schaub. Every morning they were given a pile of letters to be answered. Schaub indicated briefly what the letters should say, but left the phrasing to the ladies. I did office work for the young SS adjutants Darges, Günsche and Pfeiffer.[58] I typed out the bodyguards' reports, requests for promotion, orders for transfers, suggestions for the award of decorations. There were a great many of those; more and more men were becoming heroes, and silver and gold crosses and medals were lavishly handed out on the Eastern Front.

However, that wasn't a really satisfying occupation, and although I enjoyed the forest and the lakes I still felt discontented, like a captive. Above all, life here was unbalanced in a way I couldn't tolerate permanently. Perhaps I had been made more aware of that by my husband's ideas. He had suddenly realized how hermetically cut off from real life we were, living in Hitler's ideological sphere of influence. Once I had thought that here at the centre of events, the place to which all threads ran, you would have the best and widest view of all. But we were standing behind the scenes and didn't know what was happening on stage. Only the director knew the play, all the rest of us just learned our parts, and no one knew exactly what part anyone else was playing.

No rumours reached us, we heard no broadcasts from enemy transmitters, we knew of no other attitudes, no opposition. Just one opinion and one belief ruled here; it sometimes seemed to me as if all these people were using exactly the same words and expressing themselves in the same way.

It was not until I had gone through with it to the bitter end and returned to ordinary life that I could see it as clearly as that. At the time, I suffered from a vague feeling of dissatisfaction, an uneasiness for which I couldn't find a name, because the daily company of Hitler left no one a chance to give such ideas a firm shape.

I typed for Professor Brandt, the surgeon who was Hitler's attendant doctor and head of the health service. I began keeping a diary, and looked for intellectual stimulation and diversion among the staff of the press office. I talked to many close friends about my doubts. Many other people felt the way I did. I was especially aware of this tension in Walther Hewel, with whom I had philosophical conversations on many evenings. He too disliked the narrow-minded, artificial atmosphere here and the human inadequacies of those around us. We called our mood 'the camp megrims', and resigned ourselves to not knowing why we felt that way.

Hitler had fallen into the habit of eating his meals with Fräulein Schroeder, because she had to stick to her diet and eat no salt. After a short while he extended his invitation to all the secretaries, and from then on we too shared mealtimes with Hitler at headquarters, but thank goodness Fräulein Wolf and I could have the normal menu provided by 'Crumbs'.

Gradually I lost my shyness and timidity in Hitler's presence, and ventured to speak to him even if he hadn't asked me something first. More than ever he emphasized how much good it did him to be able to relax completely at mealtimes.

One day, when we had finished eating, I decided to seize my chance to complain to Hitler of the lack of work. It was on that very day that Hitler said, 'Dara (Frau Christian) is coming back. I asked Colonel Christian how his wife was, and he told me she wanted to go and work for the Red Cross. But in my view if she really wants to work she can work for me.'

My two colleagues looked rather downcast, even though they smiled. They had probably been just a little jealous of Frau Christian, while they didn't see me as competition or a rival. Also, and quite rightly, they felt as discontented with the lack of work as I did. We none of us liked the idea of having to share our duties with a fourth secretary.

Fräulein Wolf and I began saying our piece, protesting that we felt guilty about being little more than ladies of leisure here, when the Führer so seldom had any work for us. We thought perhaps we could be more useful in Berlin, or in some other position. After all, we said, there was a war on, and in the present circumstances our families had a lot to put up with. But we got nowhere. 'Ladies, you can't be the judges of whether your work and your presence are useful to me or not. Believe me, your duties here are much more important than if you were typing letters in some business firm or making grenades in a factory. And you are serving your people best in those few hours when you do my typing or help me to relax and gather strength.'

So a few weeks later Madame Christian rejoined us, with a great many suitcases and hat-boxes, filling the bunkers and huts with trills of laughter and causing much turmoil in the hearts of many lonely men. We now took our meals with Hitler in two shifts. Two ladies ate with him at lunch and the other two in the evening. Frau Christian was called by her old name of Dara again. When she and I were eating with Hitler the conversation often turned to marriage. To this day I don't know his feelings on the subject. He told us about an old friend of his, Hanfstaengl.[59] 'Hanfstaengl had such a beautiful wife, and he was unfaithful to her with another woman who wasn't pretty at all.' Apparently he couldn't understand that a woman's beauty alone isn't enough of a foundation for a good marriage. Yet on the other hand it wasn't just Eva Braun's beauty that attracted him. He often took his chance to talk to us about Eva. He phoned her every day, and if there were reports of an air raid on Munich he would pace up and down restlessly like a caged lion, waiting to get in touch with Eva Braun by phone. Usually his fears were groundless.

The 'little Braun house' was damaged only once, when several buildings near it burned right down. He was always talking about Eva's courage. 'She won't go down into the air raid shelter, although I keep asking her to, and one of these days that little place of hers will collapse like a house of cards. And she won't move to my apartment, where she'd be absolutely safe. I've finally persuaded her to have a little private shelter built in her house, but then she takes in the whole neighbourhood and goes up on the roof herself to see if any incendiary bombs have fallen. She's very proud. I've known her for over ten years, and when she first started to work for Hoffmann she had to scrape and save. But it was years before she would let me pay so much as a taxi fare for her, and she slept on a bench in the office for days on end so that I could reach her by phone, because she didn't have a telephone at home. It was only a few years ago that I got her to accept her little house in Bogenhausen.'

So it was mainly her human qualities that bound Hitler to Eva Braun. Once, when we were talking about weddings and marriage again, I asked, 'My Führer, why haven't you married her?' I knew how much he liked arranging marriages, after all. His answer was rather surprising. 'I wouldn't make a good father, and I think it would be irresponsible to start a family when I can't devote enough time to my wife. And anyway I don't want children of my own. I think the offspring of men of genius usually have a very hard time of it. People expect them to be just like their famous progenitor, and won't forgive them for being only average. And in fact most of them are feeble-minded.'

This was the first expression of personal megalomania that I heard from Hitler, or the first to be taken seriously. To this day I do sometimes feel as if while Hitler's fanatical ideas were megalomaniac, up till then he had kept himself as a person out of it. Indeed, he used to say: 'I am an instrument of fate, and must tread the path on which a higher Providence has set me.' But this time it did disturb me a lot to find someone describing himself as a genius.

Although Hitler didn't discuss the war or politics in our little company at table, he said more and more often that he had great anxieties. He was usually talking more to himself than to us, Ever more frequently now I would see his face wearing the grim, angry, harsh expression left on it by the preceding military briefing. 'It's hopeless making war with incompetent generals. I ought to follow Stalin's example. He purges his army ruthlessly.' And then, as if he had only just realized that we women didn't and ought not to understand such things, he would put his gloomy thoughts aside and switch to being a charming dinner companion.

Sometimes we also had interesting discussions about the church and the development of the human race. Perhaps it's going too far to call them discussions, because he would begin explaining his ideas when some question or remark from one of us had set them off, and we just listened. He was not a member of any church, and thought the Christian religions were outdated, hypocritical institutions that lured people into them. The laws of nature were his religion. He could reconcile his dogma of violence better with nature than with the Christian doctrine of loving your neighbour and your enemy. 'Science isn't yet clear about the origins of humanity,' he once said. 'We are probably the highest stage of development of some mammal which developed from reptiles and moved on to human beings, perhaps by way of the apes. We are a part of creation and children of nature, and the same laws apply to us as to all living creatures. And in nature the law of the struggle for survival has reigned from the first. Everything incapable of life, everything weak is eliminated. Only mankind and above all the church have made it their aim to keep alive the weak, those unfit to live, and people of an inferior kind.'

It's a pity that I can remember only fragments of these theories, and unfortunately I don't have the powers of persuasion with which Hitler put his ideas to us.

On the way back to our hut we were talking to each other about what Hitler had said, and I made up my mind to think more deeply about such things. Sad to say, I realized next day in

conversation with my friends that I could give only a very vague
and inaccurate account of what had impressed and moved me so
much the previous evening. If only I had been as mature and
experienced then as I am now I wouldn't have let myself just
be carried away, or have absorbed Hitler's ideas so easily and
uncritically. Then I would have been bound to wonder about the
dangers present in the power of a man whose gift for oratory
and power of suggestion could hold people spellbound, simply
suppressing their own will and convictions.

Sometimes I saw Hitler's advisors, generals and colleagues come
away from talks with the Führer looking dismayed, chewing on
thick cigars and brooding. I spoke to some of them later. And
although they were stronger, wiser and more experienced than
me, it often happened that they went to see the Führer armed
with unimpeachable arguments and documentary evidence,
absolutely determined to persuade him that an order was impossible or could not be carried out. But before they had finished
he would begin talking, and all their objections melted away,
becoming pointless in the face of his theory. They knew it
couldn't be right, but they couldn't pin down the flaw in it.
When they left him they felt despairing, crushed, with their
former firm and absolute resolve badly shaken, as if they had
been hypnotized. I think many of them tried to hold out against
his influence, but others felt exhausted and worn down, and then
just let events simply take their course to the bitter end.

But as I was saying, it took entire and total collapse, a *really*
bitter end and many deep disappointments, before I could see
clearly and with any certainty. At the time life flowed pleasantly
by. I enjoyed being beside the lakes in the great forests in summer.
My memory almost fails me today when I think of all the terrible
things going on in the world in 1943. The German Wehrmacht
was marching against Stalingrad, and our cities at home were
beginning to feel the effects of the air raids. Göring made his
great speech: 'If a single enemy aircraft appears in the skies over
Berlin then my name's Meyer.' And the sirens began wailing not

only in Berlin but all over the Reich. A great deal of building and consolidation went on at headquarters. The bunkers were reinforced, and barbed wire and mines disfigured the forest.

One day another woman appeared at the Wolf's Lair. Professor Morell brought her, introducing her as the Führer's dietician. From now on she would cook exclusively for him. Frau von Exner[60] was met with interest by the gentlemen and with icy reserve by the ladies. Only when we all moved into a hut with bright, spacious rooms, which Frau von Exner shared with us, did I come into contact with her, and we became the best of friends. Then I found out what had brought her here. She was Viennese, and had been a dietician at Vienna University Hospital when by chance she was offered a position in Bucharest by Marshal Antonescu. He had temporary stomach trouble and wanted to cure himself by following a diet. Frau von Exner's skills were so successful that Antonescu was perfectly all right again after a few months. When the two statesmen with their delicate digestions met in Salzburg in the spring, they apparently discussed the ailment they shared. Hitler turned to his physician and told him to look for a good dietician too. Morell thought his own injections and medicaments did more good than any diet, but to avoid unpleasantness he himself went to Vienna University Hospital and urged Frau von Exner to come and cook for Hitler. She had not been very enthusiastic about this offer, since she didn't want to interrupt her own work and her independent career, but in the end she accepted Morell's offer. She was a little older than me when she joined us, about twenty-four. Dark haired, well built, full of the vivacious charm of Vienna, frank and amusing, she attracted me very much. So now Hitler had a fifth female companion for his mealtimes. He liked to hear stories of Frau von Exner's family in Vienna. She had several brothers and sisters and came from a distinguished Viennese medical family. At the time when the emerging NSDAP was banned in Austria, she and her brothers and sisters had been enthusiastic supporters of National Socialism, and later joined the Party. But their enthusiasm waned once the German Gauleiter was lording it in Vienna, and Nazi government and the war came to Austria too. Frau von Exner stood up to Hitler for the interests of the Viennese: 'My Führer, you promised to give Vienna, the pearl of Austria, a golden setting. But your people are destroying more of the old culture of Vienna than they build up. Why do you prefer Linz?'

Hitler tolerated her reproaches and remained kindly and thoughtful. He liked her lively manner, was very fond of Viennese puddings, and admired her skill in making vegetarian soups that tasted better than meat broth. He couldn't guess that poor Marlene was unhappy about his modest demands. With Antonescu, despite his diet, she had been able to revel in lobster, mayonnaise, caviar and other delicacies, and she had cooked fine dinners for festive receptions. But Hitler, as usual, wanted nothing but his one-pot dishes, carrots with potatoes, and boring soft-boiled eggs. 'He'll never thrive on food like this,' she wailed, and she simmered a bone in his soup now and then. Above all, she smoked like a chimney, and I assured her that she would be Hitler's cook only until he found a cigarette end in his cocoa.

Later Antonescu paid another visit to headquarters. He was pleased to see his dietician again, and sent her a puppy by air, one of the offspring of the two fox terriers that Frau von Exner had looked after lovingly in Bucharest. He was a tiny little thing; every tuft of grass was an obstacle to him and he never grew to normal dog size, but he did become a charming, lively, clever little animal. Hitler thought him a gift unworthy of a statesman, and made haste to give Frau von Exner a dog as a present himself. 'What a Balkan like Antonescu can do, I can do better,' he said to himself, and told Reichsleiter Bormann to find the best prize-winning pedigree fox terrier he could. Frau von Exner was tearing her hair out over this proposition. 'What on earth am I going to do with *two* dogs?' she said. 'I'm in the kitchen all day.' But the pedigree dog arrived. Bormann had found a splendid specimen, the winner of several beauty contests and very expensive. Hitler proudly handed him over. The dog was called Purzel, and was a very calm, slow-moving gentleman who had never learned to do anything but stand in the proper position, well aware of his pedigree, and be admired. But he wasn't house-trained.

Hitler had had a special little diet kitchen built next to the main kitchen for the mess. When he noticed that I had made friends with Marlene von Exner, and I complained once again of not having enough work to do for him, he suggested that I might learn to cook from her. I did so, with enthusiasm, but now I was asked before every meal whether I had had a hand in cooking it. I thought this question was put with a certain amount of suspicion. But I'm sure he wasn't so much afraid of being poisoned as wondering whether I might not have added sugar instead of salt.

At the beginning of July Hitler flew to Italy for talks with Mussolini, and I accompanied him.[61] It was another of those journeys kept so secret that even the participants didn't know what was going on. We had been eating with Hitler the evening before, and he didn't say a word about his plans. Next morning I noticed a certain restlessness in the vicinity of the Führer bunker. Orderlies were hurrying about earlier than usual, carrying cases; Schaub was striding through the camp looking very important and expressing himself less clearly than ever, because he was trying to speak correct High German in honour of this important occasion. I supposed some kind of reception must be planned, and thought nothing much of it, but I did pack the office case to be on the safe side. At midday my phone suddenly rang and Linge asked, 'Do you have a uniform?' I said, 'No, why would I have a uniform? I've never needed one before.' 'Then you'll be left behind on the airfield.' Before I could ask any more questions he had hung up. I went off to Schaub, because as chief adjutant it was his business to tell us when we were needed. It was awkward for him when I asked whether the Führer was going away, and how it was that I'd learned I was to go too only by chance. He muttered something vague and said I was to be ready at two to drive to the airfield. When I asked where we were going and how long for, he said it was secret and none of my business. I just laughed and found out more from Linge. Unfortunately he was so busy that he could only tell me, briefly, it was expected that the trip would last three days. But I still didn't find out where we were going. As the situation on the Eastern Front wasn't very good, I assumed the Führer was going to visit the Army Group in Ukraine. I drove to the airfield with two of the stenographers whose job it was to take down the daily conferences verbatim in shorthand. When one of them asked me, 'Have you ever been to Italy before?' I finally knew our destination.

We flew in four large, four-engined Condor planes. I was in the same aircraft as the Führer. It was a roomy passenger plane and held about sixteen people. Hitler had a single seat just behind the pilot's cockpit, on the right-hand side of the plane. There was quite a large folding table in front of him. The other seats were arranged as they would be in a comfortable dining car, in groups of four with a little table in the middle of each group. The pilot, Captain Baur,[62] soon took the plane up to a high altitude so that the passengers would feel tired in the thinner atmosphere and go to sleep. As long as Hitler was awake, there was always someone walking up and down, disturbing the balance of the plane. Professor Morell hated flying. He sat in front in the cockpit, next to the pilot, and he was throwing up all the time. He arrived more dead than alive at the end of any flight. We stopped off for the night at the Berghof. This time I had felt upset by the flight too, and I went to bed directly after dinner. But first I asked what time we were to start next morning, and was told that we were to get into the cars and drive to the airfield at seven-thirty in the morning. I went to sleep at once, after telling the switchboard to wake me next day.

I was just sitting comfortably in the bathtub when the phone rang and an orderly asked why I wasn't ready yet, everyone was waiting for me. I was horrified, flung my clothes on, and ran downstairs still doing them up and cursing my watch which seemed to be so unreliable and said only seven o'clock. However, I was being unfair to it, for during the evening and night the weather had changed, and Hitler had decided to set off half an hour earlier. No one had thought to tell me.

We landed somewhere in northern Italy, boarded Mussolini's special train, and were taken to Treviso station. Hitler, with his entourage and their host, got into a column of cars and the motorcade roared off, surrounded by carabinieri on motorcycles, for the place where the talks were to be held, a fine old villa nearby. I didn't see Hitler or any of his entourage all day. I stayed behind in Mussolini's special train, marvelling at the mess and dirt, the old-fashioned carriages and the way the staff were got up like operetta characters, and I suffered terribly from the heat.

Late in the afternoon we started back the same way as we had come. After a wonderful flight over the Alps in the sunset we reached the Berghof, and next morning we returned to the Wolf's Lair.

Unfortunately Hitler's visit to Mussolini turned out to have done little good, for barely four weeks later Mussolini was a prisoner in another villa, and Italian Fascism was in a state of collapse.[63] Hitler swore. He was furious about the secession of Italy and Mussolini's mishap, and that evening he didn't hide his bad temper even from us women. He was monosyllabic and absent-minded. 'So Mussolini is weaker than I thought,' he said. 'I was giving him my personal support, and now he's fallen. But we could never rely on the Italians, and I think we'll win the victory better alone than with such irresponsible allies. They've cost us more in loss of prestige and real setbacks than any success they brought us was worth.'

So now I sit here thinking of what happened next. Only a few salient points stand out from the regular course of our days, and now they look like signposts along the rapid downward course of the avalanche that buried everything. All the separate small parts that added up to the great event are blurred in my mind. Hitler lived, worked, played with his dog, ranted and raged at his generals, ate meals with his secretaries, and drove Europe towards its fate – and we hardly noticed. Germany was echoing with the wail of sirens and the roar of enemy aircraft engines. Fierce battles were being fought in the East.

Then came that grey, rainy day when Fräulein Wolf, eyes red with weeping, met me on the way to the Führer bunker. 'Stalingrad has fallen. Our whole army has been annihilated. They're dead!'[64] She was almost sobbing. And we both thought of all that blood, and the dead men and the dreadful despair.

That evening Hitler seemed a tired old man. I don't remember what we talked about, but a dismal image has stayed in my memory, rather like visiting a bleak graveyard in the November rain.

Yet this gloom was temporarily dispelled by news of victories and Hitler's own unshakeable confidence. He had now made it his habit to have a nocturnal tea-party at headquarters too. As well as the secretaries he invited his doctors, adjutants, Walther Hewel, Heinz Lorenz and Reichsleiter Bormann. Göring and Himmler were never present, but Speer sometimes came, Sepp Dietrich turned up once, and of course Frau von Exner was there.

We laughed a lot, and Hitler usually tried to keep the conversation away from serious matters. But when Speer was present a technical note entered the discussion. Then we talked about all kinds of inventions, new weapons and so on, and memories of past campaigns were revived with Sepp Dietrich. I must say these evenings were much more personal and interesting than the tea-parties at the Berghof. We sat close together round a relatively small circular table, and the bright lighting in the whitewashed bunker room kept us awake.

Again, we divided tea-time duty into two shifts, because it wasn't possible to go to bed at five or six in the morning every day and then get up again at nine. Hitler entirely understood that, since he knew from Eva Braun how important a woman's beauty sleep is to her, but he didn't like it when we spoke of entertaining him as a 'duty'.

There were probably hundreds of thousands of little stories he told that I found interesting at the time, for instance about his childhood and schooldays, his time as a student in Vienna, the many pranks he played while he was a soldier, and later the early days of the Party, followed by his imprisonment and so on, but all those were such fleeting, trifling impressions in view of what happened later that I can't remember them properly any more. At the time they drew me the picture of a very human, understanding, invulnerable Führer who might think himself a genius but was also regarded as a genius by his whole entourage, and for quite a while his successes backed that idea up. In fact it was my familiarity with this sensitive, innocuous, private side of him, and my knowledge of his personal experiences, that made it so difficult to see the evil spirit inside the genius.

Once again there's a large section missing from the film of my memory. All that time in 1943 when I spent every day and every night living, talking and eating with Hitler is like a single long day. In that time bombs were dropped, the front lines changed, we flew air raids on England and tried to storm our way to victory. Christmas came, but hardly anyone took any notice, and Hitler ignored it entirely. Not an evergreen branch, not a candle marked the festival of peace and love. My husband had come back on leave; we stayed in our hut together. He was completely different; it was a stranger who had come back to me, leaving the man I'd married there at the front. He couldn't stand being back behind the lines any more; he was in despair when a conversation with Hitler showed him that the Führer no longer had a clear view of the real situation. Soon after the festive season he flew back to the army. At some time in the spring of 1944, German POWs in Russia had been induced to make confessions by injections of some kind. For reasons of secrecy Hitler immediately had everyone who had been in his immediate entourage withdrawn from the Eastern Front. That included my husband. He was transferred to the West.

Hitler spoke more and more often of the possibility of a massive air raid on Führer headquarters. 'They know exactly where we are, and some time they're going to destroy everything here with carefully aimed bombs. I expect them to attack any day,' he said, meaning the American bombers. We often heard the air-raid warning now, but it was never more than single aircraft circling above us. Our anti-aircraft guns weren't used. The planes were presumably only on reconnaissance flights, and we didn't want to attract their attention with incautious gunfire.

In spring we went to the Berghof again. Meanwhile, the head-quarters in East Prussia were to be further reinforced. Hitler wanted to have several very stable, bombproof bunkers built. Colossal structures consisting of eleven metres of concrete were to be put up, and I hated the thought that we would have to live like moles, never seeing daylight.

But for the time being our drone-like existence on the Ober-salzberg began again. Eva Braun was there once more, cheerful and sprightly with her inexhaustible wardrobe, the guests rolled up, and as far as they were concerned the war was far away.

Marlene von Exner hadn't come with us. She had stayed behind at the Wolf's Lair to pack her cases, wind up her affairs, and go back to Vienna. Hers was a tragi-comic fate. She had lost her heart to the young SS adjutant Fritz Darges, even though she couldn't stand Prussians and hated the SS. But it had happened, and there were two consequences. First, Gretl Braun was in love with Fritz Darges too, but a love affair with her was a little too dangerous and not private enough for young Fritz, so he hadn't been able to make up his mind. Second, there was something the matter with Marlene's family. She had mentioned when she first began working for Hitler that her mother's papers weren't in order. Her grandmother had been a foundling, and her origins couldn't be established. In view of the good Nazi attitude of the whole family, Hitler thought nothing much of this, until suddenly the able and industrious SD[65] found out that there really was Jewish blood in her maternal line. Marlene was horrified, not so much because she might lose her job with Hitler as because now she couldn't possibly become the wife of an SS man. Hitler had a conversation with Frau von Exner in which he said, 'I'm really extremely sorry for you, but you will understand that I have no alternative to dismissing you from my service. I can't possibly make an exception for myself personally and break my own laws just because it would be to my advantage. But when you are back in Vienna I will have your whole family Aryanized, and pay you your salary for the next six months. I would also like to invite you to be my guest at the Berghof again before you leave me.'

So Marlene said goodbye. Reichsleiter Bormann was asked, in my presence, to see about the Aryanization of the Exner family. It was a task that Bormann undertook only reluctantly, since when he himself made advances to the charming Viennese he had not had any luck, and he could never forgive her for that.

And he took his revenge, because a few weeks later I received a very unhappy letter from Vienna, saying that all the members of the family had had their Party books taken away, and they were in great distress. When I asked Bormann what was going on he said he would deal with it. But long weeks went by again, and finally I had shattering news: life for the Exners was now very hard. Marlene had to leave the University Hospital, her sister couldn't study medicine, her elder brother had to give up practising as a doctor, and the youngest brother couldn't now have a career as a military officer.

I was so angry and indignant that I sat down at the typewriter with the outsize characters, typed the letter out on it word for word, and took it to the Führer. He went red in the face with fury and called for Bormann at once. The Reichsleiter was red in the face too when he came out of Hitler's room, and he gave me a furious glance. All the same, in March I received the cheering news that everything was all right again, the whole Exner family was extremely grateful to me, and their Aryanization had finally gone through. But four weeks later the Allies were in Vienna, and their Party books were probably condemned and burnt.[66]

[. . .] Life was more irregular than ever [in the early spring of 1944: M.M.]. The conferences went on and on, meals were eaten at the most impossible times. Hitler went to bed later than ever before. The cheerfulness and light banter, and the coming and going of all the guests, couldn't hide the uneasiness in all our hearts. Hitler's entourage knew about his anxieties and the difficult situation, while those still in the dark believed his assurances of victory and so quelled their own bitter experiences and dark forebodings.

Eva Braun sought my company. She asked: 'How is the Führer, Frau Junge? I don't want to ask Morell, I don't trust him. I hate him. I was alarmed when I saw the Führer. He looks old and very grave. Do you know what he's worried about? He doesn't discuss these things with me, but I don't think the situation is good.' 'Fräulein Braun, I know less than you. You know the Führer better than I do, you can guess at what he doesn't say. But the Wehrmacht report alone is enough to make the man responsible for it anxious.'

In the tea-house, Eva told the Führer he shouldn't stoop like that. 'It comes of having such heavy keys in my trouser pocket,' he said. 'And I'm carrying a whole sackful of cares around with me.' But then he couldn't help making a joke of it. 'If I stoop I match you better. You wear high heels to make yourself taller, I stoop a little, so we go well together.' 'I'm not short!' she protested. 'I'm 1.63 metres, like Napoleon!' No one knew how tall Napoleon was, not even Hitler. 'What do you mean, Napoleon was 1.63 metres tall? How do you know?' 'Why, every educated person knows that,' she replied, and that evening, when we were in the living room together after dinner, she went to the bookcase and looked in the encyclopaedia. But it didn't say anything about Napoleon's height.

It snowed without stopping during these weeks. Walls of snow towered up on the terrace, huge quantities of it had to be shovelled away every day to make a narrow path to the tea-house and leave the entrances free. Eva would have loved to go skiing, but Hitler wouldn't let her. 'You could break a foot, it's too dangerous,' he said. So she made do with long walks and often wasn't in for lunch.

It was still snowing in April. At a thousand metres above sea level, the snow was nine metres deep. Then at last spring came, and with the spring enemy aircraft appeared above the Berchtesgadener Land. The Allies had captured so many bases to the south that large squadrons could keep taking off from them, flying over Austria and on to Bavaria. And they all flew over our area. The sirens always wailed just as we were dropping off to sleep in the early hours of the morning. Then the smoke mortars were set off in the valley and on the slopes of the Führer's grounds, and the whole area was hidden by thick clouds of artificial mist.[67] Hitler was expecting an attack on the Berghof and his headquarters, and men had been working on a huge complex of shelters in and around the Berghof for months. The rock had been hollowed out in many places, machinery was eating its way into the mountain, threading a whole network of tunnels through it. But only the Berghof bunker was ready. A large gate led deep into the rock opposite the back door beside the living room. You had to climb down sixty-five steps, and then you reached an air-raid shelter which contained everything useful and necessary to sustain life for the Führer and a large number of other people. I only saw the two shelter rooms themselves, not the storerooms and archives accommodated there. Almost every day the sleepy guests assembled in the cave under the mountain with their cases. But no raid ever came.

We were only on the bombers' flight path, and the raids were usually aiming for Vienna, targets in Hungary or cities in Bavaria. When the clouds of mist had dispersed we often saw the red reflection of fires in the sky over Munich. It was hard to restrain Eva then. She begged for permission to drive to Munich and see if her little house was all right. Usually Hitler wouldn't let her. Then she would be on the phone, giving instructions, getting detailed information from everyone she knew. And when one of her best friends, the Munich actor Heini Handschuhmacher, died in an air raid there was no holding her. She went to the funeral with her friend Herta Schneider and her sister Gretl and came back badly shaken, with terrible accounts of the misery of the people who had suffered in the bombing. Hitler listened to her description with a gloomy expression.

Then he vowed revenge and retaliation, and swore that the new inventions of the German Luftwaffe would pay the enemy back for this a hundred times over.

Unfortunately these threats never came to anything. Swarms of Allied planes kept flying over the Reich, and although V1 and V2 bombers flew in the opposite direction to London, what good did that do the German cities? Hitler was full of enthusiasm for the V1s and V2s. 'Panic will break out in England. The effect of these weapons will wear their nerves down so badly that they won't be able to hold out for long. I'll pay the barbarians back for shooting women and children and destroying German culture.' But the reports he received of the Luftwaffe defence measures were devastating. I remember one daylight raid on Munich. Hitler wanted to know exactly what forces were being used in defence, and Colonel von Below was on the phone all the time, getting news. Finally he had to report: 'My Führer, it was planned for six German fighters to take off, but three never got off the ground, two had to turn back because of engine trouble, and the last plane felt so isolated it didn't attack.' Hitler was furious. Although his guests were with him he couldn't help ranting and raging at the German Luftwaffe.

So we went on being routed out of bed almost daily and having to climb down into the underground dungeon. But after we had played this game dozens of times and no bomb had fallen anywhere near us, our willingness to leave our beds gradually faded. Hitler himself never climbed down the sixty-five steps until the anti-aircraft guns were firing or we were sure there was a genuine raid on nearby targets. But he stood close to the entrance keeping watch, like Cerberus, to make sure that no one left the bunker until the all clear went. He was particularly strict with Eva Braun about that.

One day, when the sirens were wailing again, and I was already up and had eaten breakfast, I went down to the tunnels to see if the Berghof party had assembled down there. There wasn't a soul in sight. But when I reached the top steps and my head was already coming up to surface level I saw the Führer standing outside the entrance. He was talking to Adjutant Bormann and the liaison officer Hewel. When he saw me he wagged his finger and said, 'Now don't be so reckless, young woman, just go back down again, they haven't sounded the all clear yet.' Since I didn't want to say that neither Eva nor the other guests had even got out of bed, let alone gone down to the bunker, I obediently withdrew. I tried to escape again twice, but each time I was turned back, and not until the siren sounded the all clear could I leave the dungeon.

At table Hitler delivered a lecture, saying it was absolutely essential to go down into the bunker when there was an air-raid warning. 'It's stupid, not brave, for people not to get into safety. The duty of my staff is to go into the bunkers – some of you are irreplaceable. It's idiotic to imagine you show courage by running the risk of being hit by a bomb.' He didn't mean me so much as many of the men in his entourage, and the officers who didn't believe an attack on headquarters was likely, and didn't feel like spending hours of their time doing nothing down underground.

During our stay at the Berghof in the spring of 1944, Hitler assembled the army commanders, staff officers and the leaders of all divisions of the troops at the Platterhof and made inspiring speeches to them. Industrialists and political leaders were summoned too and given Hitler's instructions. Although he made long speeches he didn't dictate the text to me. On such occasions, when he was addressing an internal audience, he didn't need notes. His speech wasn't for the general public, and he much preferred speaking off the cuff. The top brass included Field Marshal Dietl, commander of the mountain troops in Norway.[68] He had come straight from the front, and was awarded the brilliants to the Knight's Cross on this occasion.[69] Hitler thought very highly of him, and they talked for a long time. Of course Dietl wanted to seize the chance of seeing his wife. Hitler advised him not to take off in a plane until next morning, since weather conditions around Salzburg were usually very bad for take-off in the evening. But Dietl couldn't wait. He set off very early in the

morning, in spite of the fog, and Hitler was woken with the news
that his outstanding commander had died in a crash, brilliants
and all. Hitler was very upset. I can't imagine he was just pretending. We all liked Dietl and were very sorry about his sudden
death. But at the same time Hitler was furious that Dietl had
been so reckless as to put himself in danger, flying in poor
weather conditions. He repeated yet again that it was the duty
of his irreplaceable colleagues to avoid danger.

A few weeks later, however, there was another plane crash
near Salzburg, and another commander was killed, General
Hube.[70] This time Walther Hewel had been in the crash too, and
was taken to the Berchtesgaden hospital badly injured. I never
found out how the accident happened.

I quite forgot to say that meanwhile a new face had appeared in
Hitler's circle, that of Gruppenführer Fegelein.[71] He acted as
liaison officer between Himmler and Hitler and was on Hitler's
staff. At first you only saw him arriving for the military briefings,
but soon he made friends with Reichsleiter Bormann, and before
long he was setting the tone at the Berghof.

Hermann Fegelein was the daring cavalryman type. He had a
very large nose, and wore the Knight's Cross with oakleaves and
swords. No wonder he was used to women flocking around him.
In addition he had a refreshing, sometimes very dry wit, and
never minced his words. You felt he was a naturally frank and
honest person. That helped him to forge a remarkable career
quickly and unexpectedly. No sooner had he appeared than he
was sitting with us at table in the Berghof. He went to Bormann's
nocturnal parties, drank to the health of all the important men
there, and all the women were at his feet. Those who were not
his friends were his enemies until he was firmly in the saddle.
He was clever but ruthless, and had some very attractive qualities, such as the honesty with which he admitted that at heart
he was a terrible coward, and had won his decorations doing
heroic deeds out of pure fear. He also frankly admitted that
nothing was as important to him as his career and a good life.

Unfortunately differences of opinion and intrigues surfaced in Hitler's entourage soon after he had joined us. Fegelein, who was an entertaining, sociable person, soon attracted the attention of Eva Braun and her sister Gretl. The latter in particular was the object of handsome Hermann's attentions. It's true that before he knew she was Eva's sister he had said, 'What a silly goose!' But he was quick to change his mind in view of her family connections. Everyone was surprised when Fegelein's engagement to Gretl Braun was announced. It reinforced Fegelein's position personally too. Hewel the liaison officer, who had married now himself and was at present in hospital, injured, after his plane accident, was the only man to have a good enough personal relationship with Hitler to be an obstacle in Fegelein's way. So Fegelein used Hewel's absence to slander him to Hitler, and he succeeded. Hewel, who couldn't defend himself, fell into disfavour, and Hitler refused even to meet his wife.

But all these personal human experiences became unimportant in view of the American invasion in the West. It came suddenly, although it had long been expected and was supposed to be doomed to failure from the start. My husband, who was just enjoying a short leave with me in Berchtesgaden, had to return to the front immediately. The war conferences went on and on. We saw Hitler's grave and rather careworn face. His hopes that the enemy would be decisively defeated when they attacked in the West didn't seem to be being realized very quickly. Guests came and went at the Berghof, the sun shone down over the peaceful landscape, we chatted, laughed, made love and drank, yet the tension still grew from day to day. Julius Schaub's lower lip was hanging right down to his chin: it was his job to go through the Luftwaffe reports. The reports of losses and injuries were coming in so thick and fast that we could type out only brief notes of them in the reports for the Führer. Göring and the Luftwaffe officers were angrily reproached at every military briefing. Large quantities of photographs came in from Gauleiters all over the Reich showing the destruction of their cities. Hitler looked at them all and snorted with rage. But he never saw the extent of the devastation with his own eyes.

One day, when I came back from Munich, which I had left just after a bad air raid, I told him, 'My Führer, all those photographs you're looking at are nothing to the misery of the real thing. You ought to see the people standing outside the burning buildings, weeping and warming their hands on the glowing, charred beams, watching their homes collapse and bury everything they have.' He replied, 'I know what it's like, but I shall change things. We've built new planes now, and soon all these horrors will be over!'

Hitler never saw what the war looked like in his own country, never realized the full extent of the destruction and devastation. He spoke of nothing but retaliation and the success to come, the certainty of the final victory. I couldn't help it, I thought he really did have some certain method, some last reserves in the background that would free the people from all their suffering one day.

Life would have been good but for the feeling that we were sitting on a powder keg, while our secret nervousness kept spreading. Among his guests, Hitler was still trying to show his confidence and certainty of victory by making light conversation to the ladies, walking to the tea-house, and playing records and telling stories by the fire in the evening. But I thought he sometimes sat there [...] looking old and tired, his mind elsewhere. He, the gallant cavalier who never wanted to look old, asked the ladies whether they minded if he put his feet up on the sofa. And Eva Braun's eyes looked anxious and sad. She was trying harder than ever to keep Hitler's guests in a good mood, desperately and with touching efforts doing her best to provide cheerfulness and relaxation. She was never absent from meals or the hearth in the Great Hall these days.

By now it was July. Hitler was not planning to stay on the Obersalzberg any longer. His bunker at headquarters wasn't ready yet, but all the same he gave orders for a return to the Wolf's Lair. For the time being he would live in the former adjutants' and guest bunkers, which we secretaries had once occupied. So in the first week of July, like migratory birds, we returned to East Prussia.

The place was barely recognizable. Instead of the low-built little bunkers, heavy, colossal structures of concrete and iron rose above the trees. There was nothing to be seen from above. Grass had been planted on the flat rooftops, trees grew from the concrete, some of them real and some artificial, and from the plane you would have thought the forest stretched on unbroken. The rooms in the new bunker were small and their furnishings makeshift. Hitler set aside the hut next to it for conferences; the place had been intended for guest accommodation and had a large sitting room. Several large tables were set up here so that the huge maps could be spread out, and now the place was ready for use as a conference room. All four secretaries were together again here at the Wolf's Lair. We had more social duties now and plenty of work to do as well.

It was a hot summer. The sun blazed down from the sky and each day was finer than the last. The huts gave no cool shelter, and once again the bunkers became our favourite places to work. Swarms of midges and mosquitoes hovered over the marshy meadows, making our lives a misery. The guards had to wear mosquito netting over their faces, and the windows were fitted with mesh to keep flies out. Hitler hated this kind of weather. Blondi was exercised almost exclusively by Sergeant Tornow the dog-walker, while Hitler stayed in the cool of the concrete rooms. He was bad-tempered and complained of insomnia and head-aches. He needed distraction and relaxing company more than ever, and the worse the war was going the less anyone talked about it. We depended on the reports of Wehrmacht High Command, which were hung up in the anteroom of the mess next to the day's menu and the cinema programme. The news was not cheering.

But Hitler went on with the war, and with his nocturnal tea-parties too. He even invited guests who were not part of his usual entourage. 'I'm so tired of being surrounded by soldiers,' he said. The adjutants racked their brains, wondering who might provide the Führer with suitable entertainment. Heinrich Hoffmann was always available as a last resort, but he had become so senile and was so addicted to the bottle that Hitler didn't really enjoy talking to him any more. However, the builder and architect Professor Hermann Giesler was just the man Hitler needed. He was not only an artist in his profession, but he also had a talent that made him something of a court jester: he could imitate the voice and almost the appearance of Reich Organization Leader Robert Ley. Ley had a speech impediment that meant he could form words only with difficulty, and in addition he talked such sheer nonsense that you could hardly take him seriously.

Since Ley, as leader of the German Labour Front, had given Professor Giesler many commissions for buildings, Giesler knew all his weaknesses quite well, and he had noted Ley's howlers with special relish. 'I have become more beautiful, and Germany is pleased to see it,' the Reich Organization leader had once announced to a meeting of workers in the fervent tones of conviction, meaning exactly the opposite: 'Germany has become more beautiful, and I am pleased to see it.' When Giesler laboriously uttered such comments in Ley's own manner Hitler roared with laughter. [. . .] Giesler put on a wonderful comic act. But Hitler must have felt rather awkward, in view of the fact that his Reich Organization Leader had uttered these howlers publicly and as a leading personality, and there was always the chance that other people too might laugh at Hitler's colleague. 'Ley is a faithful old Party comrade, and a real idealist. He has created a unique organization. And above all I can rely on him one hundred per cent.' Such were the excuses Hitler made for him. He showed similar tolerance to other old comrades from the Party's early days, but failed to show any to the clever folk who ventured to contradict him.

The Reich Stage Designer Professor Benno von Arent[72] from Berlin was often invited to headquarters too. Today it strikes me as really comic that all these gentlemen were called Reich something-or-other and were professors. No wonder we gave the sergeant who exercised the dog the title of Reich Dog-Walker, christened Professor Morell the Reich Injections Impresario, and Heinrich Hoffmann the Reich Drunk. As I was saying, the Reich Stage Designer was one of our party at night, although he really had no business at headquarters while the war was in the middle of its worst phase. All the same, he helped to keep up the strength of the Supreme Commander, which was important war work. Even in the Third Reich, theatre people didn't wear uniform, but secretly, backstage, leading artists did have some kind of Party or military rank so that they could appear in 'full dress German uniform' if necessary. So it wasn't surprising that Benno von Arent went around in an elegant field-grey uniform with quite a lot of silver braid on it. I must say he was a really charming, amusing, witty man, not a very strong character but fun. Whether he was any good as a stage designer I don't know, but he was excellent company, and when he and Giesler were together there was so much laughter, relaxation and amusement that I really sometimes forgot Hitler had to wage a merciless war, and the fate of Europe was embodied in him.

Then came 20 July 1944.

I can still feel the oppressive, sultry heat of that day. It made the air quiver slightly, and wouldn't let us sleep in the hot huts although we hadn't gone to bed until sunrise. Frau Christian and I cycled to the Moysee, the little lake outside the camp. Lying in the water, we dreamed of peace and quiet. We were half asleep, trying to get some more rest. I had such lovely, soothing thoughts in all that silence. There wasn't another human soul anywhere, and we didn't speak to each other until the sun began blazing down right overhead, telling us it was midday. We didn't know when the conference was to be held, and thought we might be needed before it. So we tore ourselves away from our other world and went back to the busy complex in the forest, at the heart of the war. Apparently the conference had already begun. The cars of officers who had come from other staff bases were in the car park, but otherwise all was noonday peace. All the secretaries were in their rooms. Then, suddenly, a terrible bang broke through the quiet. It was unexpected and alarming, but we often heard bangs near by when deer stepped on landmines, or some kind of weapon was being tried out.

I was writing a letter and didn't let the bang disturb me. But then I heard someone outside shouting for a doctor in urgent, agitated tones. Professor Brandt wasn't at headquarters. The voice calling for Professor von Hasselbach sounded distraught and full of panic.

So it wasn't the bang that suddenly made my heart stand still. As I said, we were used to hearing sudden shots or explosions echoing through the forest. People tested weapons in the forest, there were buildings going up everywhere, the anti-aircraft guns practised firing, and we accepted these sounds as natural. But what had just happened made me terribly anxious. I ran out. My colleagues came rushing out of the other rooms with pale, frightened faces. Outside we saw the two orderlies coming from the Führer bunker with distraught expressions, looking for the doctor. 'A bomb has exploded, it was probably in the Führer bunker,' they stammered.

We didn't know if Hitler was in his bunker or if the conference was still in progress. We stood there like sheep in a thunderstorm, paralysed by terror. Was the terror for our own lives or for Hitler? 'What will become of us if Hitler's dead?' Fräulein Schroeder suddenly asked in the oppressive silence, and that set us all moving. The spell was broken. We scattered wildly in different directions. Fräulein Wolf wanted to help look for the doctor, Fräulein Schroeder went in search of someone who could give precise information. Frau Christian and I ran towards the Führer's bunker and the hut next to it.

The dense trees still hid the site of the incident from view. On the narrow footpath that wound through them I saw General Jodl and Lieutenant Colonel Waizenegger[73] coming towards me. There was blood all over Jodl's face and his uniform was torn. Waizenegger's white uniform tunic showed spots of red too. They were swaying.

Frau Christian ran to meet them, and we were sent back and

told not to go any further, because the place was barricaded off. We learned no more. The two officers scarcely heard us, which wasn't surprising; the explosion had not only concussed them but burst their eardrums.

We went back to our hut. We still knew nothing about the cause of the accident, or its nature and effect. If only we could know what had happened! Was Hitler still alive? We hardly dared ask, but vague ideas of what might happen if Hitler was dead haunted my mind. I couldn't think straight. Was there anyone among Hitler's colleagues who could take over as his successor? Himmler, Göring, Goebbels? The idea struck me as impossible. They were just moons who drew their radiance from the sun and had no power of their own to give light. Or was there someone else in Germany, some opponent of Hitler, who might now seize power for himself?

Confused suppositions were going round and round in my head, yet it was only minutes since we'd heard the explosion. At last Otto Günsche passed our window. He must have been at the conference too, but he seemed to be all right and uninjured. We ran to him. 'What's happened? Is the Führer alive? Was anyone killed? What caused it?' He couldn't answer all our questions at once. 'The Führer is all right. He's back in his bunker, and you can go and see him. But the whole hut was blown up. It was an explosive device – probably hidden in the floor by the OT people.[74] We don't know any details yet.'

Curiosity drove us to the Führer bunker. I almost laughed at the sight of Hitler. He was standing in the little anteroom surrounded by several of his adjutants and servants. His hair was never particularly well cut, but now it was standing on end so that he looked like a hedgehog. His black trousers were hanging in strips from his belt, almost like a raffia skirt. He had thrust his right hand between the buttons of his uniform tunic; his arm was bruised. Smiling, he greeted us with his left arm. 'Well, ladies, everything turned out all right again. Yet more proof that Fate has chosen me for my mission, or I wouldn't be alive now.'

Of course we asked what had caused the explosion. 'It was a cowardly assassination attempt,' said Hitler. 'The explosives were probably laid by a craftsman working for the OT. I don't believe in the other possibility,' he said, turning to Bormann, who nodded in agreement. Bormann was always nodding in agreement. We would have liked to know more details. But Linge looked at his watch and said, 'My Führer, I think you'll have to change your trousers. The Duce will be arriving in an hour's time.' Hitler looked down at his rags. 'You may be right.' He left us and went to his room, his stance more upright and erect than I had seen it for a long time.

We would have liked to see the scene of the incident at close quarters, but we weren't allowed into it yet. All we could see from the entrance to the Führer bunker was that the part of the lightly built hut containing the big conference room had collapsed.

However, Grenadier Mandl, the youngest and most junior soldier in the Führer bunker, was happy to show off his importance by giving us a full description of what he had seen on orderly duty in the hut while the conference was in progress. 'The explosives went off only two metres from the Führer, but General Bodenschatz, who was standing next to him and was just bending over the table, took the main force of the blast just as the device exploded. He's very badly injured. So is General Schmundt. He lost large chunks of flesh torn out of his back, and he has a lot of burns. The stenographer sitting at the end of the table died instantly. Both his legs were torn off. Keitel and Jodl are wounded too, but the Führer wasn't injured. Sturmbannführer Günsche and Major von John[75] were flung out of the open window by the blast and landed in the grass several metres from the hut. Most of the men who were at the conference have splinter wounds, burns or minor injuries.' Grenadier Mandl knew all about it.

There was feverish tension and excitement all over the camp. Whenever two people met they discussed the assassination attempt. Hours passed like minutes and minutes like hours. As soon as the last smoke from the explosion had dispersed, they managed to identify the assassin. And in Berlin, Fate came down on Hitler's side.

While Hitler was returning to the scene with his companions after the assassination attempt, and they were going over all the details again, someone mentioned that Colonel von Stauffenberg[76] was the only officer who hadn't been present when the explosion occurred, because he had just left the room to make a phone call.

Suddenly Lance Corporal Adam from Intelligence came up to the Führer. He had been on telephone duty in the conference room, and suddenly announced, 'My Führer, yes, Colonel von Stauffenberg did leave the conference room just before the explosion, but not to make a phone call. He left the hut instead. He had such an odd expression on his face that I feel it's my duty to tell you he could have been the one who did it.'

Hitler was silent for a while. No one said anything. Up to now no one had suspected that an officer on Hitler's own staff could be the assassin. This was a second bombshell. Hitler still didn't want to believe it, but he gave orders to have Stauffenberg traced. The avalanche began to roll and the tragedy took its course. Not until that evening when we joined Hitler for tea did we hear the full story.

It really had been Colonel von Stauffenberg who brought a bomb in his briefcase and left it by the table leg, just two metres from where Hitler was sitting. Stauffenberg did not often attend the military briefings. This time he had volunteered to General Buhle for the duty. Major von John usually carried Stauffenberg's briefcase for him because he had only three fingers on his right hand. Now John suddenly remembered that on this occasion Stauffenberg had refused to hand over his briefcase. With its fatal contents, it had been standing right next to Hitler for over an hour. Then Colonel von Stauffenberg left the scene of the crime and set off to join General Fellgiebel, one of his fellow conspirators, and wait for news that the plot had succeeded. The bomb went off just as he had planned. Stauffenberg got into his car and drove through the camp, past the ruined hut. He saw the wounded officers lying in the grass, no sign of Hitler, just the smoking, shattered wooden remains and bleeding men. He must have thought his mission had succeeded, and he drove to the airfield convinced that Hitler was dead. But by the time Stauffenberg drove past the hut the Führer was already back in his bunker, uninjured and fit and well.

Of course Goebbels was immediately informed of the failed assassination, but it wasn't made public knowledge. No one knew yet how many accomplices Stauffenberg had and what was going on in Berlin. But soon there was much hurry and bustle, with a great many confused orders and counter-orders. All hell was let loose at OKW.[77] None of them there knew where their allegiance lay – with the resistance movement in the Wehrmacht, or with those loyal to Hitler? The circumstances of what went on in Berlin were never quite clear to me. All I know is that the commander of the 'Greater Germany' regiment, Colonel Remer,[78] decided the matter when he placed himself under the orders of Goebbels, ordered his men to occupy the Reich Chancellery and the radio station, and denied entrance to the resistance officers. This action earned him the award of the Knight's Cross from Hitler next day, and peace was restored to the streets of Berlin without a shot being fired.

But it took a long time for the waves of excitement to die down at headquarters. When I saw Hitler that evening he was still full of fury and indignation over such treachery at the most crucial phase of the war. 'What cowards they are! They could at least have shot at me – then I might feel some respect for them. But they daren't put their lives at stake. There can't be many people stupid enough to think they could do better than me. Those fools don't know what chaos there will be if I let go of the strings. But I'll make an example of them that will stop anyone else wanting to commit such treachery against the German nation!' Hitler's eyes were flashing. He was livelier than I'd seen him for a long time, although his right arm was causing him pain. He held it motionless between the buttons of his tunic.

The table top had wrenched his arm when the bomb blast sent it up in the air.

I don't know what would have happened if the assassination had succeeded. All I see is millions of soldiers now lying buried somewhere, gone for ever, who might instead have come home again, their guns silent and the sky quieter once more. The war would have been over.

But that vision is quickly banished by what really happened: the assassination attempt of 20 July was the greatest possible misfortune for Germany and Europe. Not because it was made but because it failed. Hitler saw all the unfortunate coincidences that foiled the plot as his personal success. His confidence, his certainty of victory and his sense of security, his consciousness of power and his megalomania now really passed beyond all the bounds of reason. If recent military defeats might perhaps have made him ready to compromise, if his inmost heart had sometimes wavered in its belief in victory, now he thought that Fate had confirmed his own worth, his ideals, his power and all that he did.

'Those criminals who wanted to do away with me have no idea what would have happened to the German nation then. They don't know about the plans of our enemies who want to destroy Germany so that it can never rise again. If the Jews, with the hatred they feel, ever get power over us, then all will finally be over for German and European culture. And if they think the Western powers are strong enough to hold back Bolshevism without Germany they're wrong. This war must be won or Europe will be lost to Bolshevism. And I shall make sure that no one else can keep me from victory or do away with me. I am the only one who sees the danger and the only one who can stop it.' Hitler thought it necessary to address the German people that same day. While we were still in the bunker a radio car was ordered from Königsberg, and the transmission line was set up in the tea-house.[79] We went over there with Hitler just before midnight. The officers who had survived the assassination attempt with only slight injuries were in the tea-house as well.

General Jodl had a bandage round his head, Keitel's hands were bandaged too, and other officers wore plasters. It looked like the aftermath of a battle. For the first time you got the impression of a field headquarters. Men had really been wounded.

They were acting as if they had won a hard battle and a great danger had now passed. They congratulated the Führer on his miraculous survival, and we stood there and let their mood infect us, we went on believing in him, never realizing that the die had been cast to decide our fate that day.

Then Hitler spoke. He made a short speech intended to show the German nation that he was uninjured. He thanked Providence for averting a great misfortune from the German people, and urged them to go on believing in victory and work for it with all their might.

We listened, isolated and dazed by the frenzied aura of superior confidence radiating from these heroes of 20 July, and it never occurred to us that thousands of listeners out there were groaning in disappointment, burying their hopes and cursing the fate to which Hitler was so grateful. I still thought we had to win the war because otherwise all the terrible things Hitler had mentioned would happen, and they meant the end.

After the speech we went back to the bunker. Hitler summoned Professor Morell to come and examine him. He had had his pulse taken directly after the assassination attempt, and was very proud that it was perfectly regular and had been no faster than usual. Now, before he went to bed, he wanted confirmation that he was uninjured. We sat there for a while until the fat doctor made his way through the door, and then we went to bed ourselves. The morning sky was already showing pale through the trees. The sun would soon rise.

Of course the assassination attempt was the main subject of every conversation for a long time to come. Eva Braun was dreadfully upset, and wrote Hitler an anxious, desperate letter. He was very moved by her affection, and sent his wrecked uniform to Munich as a memento. Once he said, 'I can rely absolutely on my presentiments. I once had such a restless, odd feeling at the Berghof that I just had to leave. And now I know an assassination attempt was being planned on the Obersalzberg. There was new equipment for me to look at, and one of the soldiers involved in the display was to have an explosive device put in his knapsack without his knowledge. But by chance a general who was one of the conspirators was present, and they wanted to spare him, so the attempt had to be called off. However, if that bomb had exploded at the Berghof or in the new bunker none of us would be alive now. I don't fear death. My life is so full of care and so hard that death would come merely as a release. However, I have a duty to the German people, and I will do that duty.'

Although he said he felt 'uninjured', Hitler did summon an ear specialist from Berlin, because his hearing was giving him trouble and he was suffering from headaches. Dr Giesing[80] found out that one eardrum was burst and the other damaged. Professor Brandt, who hadn't been present when the assassination attempt took place, did not come. We wondered why not. There was nothing Professor Morell, a specialist in internal medicine, could do with his injections. After his treatment the badly injured men in hospital in Rastenburg recovered only with difficulty. There was no saving General Schmundt. He died of his injuries a few weeks later, although Morell had tried out his newest sulphonamides on him.

Gruppenführer Fegelein had been detailed to investigate the assassination attempt and track down the guilty men. He was personally indignant to think of anyone wanting to blow up such a splendid fellow as himself. I think he thought that was more criminal than any plan to get rid of Hitler, and he flung himself into the investigation with the zeal of his desire for revenge. Finally it became obvious even to Hitler that the resistance movement had spread more widely in the army than he had supposed. Distinguished names of men holding high rank were mentioned. He raged and shouted and said a great deal about traitors and scoundrels.

Hitler did not look well, and was leading an unhealthier life than ever. He hardly went out into the fresh air at all now, he ate little and had no appetite, and his left hand was beginning to tremble slightly. He remarked, 'I had this trembling in my right leg before the assassination attempt, and now it's moved to my left hand. I'm glad I don't have it in my head. I wouldn't like it at all if my head kept wagging.'

There was a new subject of conversation for the evening tea-parties: Blondi was to have a family. Hitler was looking for a suitable mate for her. His choice fell on Frau Professor Troost's German shepherd, a dog he had once given her as a present. So one day Gerdy Troost, the only woman visitor to Führer headquarters, turned up with her dog Harras. Blondi, whom we expected to be pleased by a male companion, took no notice at all of the visitor, and when he first tried getting closer bared her teeth furiously at him. Hitler was disappointed, but he didn't give up hope that after a while the two animals would learn to value and love each other, and then he could bring up a puppy one day.

We were sitting over tea with Frau Troost in the evening. She told Hitler he ought to go for more walks. 'This is no kind of life, my Führer. You might just as well have the landscape painted on these concrete walls and never leave the bunker at all!' He laughed and said he found the Prussian climate so unpleasant in summer that it was much healthier for him to stay indoors in the cool. However, when Frau Troost said he ought at least to have massages, they would do his arm good too, he was very firmly against it. He hated to be touched. He had dislocated his shoulder in the November putsch in Munich in 1923, and it had been massaged by a sergeant who did him more harm than good, and whose treatment was still a painful memory to him.

Frau Professor Troost left again, leaving her dog behind. Rudely rejected by Blondi, he now took a lively interest in my tiny fox terrier bitch, who was in heat for the first time. I was rather alarmed when a big grey shape leaped through my window in the hut one night, but I soon realized that this was a visitor for my little dog.

Harras was getting obviously thinner as a result of the constant excitement. Finally Blondi became friendlier and more forthcoming, and at last Hitler told us one day, beaming, that the two of them had mated! Harras stayed a few weeks longer to eat his fill from the fleshpots at headquarters.

While life flowed by at a regular pace for us at headquarters, and Hitler was always friendly, confident, amusing and charming, there was fierce fighting on all the fronts. In the East, the only victories won were defensive, and the front was contracting while the Russians kept advancing and coming closer. And in the West the invasion had spread out, forcing the German troops into defensive manoeuvres. My husband's division had seen bloody battles in the East, and had then been transferred to France to wait for more tanks and reinforcements. Hans Junge was sent to the Führer headquarters as a courier just as I was about to go to Munich to help my family, who had been bombed out. We spent a few days together in the ruined, bleak city of Berlin, and then parted. I went to Bavaria, he returned to his unit.

I found Munich a picture of destruction too. The building where we had lived was completely flattened. Nothing could be saved. People were desperate and hopeless. I met few who still believed in victory. When I repeated what Hitler said I lacked his own conviction and sense of security, and my heart was full of doubts and conflict. On going back to headquarters after three weeks, at the end of August, I asked the officers, the adjutants and everyone who ought to know, 'Tell me, how is the war going? Do you really believe we shall win?' And I always got the same answer. 'It looks bad, but not hopeless. We must hold on and wait for our new weapons to come into play.'

Once again we sat with Hitler in the evenings. Now that most of the German cities were rubble and ashes, he was devoting himself with passionate intensity to plans for rebuilding them. When Giesler was there, he discussed the reconstruction of Germany in minute detail. The rebuilding of Hamburg, Cologne, Munich, Linz and many other cities had taken firm shape, not just in Hitler's head but as complete architectural plans on paper. Hitler tended these plans lovingly, the way a gardener tends his roses. Sometimes we listened, uncomprehendingly, as his descriptions brought the finest cities in the world into existence before our eyes, the broadest streets, the tallest towers on earth. Everything was to be much better than it had ever been before, and he lavished superlatives on it all. Did he believe in his own words? I never stopped to wonder about that at the time. [. . .]

I didn't want any monumental buildings, I wanted peace and quiet. I certainly had a better life than most other people in wartime, I didn't have to sit in a boring office and I had hardly been in any air raids. But I felt like a prisoner in a golden cage, and I wished I could finally get away from here and go back to other people where I belonged. After all, I'd been married for over a year, and I hardly noticed. Hitler still treated me like the baby of a family. He particularly liked joking with me. I would be asked to imitate a comic Viennese film actor, or speak in Saxon dialect and reply to his jokes. Frau Christian was the object of Hitler's gallant attentions. It sometimes looked like a little flirtation, but almost every day the conversation would come round to Eva Braun, and then I could see Hitler's eyes take on a deep, warm glow, while his voice grew soft and gentle.

But when he called an officers' meeting again around the middle of August, and addressed the top military leaders at headquarters, there was no tolerance and softness about him now. I wasn't at the meeting, but I saw the grand uniforms locked in violent and agitated discussion in the mess afterwards. There seemed to have been angry words. Hitler had given full expression to his indignation over the treachery of 20 July, and he imposed the 'German greeting' on the whole German Wehrmacht. At the same time he called on the loyalty and conscience of the officers and their unreserved obedience. Later, by chance, I saw the minutes of this meeting. I had no right to read them, but I did cast a quick glance at some of the pages. They said: '. . . and I thought that at my last hour, my officers would gather around me in unshakeable loyalty, their daggers drawn . . .' Here

General Manstein[81] called out: 'And so they will, my Führer.' In brackets, after that, the minutes said: Loud applause.

Hitler also awarded decorations to the men wounded on 20 July around this time. Several had now died of their injuries, including General Schmundt. The survivors were solemnly given the award for the wounded. The newsreels and photo-reports recorded this great moment. I saw that Hitler kept his left hand motionless behind his back all the time. He was very anxious that no one should see its constant tremor. I noticed that his state of health wasn't very good anyway. He was taking any amount of medication. Either before or after meals Linge had to give him at least five different pills. One was to stimulate the appetite, another to aid digestion, a third to prevent flatulence, and so on. In addition Professor Morell, grunting and groaning, turned up in person every day to administer his usual miracle-working injections. The doctor had been suffering from particularly bad heart trouble recently. Once again he tried to lose weight by going on a diet, but his voracious appetite made it very difficult. When he came for tea in the evening it was usually only a few minutes before we heard his quiet snoring, which didn't stop until Hitler went to bed. Then Morell would assure us he had enjoyed the evening very much, but he was extremely tired. Hitler was never angry with him, but as solicitous as if he were a child. There was much gratitude and something like pity in his eyes when he spoke of Morell. He trusted him so completely that he said, 'But for Morell I might have died long ago, or at least have been unable to work. He was and still is the only person who can help me.' However, no one knew what Hitler was really suffering from. No definite diagnosis was ever made.

V

We were sitting together at lunch again; this was the end of August [1944]. Hitler's manner to me was very strange. He seemed almost unfriendly. He never said a word to me all through the meal, and when I happened to meet his eyes by chance they bent a serious, questioning gaze on me.

I couldn't imagine what I might have done or how I could have annoyed him. I didn't worry about it any further, and thought he was probably just in a bad mood.

That same day Fegelein phoned me. 'Can I come and have coffee with you this afternoon?' he asked. I wondered why he suddenly wanted to come and see me, he'd never done that before, but I said yes. Coffee time came and went but Fegelein didn't turn up. Finally the phone rang again. He said the briefing had gone on a long time and now he had to get some work done, but could I just drop in on him for a moment? All right, I thought, I might as well take my dog for a walk, and I set off for Fegelein's new hut, the last building in the headquarters complex. Fegelein greeted me. 'Hello, nice of you to come, would you like a schnapps?' Goodness me, I thought, what's he after? I'd assumed he had something he wanted to discuss with me. 'No,' I said, 'I don't want a schnapps at the moment, but you were going to come and have coffee with me, weren't you? What's up? I mean, why are you doing me this honour although you know I'm faithful to my husband?' Then he came over to me, put his arms round me in a paternal way and said, 'I'd better tell you straight out. Your husband has fallen.[82] The Führer has known since yesterday, but he wanted to wait for confirmation, and then he found he couldn't tell you himself. If you're in any kind of trouble come and see me, I'll always help you.' With these words he let me go and poured me a schnapps after all, and now I did drink it. For the moment I couldn't think at all, and Fegelein gave me no time for it. He went on talking, and as if from a great distance I heard him saying what 'a terrible mess', everything was, this war and the Bolshevists and absolutely everything, but one day it would all be different . . . Funny how I still remember that, although I was hardly listening to him.

Suddenly I was out in the open air again. Warm summer rain was falling very gently, and I walked on down the road, out of the camp and over the fresh green meadows, and it was very quiet and lonely. I felt very much alone, and it was all so terribly sad. I got back to my room late. I didn't want to see or hear anyone. I wasn't anxious to hear any condolences and sympathy. Then a call came from the Führer bunker. 'Are you coming to dinner today, Frau Junge?' I said, 'No, I won't be there at dinner today.' The orderly hung up. But the phone rang again. This time Linge himself was on the line. He said, 'The Führer would like a quick word with you all the same, so come on over even if you don't stay for dinner.' Finally I thought well, the sooner the better, and then I'll have it behind me.

I was taken into the little room that had once been Fräulein Schroeder's living room. Now it was a temporary study for Hitler. How gloomy and sober the room looked now. Once Linge had closed the door behind me Hitler came towards me without a word. He took both my hands and said, 'Oh, child, I'm so sorry. Your husband was a splendid fellow.' His voice was very soft and sad. I almost felt sorrier for Hitler than for myself, because it's so difficult to express sympathy. 'You must stay with me, and don't worry, I'll always be there to help you!' Suddenly everyone wanted to help me, and I felt like running away.

Soon I was sharing mealtimes with Hitler again. He was feeling very unwell, he was silent, and looked old and tired. It was difficult to arouse his interest in a conversation. Even when Speer was talking Hitler sometimes didn't listen. 'I have so many anxieties ... If you knew what decisions I have to take, all by myself, no one shares the responsibility with me.' This was the kind of thing he said every time we asked him how he was feeling. The doctors went in and out of the bunker. The senior doctor from Berlin was always there, and Brandt was consulted too and examined Hitler's painful arm and trembling hand. Finally Professor von Eicken[83] was summoned from Berlin. He had once carried out a successful operation on Hitler's larynx, and had his full confidence. And Morell was ill himself; there was nothing for it, he had to go to bed and leave the care of Hitler to his deputy Weber. It was the worst blow in Morell's ambitious life to find that Hitler was happy with his deputy. He suddenly realized that there were other doctors who could give injections as well as Morell. Hitler claimed it was positively a work of art to find a vein of his to inject, and it was rare for a doctor to be able to treat him well. Morell was wildly jealous and ambitious, but now he had to leave the field temporarily, just when Hitler needed him most. Dark clouds were gathering above his own fat head. Brandt and his colleague von Hasselbach had found out that the tablets Morell was giving Hitler contained a certain percentage of strychnine, which was bound to be deadly one day if Hitler went on taking such large doses.

No one checked up on the medicaments that Hitler took in the course of a day. Linge had a certain amount of supplies in his cupboard, and when Hitler wanted something Linge would take it to him without asking Morell first. Finally the two surgeons wrote a memo and handed it to Hitler. The result was an outbreak of fury on the Führer's part and Brandt's dismissal from his post as attendant doctor. He had lost Hitler's confidence, although he had previously been quite friendly with Eva Braun. But it was a dangerous and almost hopeless undertaking to criticize Morell.

A few days later we were told, 'The Führer sends apologies but he will eat alone.' There was no tea-party either. And finally the Führer spent a day in bed. This was a great sensation. No one had ever seen Hitler in bed. Even his valet woke him through the closed door, and put the morning news down on a small table outside. Hitler had never even received any of his colleagues in his dressing-gown. Suddenly he was ill, and no one knew what the trouble was. Had the assassination attempt not left him uninjured after all? The doctors thought it might be the after-effects of concussion only just showing. Anyway, we didn't see Hitler for days. The adjutants were in despair. The Führer wouldn't see anyone. Once Otto Günsche came to me and said, 'The Führer is completely listless. We don't know what to do. Even the situation in the East doesn't interest him, although things are going very badly there.'

Speaking by phone from his sickbed, Morell gave his assistant instructions for treating Hitler. And lo and behold, suddenly Hitler's spirits revived, he gave orders from his bed, had the situation at the fronts described to him, and after a few days he even began the nightly tea-parties again. I think it was the only time in his life that Hitler received guests in his bedroom, lying in bed. I must say it was very uncomfortable.

The little room in the bunker was very shabbily furnished, just like a soldier's cubicle in a barracks. In addition Hitler had a huge wooden crate in the room, which was meant for Blondi and her family, so there was really very little room. I couldn't help thinking of Eva Braun's worries — she could never think what to give Hitler for his birthday or Christmas. He wore an ordinary grey flannel dressing-gown, no coloured ties, just ugly black socks and not even modern pyjamas. He lay in bed, well shaved and with his hair brushed, in the kind of plain white nightshirt that only the Wehrmacht could design. He hadn't buttoned up the sleeves, because they chafed him, so we could see the white skin of his arms. Bright white! We could understand why he didn't like wearing shorts! A small table had been pushed up to his bed, so we drew up a few chairs and with some difficulty formed a group round the bed. If one of the guests wanted to go out – and there weren't many of us, just two secretaries, Adjutant Bormann and Hewel – we all had to stand up, and serving tea was difficult.

Hitler wasn't talking much yet. He got us to tell him what we had been doing these last few days. There wasn't much we could say. Our main activity had been typing out whole reams of reports of losses. It was wretched work, and seemed to us so pointless. Hitler hadn't even looked at the reports over the last few days. It was a desperate feeling to see how the only man who could have ended all this misery with a single stroke of his pen lying almost apathetically in bed, staring into space with tired eyes, while all hell was let loose around him. It seemed to me as if his body had suddenly understood the pointlessness of all the efforts made by his mind and his strong will and had gone on strike. It had just lain down and said, 'I don't want any more.'

Hitler had never known such disobedience before, and he had been taken by surprise.

But it wasn't long before he overcame this weakness. News that the Russians were about to invade East Prussia got him on his feet and cured him overnight. By now the new bunker was ready too. It was a positive fortress. Hitler moved in. This huge new concrete building contained a maze of passages, rooms and halls. A kitchen for Hitler's diet food had been installed in the bunker too, and all his close colleagues had their own rooms there. He was expecting a well-targeted air raid on his headquarters any day, and when it came all the important people must be together. All the other bunkers were reinforced at the same time. It's true that we had air-raid warnings every day now, but there was never more than a single aircraft circling over the forest, and no bombs were dropped. All the same, Hitler took the danger very seriously, and thought all these reconnaissance flights were in preparation for the big raid he was expecting.

The Russians were advancing with uncanny speed. Dreadful reports came from the villages that they had occupied. Hitler was no longer in a good temper. When we came for tea in the evening he looked gloomy and full of cares, and he had to make a great effort to forget, at least for a few hours, the pictures and reports coming in from the East. Raped women, murdered children and mistreated men, death, misery and despair rose up to accuse him.

He swore revenge and fanned the flames of hatred. 'They're not human beings any more, they're animals from the steppes of Asia, and the war I am waging against them is a war for the dignity of European mankind. No price is too high for victory. We have to be hard and fight with all the means at our disposal.'

But it did not look as if victory was coming any closer. The enemy troops, on the contrary, were. In the West too the Allies were gradually approaching the borders of Germany. And we were still here in East Prussia. It couldn't be long before the Russians drove us out. On many clear autumn days we heard the thunder of the guns. And Hitler was having buildings erected and fortified and made ready for defence. By now a huge apparatus had been constructed. There were barriers and new guard posts everywhere, mines, tangles of barbed wire, watchtowers. The paths along which I had walked my dog one day would suddenly be blocked the next, with a guard wanting to see my pass. If the enemy had known what chaos the air-raid warnings always set off in our camp they would surely have attacked.

The warnings were terrible at night. All the lights were suddenly switched off, everyone had to make haste to the bunkers, but there were trees in your way everywhere and it was difficult to get your bearings. In addition we all had to know the password and the counter-password, for the guards weren't taking any nonsense and would shoot faster than you could think. But normally no one bothered about that, because your pass was enough by day, and no one went walking outside the restricted area any more by night.

Hitler was trying to pluck new divisions out of thin air and send them to the East. When the front line was shortened and to some extent stabilized, Hitler decided to go to his western headquarters in the Taunus to control the Western Front from there. We moved out of the Wolf's Lair in early September, taking all our possessions with us, for the Russians were coming close.

We left the Wolf's Lair with the rather melancholy feeling of saying a final farewell, and one morning in November we boarded the special train, which was to take us to Berlin. I had enjoyed life in the forest, and had taken the landscape of East Prussia to my heart. Now we were leaving it — for ever. Hitler probably knew that himself. And although he went on with the building works there as if he intended to come back some day, he too was in valedictory mood. Hadn't he himself always said that as long as he personally held a section of the Front he would not give up? He was obsessed by the belief that his personality made the impossible possible.

The special train was full. The rest of the staff had already left in another train an hour earlier. This time we were travelling by day. Hitler wanted to arrive in Berlin after dark so as to keep his presence there a secret. Slowly, the sun came through the mist and gave us yet another bright, clear autumn day.

But the windows of Hitler's carriage were darkened. He sat in his compartment by artificial light. Lunch in his saloon car was very gloomy! Outside, the sun was shining brightly, but here the twilight of a mausoleum reigned. Morell, Bormann, Hewel and Schaub joined the meal. Fräulein Schroeder and Frau Christian were already in Berlin. And Fräulein Manziarly,[84] the young dietician from Innsbruck who really wanted to be a teacher and had entered Hitler's service only temporarily, was still too new to be a part of the inner circle. So Fräulein Wolf and I were the only women there.

I never saw Hitler so depressed and distracted as he was that day. His voice hardly rose above a loud whisper; his eyes were lowered to his plate or stared absently at some point on the white tablecloth. An oppressive atmosphere weighed down on the cramped, rocking cage in which we were gathered together, and an eerie feeling came over us all. Suddenly Hitler said something about an operation. At first I didn't know what he was talking about. He mentioned his great confidence in Professor Eicken's skill. 'He bears a great responsibility, but he's the only man who can do it. An operation on the vocal cords isn't exactly life-threatening. But I might lose my voice ...' He left the sentence unfinished. And we saw the dark cloud of silence hanging over his head. You could almost touch it. He knew very well that his voice was an important instrument of his power; his words intoxicated the people and carried them away. How was he to hold crowds spellbound if he couldn't address them any more?

His colleagues had been telling him for weeks: 'My Führer, you must address the German people again. They've lost heart. They have doubts about you. There are rumours that you're not alive any more.' The adjutants had asked us secretaries to try to get the Führer to dictate a speech to us. But he had always replied, 'This is no time for making speeches. I have to take decisions and act. And I have nothing to say to the German people. First I must achieve success, then I can give them strength and courage again.' And now, soon after he had escaped the assassination attempt, a new sword of Damocles was hanging over his head. The fronts were ablaze everywhere; he would have needed to be on both the Western and the Eastern Fronts at the same time. He decided to stay in Berlin for the time being.

We arrived in Berlin that evening without hearing any air-raid warnings. We had to use Grunewald Station; the Silesian Station had come under fire the day before. When we got out of the guest carriage, Hitler had already left. The tail lights of his car were just turning the corner as we drove out of the station. In black-out, the city looked darker and bleaker than the forest by night. As far as possible, the column of cars tried to drive down streets that were still intact. Once again, Hitler had no chance to see Berlin's wounds as they really were. The dipped headlights of the cars merely touched on mounds of rubble to right and left of the road.

When we reached the Reich Chancellery there was already quite a large company assembled in the Ladies' Room. It was some time since the Ladies' Room had had anything to do with ladies. It was a large room with a fireplace, tall mirrors, several comfortable nooks for sitting in, and its title came from the days of brilliant parties when Hitler received a great many artists here. Now the thick carpets had been taken down to the bunkers, and the valuable furniture replaced by comfortable but simple tables and chairs.

Hitler did not sit with us for long. We had already eaten our evening meal in the train. He told Linge to get his bedroom ready and take Blondi out. He himself withdrew very early. There was no mistaking his nervous state. He was to have his operation tomorrow.

I had never been in Berlin for very long with Hitler and his whole staff. For the first time since the beginning of the war, headquarters had now been moved to the heart of Germany, to Berlin itself. The huge complex of the Reich Chancellery, which stood between what had once been Hermann-Göring-Strasse,

Voss-Strasse and Wilhelmstrasse, was always a maze to me. I couldn't get the hang of it. I did know Hitler's apartment in the old palace looking out on Wilhelmstrasse, but the rooms were dead and empty, like a gentleman's town house when its owner has gone into the country.

By now several bombs had fallen here too, and the old building had suffered a good deal of damage. It was a very remarkable old structure, and even Hitler's conversion could never make it really practical and useful. There were any number of flights of front stairs and back stairs, and an astonishing amount of forecourts and halls that had no purpose except to make it more difficult to find important people who were needed urgently.

Hitler's library and study, his bedroom and Eva Braun's apartment were on the first floor. There was also a large and very handsome Congress Hall, which Hitler said he had saved from collapsing. 'The old gentleman' – that was what he called Hindenburg – 'received me in this hall when he appointed me Reich Chancellor. "Keep to the walls if you can, Hitler," he said in his deep voice. "The floor won't hold up much longer!" I think the building would gradually have fallen into ruin if nothing had been done.' It was true that Hitler had had new ceilings put in, but a bomb had fallen in this very hall, and now it was empty and abandoned, and no more repairs had been carried out. Three different flights of stairs led to this upper floor.

Directly opposite the door of Hitler's study, a few steps led to a long passage with the rooms of Hitler's entourage opening off it. The first room, at the foot of some steps, was called the Staircase Room. It was now our sitting room, the adjutants' waiting-room, and was sometimes used as a bedroom by some unexpected visitor. Schaub's room was next to it, then came a room for Dr Otto Dietrich the press chief, then the room really meant for Sepp Dietrich but now occupied by Adjutant Bormann, and finally there was the living room always used by Gruppenführer Albrecht, the permanent Berlin adjutant.

The corridor went round a corner and led to rooms for Morell, Colonel von Below, General Burgdorf[85] and Professor Hoffmann.

The ground-floor rooms were arranged in the same way. They included the office of the household manager Kannenberg,[86] a small room furnished in rustic style as a staff dining room, the valet's room, a medical room, and a shower and bathroom. The cook and housemaid lived down here too, and the laundry rooms and ironing room were also on the ground floor.

The rooms of state were under Hitler's private rooms. Even with carpets, furniture and pictures less valuable than usual, the huge room through which you entered them was still handsome and pleasant, but it was never used. You reached the salon through a small anteroom. On its right was the Ladies' Salon, on its left the cinema and concert hall. Three handsome, wide doors led straight into the grounds of the Reich Chancellery. The Winter Garden was the finest room in the whole place. It was a building in itself, extending a long way and with a semi-circular bay which contained many tall windows and doors and looked out on the park. The word 'garden', however, didn't suit it any more; the beautiful plants, flowers and shrubs that used to stand here had gone long ago. There were two round tables in the curved bay of the room, where we took breakfast, and Hitler also held his usual military briefing here if he didn't need a particularly large staff. If he did, he used the huge study in the New Reich Chancellery. Now these long-deserted rooms were suddenly full of life again.

During the first days of our stay there was an atmosphere of suppressed nervousness everywhere. Hitler had come through his operation all right. Professor Eicken had removed a nodule from his vocal cords. I don't even know if the operation took place in his bedroom or in a hospital, but anyway we didn't see him for three days. Then he suddenly and quite unexpectedly appeared at the breakfast table one day. There had been an air-raid warning in the morning, and now we had all come out of the bunker and gathered for breakfast. Hitler had got up sooner than he meant to because of the air-raid warning, and didn't know how to occupy his time until the conference. He looked for company, followed the sound of voices, and found us at breakfast. Of course several cigarettes were immediately stubbed out, and the windows were opened. Most of us hadn't seen Hitler since his operation. The new attendant doctor who had joined us to replace Professor Brand was so self-conscious that he stumbled over his own chair-leg when he rose to greet Hitler, got entangled in the tablecloth and knocked his cup over. He went terribly red, looking embarrassed, and I felt really sorry for him when he was standing helplessly before his Führer at his full height of almost two metres. He had hardly come into social contact with Hitler at all before.

The Führer could only whisper. He had been told not to speak out loud for a week. After the conversation had gone on for a short time we all began speaking in whispers too, until Hitler pointed out that there was nothing the matter with his hearing, and we didn't have to spare it. We burst out laughing, and Hitler laughed too. He also had to report a sad disappointment about Blondi's condition: 'She's not in pup after all,' he said. 'She certainly got fatter and looked as if she'd soon be able to suckle a litter, but I think she just put on weight because she was getting more than usual to eat and didn't have so much exercise. Tornow the dog-walker told me it was a phantom pregnancy, but I think she was just having us on!' The Führer thought that her mate might have been undernourished, and next time there was a chance he was going to try again.

One by one people rose from the breakfast table. Schaub had to go to his position by the telephone. The Wehrmacht and SS adjutants had to prepare for the conference. Lorenz and Dr Dietrich were going to catch up with the latest press reports. Finally no one was left except Frentz the photographer, Frau Christian, me, and Dr Stumpfegger.[87] We talked about Christmas. Would we be spending it in Berlin this year? Hitler shook his head. 'I must go to the West. We shall probably spend Christmas in our "Eagle's Eyrie" in the Taunus.' I took the opportunity to ask if I could go on leave at Christmas this year. [. . .] Frau Christian could stay with Hitler, together with her husband.

I was given permission. Christmas wasn't so far off now. In

four weeks' time it would be Christmas Eve. We four secretaries were using the time in Berlin to draw up lists of Hitler's Christmas bonuses and pack up parcels. 'Yes, one ought to spend Christmas with one's family,' whispered Hitler, sounding sad and wistful. 'Eva writes to me too – urgent pleas to go to the Berghof this year. She says I must be in bad need of recuperation after the assassination attempt and my illness. But I know it's mostly Gretl behind all this, wanting her Hermann with her.' For Fegelein really had married Eva's sister in the spring.[88] We had still been in Berchtesgaden, and the wedding was celebrated magnificently 2000 metres above sea level at the Kehlstein house. I myself wasn't invited. And now Gretl was already expecting her first child in the spring [of 1945]. Surprisingly, handsome Hermann had succeeded in making friends with Eva, or perhaps it wasn't so surprising when you think how lively, funny and amusing Fegelein could be. And Eva, who was young and loved life but had to live in such a prim and proper, retiring way was glad to have a brother-in-law with whom she could dance and joke to her heart's content without losing prestige.

But Hitler remained firm. If he thought it would be irresponsible for him to go away, then Eva could not sway him, for all her charm and the great things she promised. And Hitler gave himself no peace. He had to go to the West. He meant to spend only two weeks in Berlin. But I had a wonderful opportunity of getting to Munich sooner than I had expected. Captain Baur was flying a plane from Berlin to Munich on 10 December. I asked if he would take me with him, and of course he said yes. So at least I didn't have to worry about whether my little fox terrier would be all right while I was away. I could take her with me in the plane, whereas dogs in trains had been forbidden for several years.

I had a lot of cases full of presents and delicacies to give my family and a great many friends pleasure. I had searched the big warehouse full of Hitler's birthday presents and found lots of useful things for my mother, who had been bombed out and was now living with my sister in a little village by the Ammersee

Traudl aged about two with her mother Hildegard Humps

Summer holidays by the Ammersee, c. 1927: (left to right: Traudl Humps, a playmate, Inge Humps, in the background Traudl's grandmother Agathe Zottmann)

With her friend Ulla Kares, 1940

Traudl when working at the Reich Chancellery in Berlin, 1942

Wedding to Hans Junge, 19 June 1943

The newly-weds: Traudl and Hans Junge with the witnesses to
their wedding, Otto Günsche (left) and Erich Kempka (right)

In the Führer's special train: Traudl and Hans Junge with Johanna Wolf (right) looking at their wedding photographs (photo: Walter Frentz)

Adolf Hitler with his orderly Hans Junge, early 1940s

On the Berghof terrace, 1943, seated left to right: Lieutenant Colonel Gerhard Engel, Heinrich Hoffmann (with Traudl Junge behind him), Walther Hewel, Gerda Bormann (back view), State Secretary for Tourism Hermann Esser (photo: Walter Frentz)

In conversation with Sepp Dietrich, 1943 (photo: Walter Frentz)

The evening ritual: darning stockings in her room
at the Wolf's Lair Führer headquarters, 1943

Only Adolf Hitler's meals were cooked in the diet kitchen at the Wolf's Lair. From left to right
Marlene von Exner, kitchen assistant Wilhelm Kleyer, Traudl Junge, late 1943

Photograph for her new identity card,
Berlin, November 1945

Traudl Junge with her fiancé Heinz Bald, 1955

II.

In der "Wolfschanze"

Es dauerte verhältnismässig kurze Zeit, bis ich mich
in dieser neuen, fremden Welt eingewöhnt hatte. Allerdings
war die Natur, der Wald und die Landschaft eine grosse Kuppleri
in meinen Beziehungen zur neuen Arbeitsstätte. Es gab keine Bür
atmosphäre, keine feste Arbeitszeit, ich machte weite Spazier-
gänge und genoss den Wald. Keine Sekunde hatte ich Sehnsucht
nach der Grosstadt.

Hitler selbst behauptete zwar, man habe das billigste,
sumpfigste, mückenreichste und klimatische ungünstigste Gebiet
für ihn ausgesucht, aber ich fand es herrlich. Zumindest im
Winter hatte die Ostpreussische Gegend einen unbeschreiblichen
Reiz. Die verschneiten Birken, den klaren Himmel und die Weite
der Ebenen mit ihren Seen werde ich nie vergessen. Im Sommer al
lerdings musste ich meinem Chef zu einem grossen Teil recht
geben, denn Myriaden von Mücken hausten mit uns und ernährten
sich von unserem Blut. Die Luft war dumpf und feucht und manch-
mal atembeklemmend. Bei solcher Witterung war es schwer, Hitler
zu seinem täglichen Spaziergang zu bewegen. Er verkroch sich in
seinem kühlen Bunker und nur seinem Hund Blondi zuliebe unterna
er nach dem Frühstück einen Rundgang in dem kleinen Gelände, da
anschliessend an seinen Bunker für diesen Zweck reserviert war
Hier musste die Schäferhündin ihre Kunststücke zeigen und wurde
von ihrem Herrn zu einem der gelehrigsten und gewandtesten Hund
ausgebildet. Hitler hatte das grösste Vergnügen, wenn Blondi
ein paar Zentimeter höher springen konnte, wenn sie ein paar
Minuten länger auf einer schmalen Stange balancieren konnte und
behauptete, dassseinseinediedie Beschäftigung mit seinem Hund sei
seine beste Entspannung. Es war auch erstaunlich, was Blondi le
stete. Sie sprang durch Reifen, überwand eine 2 m hohe Holzwand
spielend, kletterte eine Leiter hoch und machte oben auf der
kleinen Plattform ihr schönstes Männchen. Es war wirklich eine
Freude, zu beobachten, mit welchem Vergnügen Herr und Hund die
Übungen verfolgten. Am Rande des Geländes fanden sich manche Z
schauer ein, die das Spiel beobachteten und auch für mich war
es wochenlang die einzige Gelegenheit, bei der ich mit dem"Füh
in Berührung kam. Wenn er mich sah, begrüsste er mich freundli
mit Händedruck und fragte mich, wie es mir ginge.

Traudl Junge's original typescript of 1947

outside Munich. They included underwear, crockery, clothes, etc., and I was also taking my husband's entire wardrobe, quite forgetting that the plane was flying only to Munich, and then I would have to get myself and all my things by normal means to Breitbrunn, which didn't even have a railway station. I had also forgotten that there was no shipping traffic on the lake in winter, so after a great deal of trouble I had to leave my cases in the nearest good-sized place on the railway line and set out on foot with my dog and my travelling bag. But the pleasure my early, unexpected arrival gave was enormous. At last we had a Christmas tree again, with our dear old decorations, the traditional Christmas baking, and a few little things saved from the old days.

Hitler was now at the Eagle's Eyrie with his staff, ignoring the fact that even in these times of great distress a festival of love and reconciliation was being celebrated all over the country. I was rather uneasy in our cramped little kitchen-cum-living room, without a telephone or anything but a radio that broadcast the Munich station very indistinctly. And usually the broadcasts were interrupted by that quiet, uncanny ticking that was called 'the Gauleiter's groans' and meant there were enemy aircraft nearby. Shortly before I had to get ready to return to headquarters, on 8 January 1945, Munich suffered one of its worst air raids. From our little village, about 40 kilometres outside the city, we saw the blood-red sky and the glaring white explosions of heavy bombs.

Next day all connections to Munich were cut off. The railway line was damaged, the phones weren't working. But I had to be in Berlin on 10 January. My mother was worried and unhappy. She asked me to stay; she had a foreboding of something terrible that threatened us. But I couldn't wait. I left my dog and my suitcase behind and went into Munich on a lorry. Making my way through the smoke, rubble and crowds of people I finally reached the Führer's apartment on Prinzregentenplatz, picked up my ticket and travelled to Berlin that night. Once again my heart was very heavy as I saw bleak scenes of the horrors of war.

Fräulein Wolf, who had also spent Christmas in Munich but had returned to Berlin a few days earlier, was waiting for me, and next day the two of us boarded the train to the Führer headquarters, this time going west.

Once again the courier train was taking me to a part of Germany I had never seen before. We arrived at a small, snow-bound station in Hesse in the morning. The place was called Hungen.

There were cars here to take any new arrivals to Führer headquarters. We drove through Bad Nauheim, which was still sleepy and lifeless this early winter morning, and forged our winding way through deep snow up the wooded hills of the Taunus, until we saw the Führer headquarters well camouflaged on one of the mountain crests. It was a beautiful place. Little log cabins clung to the wooded slopes, each of them with a deep, solid bunker underground. The rooms were small, but better furnished than at the Wolf's Lair. The Führer lived in two rather larger rooms in the log cabin situated lowest down.

I went for a little walk round the place on the first day. There was a castle quite close, on the nearest hill. This was the headquarters of General Rundstedt, who at the time was commander of the Army Group West.[89] Hitler was holding important talks with him. He had come here to calm the situation on the Western Front and hold up the American advance.

All day there was feverish coming and going in the Führer bunker. The conferences went on for hours. We didn't see Hitler until dinner in the evening. He had recovered and looked better than in Berlin. I told him about the heavy raid on Munich. He listened to my description and then said, 'All these horrors will come to a sudden end in a few weeks' time. Our new aircraft are now in production, whole series of them, and then the Allies will think better of flying over the Reich.' Blondi was lying beside Hitler's chair as we sat drinking tea together. She tried to attract his attention once or twice, but he indicated that she was to keep still, and she obediently lay down again. If I could trust my nose the dog really did badly need to go out. But Hitler didn't

notice. Although he claimed he could infallibly smell any cigarette, he was completely unaware of the smells his beloved dog
made. Finally I said, 'My Führer, I really do think Blondi needs
to go out.' She reacted to my words by gambolling with joy, ran
to the door, jumped up at it, and rushed out when Hitler had
rung for Linge. We were all rather relieved when fresh air came
in through the door. I said, 'My Führer, it's amazing what pleasure you can give a dog with such a little thing.' At that he
laughed and said, 'Have you any idea what pleasure a little thing
like that can give human beings too? Once I was on a long tour
with my staff. I used to take many car journeys all over Germany.
At the end of this one I still had to go to Magdeburg to open the
first stretch of the completed autobahn. When my motorcade
was recognized on the roads cars kept joining it and following
me, and I often had great difficulty in getting away. Sometimes
it was impossible to disappear into a wood and be alone, much
as I needed to. But on that occasion, as we came to the autobahn,
there was nearly an accident. We'd been driving for hours and
were longing for a break. But there were crowds lining the route
everywhere. First the Hitler Youth, then the BDM, the SA, the
SS, all the formations. I hadn't realized how many formations
there really were in my Party, and on that occasion I thought
there were far too many. I had to stop and look friendly. Brückner
and Schaub were sitting there, stony-faced, until suddenly
Brückner had a wonderful idea: "My Führer, I had the special
train left at Magdeburg, just in case. Couldn't we . . . ?" So we
raced to the station and were delighted to see our train.' Schaub,
who was sitting at the table with us, cupped his ear round his
hand and grunted with pleasure when Hitler told this story.
Then he added, 'My Führer, do you remember Weimar? When
you stayed at the Elephant?' 'Yes,' said Hitler, smiling. 'That
was another tricky moment. I used to go to Weimar often, and I
always stayed at the Elephant Hotel. It was quite an old hotel,
but very well managed. I had my usual room, which did have
running water but no bathroom and no lavatory. I had to go
down a long corridor and through the last door. And that was

quite a trial every time, because when I left my room word ran like wildfire right through the hotel, and when I came out of the smallest room again people were giving me ovations, and I had to run the gauntlet back to my own room with my arm raised in a salute and a rather embarrassed smile on my face. I had the hotel modernized later.'

It was a very lively conversation that evening. You might have thought there wasn't a war on and Hitler hadn't a care in the world. But anyone who knew him as well as we did realized that he was just anaesthetizing himself with such talk, taking his mind off the losses of land, men and war *matériel* that were reported to him daily, indeed hourly. And the planes constantly flying over his western headquarters and setting off air-raid warnings all day long showed that peace and freedom from care were a long way off.

I didn't even have a chance to get to know the camp properly before we had to leave. Hitler was urging us to return to Berlin. He wanted to be closer to the Eastern Front again. He really needed to be on both fronts at once, and best of all have the southern section under his direct control too. He couldn't go back to East Prussia. The Wolf's Lair was too close to the front line now. I was at the western headquarters for only three days. On 15 January 1945 the Führer's special train went back to Berlin, towards catastrophe. People were still cracking jokes. Someone said Berlin was a very practical spot for headquarters, because soon we'd be able to travel between the Eastern Front and the Western Front by suburban railway. Hitler could still laugh at that.

By now the Führer's huge underground bunker in the grounds of the Reich Chancellery had been made ready. Eleven metres of thick reinforced concrete covered the little cabins and rooms inside. But only a flat roof emerged above ground level. The bunker was intended only for temporary accommodation during an air raid, but when an incendiary bomb made the living rooms above ground uninhabitable, particularly the library, it became permanent living space for Hitler and his staff. The adjutants' wing, as it was called, which contained the little Staircase Room, had not been damaged. This was where we had our typewriters and did our office work, and now we ate lunch there with Hitler too.

But in the evening, punctual as clockwork, enemy aircraft came over, and we had to dine with Hitler in the little room in the bunker where he lived and worked. It was a tiny place in the very heart of the new Führer bunker. If we didn't climb straight down the stairs from the park into this underground fortress, we had to go through the kitchen of the Führer's apartments and make our way along several winding corridors to what had once been the air-raid shelter. Then you reached a wide corridor with several rooms for the men on duty to left and right of it, and from there down several more flights of steps, deeper into the real new Führer bunker. Heavy iron doors led to a broad corridor. On the left there was a door leading to the lavatories, on the right the engine room with the lighting and ventilation equipment, then the door to the telephone switchboard and the valet's room. From here you went on to a general common room which you had to cross to reach Professor Morell's room, the medical room, and a small room where the men on duty could sleep. This part of the bunker could be closed off by more heavy iron doors, but they were usually left open. Then came the section of corridor leading to Hitler's rooms. It was also used as a waiting-room and sitting room. A broad red carpet runner covered the stone flags on the floor. Along the right wall of the corridor hung the valuable paintings that had been brought down here for safety from the upper rooms of the Führer's apartments and the Reich Chancellery. Handsome armchairs were ranged below them. And doors off this corridor led to Hitler's rooms. You entered his study from the corridor through a small anteroom outside it. The room was about three by four metres with a low ceiling, which had a depressing effect. There wasn't room for much furniture. A desk stood against the wall to the right of the door, opposite it was a small sofa, more of a bench really, with blue-and-white linen upholstery. In front of that was a small rectangular table and three armchairs. A little table with a radio on it to the right of the sofa completed the furnishings. On the right a door led to Hitler's bedroom, which had no entrance of its own from the corridor. I never saw inside it. On the left you reached Hitler's bathroom, and from there you came to a small dressing room which also adjoined Eva Braun's accommodation in the bunker. There was access to this room too from the little anteroom, which the servants used as a place to store provisions and put things down while they were serving, but the mistress of the place had never stayed here before.

Next to Hitler's bedroom there was another small room that was used for conferences, talks and military briefings. There was nothing in it but a large table, a bench running round it, and a few chairs and stools. Then came the door at the end of the corridor, which again led to a little forecourt through which you could reach the staircase and finally emerge into the park. Here, in this relatively small complex, which was laid out in such a bewildering way that it's difficult to describe it clearly, the last act of the drama took place.

Today it seems to me almost incredible that we still trusted Hitler's confidence and his belief in victory at the beginning of that February. Cheerful, light-hearted conversations were still conducted at meals, and we seldom discussed the gravity of the situation. But anxious doubts began to stir in my heart, for the Russians were coming close and closer. The Wolf's Lair had been blown up some time ago, even before the OT construction troops had finished work on the mammoth bunkers. The Russians had come flooding into East Prussia, and there were terrible tales from the villages that had fallen into enemy hands. Murdered men and children, raped women, burning villages cried out to heaven for vengeance. Hitler's features were set hard and full of hatred, and he kept saying, 'These uncivilized brutes cannot, must not be allowed to swamp Europe. I am the last bulwark against that danger. If there is any justice we shall prevail, and one day the world will understand what this struggle was about!' He often quoted some remarks by Frederick the Great, whose picture hung over his desk: 'The commander who flings his last battalion into the fray will be the victor!' And the battle of Kunersdorf* was a fiery memorial and warning in Hitler's mind.

20 April 1945 – Hitler's birthday! The first Russian tanks stood outside Berlin. The thunder of the infantry guns reached the Reich Chancellery, and the Führer received birthday wishes from the faithful. They all came, shook his hand, promised to be loyal, and tried to persuade him to leave the city. 'My Führer, the city will soon be surrounded. You will soon be cut off and unable to reach the south. There's still time to take command of the southern armies if you go by way of Berchtesgaden.' Goebbels, Ribbentrop, Himmler, Dönitz[90] – they all tried, but in vain. Hitler intended to stay and await developments. Out in the park, he pinned decorations on boys of the Hitler Youth, children who had distinguished themselves in battle against Russian tanks. Was he planning to rely on that kind of defence? He did at least say he was prepared to move all the staffs south, all the personnel, ministries and departments that were not indispensable here.

In the evening we sat crammed together in the little study. Hitler was silent, staring into space. We too asked him if he wouldn't leave Berlin. 'No, I can't,' he replied. 'I should feel like a Tibetan lama turning an empty prayer mill. I must bring things to a head here in Berlin – or go under!' We said nothing, and the champagne we were drinking to Hitler's health tasted insipid.

For Hitler had now said out loud what we had long seen, with terror, as a certainty: he himself no longer believed in victory. He retired early, and the birthday party broke up. But Eva Braun came back once she had led Hitler to his room. A restless fire burned in her eyes. She had on a new dress made of silvery blue brocade; it was meant to be worn to a party at the side of the

* Where Frederick the Great suffered a heavy defeat.

man she loved. Hitler hadn't noticed it. And he hadn't noticed that there were four young women at his table who wanted to live, who had believed in him, who had hoped for victory from him.

Eva Braun wanted to numb the fear that had awoken in her heart. She wanted to celebrate once again, even when there was nothing left to celebrate, she wanted to dance, to drink, to forget . . . I was only too willing to be infected by the last stirrings of lust for life and get out of the bunker where the heavy ceiling suddenly weighed down so palpably on our spirits, and the walls were white and cold.

Eva Braun carried off anyone she met, all who crossed her path, sweeping them away with her up to her old living room on the first floor, which was still intact although the good furniture was down in the bunker now. The large round table was laid festively once again for any of Hitler's entourage who were still in Berlin. Even Reichsleiter Bormann left Hitler's side and his own desk, and fat Theo Morell came up from the safety of his bunker in spite of the constant thunder of the artillery fire. Someone produced an old gramophone from somewhere with a single record. 'Blood-Red Roses Speak of Happiness To You . . .' Eva Braun wanted to dance! Never mind who with, she whirled everyone away in a desperate frenzy, like a woman who has already felt the faint breath of death. We drank champagne, there was shrill laughter, and I laughed too because I didn't want to cry. In the midst of this an explosion silenced the party for a moment, someone hurried to the phone, gleaned more important news. But no one said anything about the war, no one mentioned victory, no one spoke of death. This was a party given by ghosts. And the red roses kept on speaking of happiness . . .

I suddenly thought I might throw up any minute. I felt terrible. I could hear nothing but the dull roar of the guns. I'd come round from the anaesthetic. Quietly and inconspicuously I left this last wild party and slipped through the labyrinth of corridors in the bunkers and cellars over to the New Reich Chancellery. What would the next few days bring? I fell asleep before I found an answer.

Next morning our ranks had thinned out. The prominent people who had come with birthday wishes had left the sinking ship, slipping through the last narrow escape route to the south. Ribbentrop had tried to use one last way of persuading Hitler to set out too. He talked to Eva Braun. She told me about it later. 'You are the only person who can get the Führer away from here,' he begged her. 'Tell him you want to leave Berlin with him. You will be doing Germany a great service.' But Eva Braun replied, 'I shall not pass on a word of your proposition to the Führer. He must decide alone. If he thinks it right to stay in Berlin, then I will stay with him. If he leaves, I shall leave too.'

Aircraft and columns of vehicles were setting off south all the time. Fräulein Wolf and Fräulein Schroeder, the other two secretaries, were among those who left. Fräulein Wolf had tears in her eyes when she said goodbye, as if she sensed that she would never again see Hitler, who had been her boss for 25 years.[91] One after another, people shook hands with Hitler as they said goodbye. Only the most important liaison officers stayed behind.

VI

22 April 1945. Feverish restlessness in the bunker. All hell is let loose outside. We've heard shooting and thunderous gunfire all day, you can hardly put your head out of doors. The Wilhelmsplatz looks bleak, the Kaiserhof has collapsed like a house of cards; its ruins reach almost all the way to the Reich Chancellery. All that's left of the Propaganda Ministry is its white façade standing symbolically in the empty square.

I ask everyone I meet how the attack is going. It should be in full swing now. Are those German guns and tanks that are making such a noise? None of the officers know. They are all chasing around like waxwork figures pretending to be busy and deluding themselves.

The doors of Hitler's conference room are closed. There's an agitated discussion in progress behind them. My colleague Frau Christian, Martin Bormann's secretary Fräulein Krüger[92] and I are sitting in the dietician's kitchen drinking strong coffee. We are talking about trivial things just to quell the desperate fear we feel. Each of us is trying to deal with the situation in her own way. No one thinks of eating lunch, although it was lunchtime long ago. Our restlessness makes us go to the door of the conference room again. We hear voices rising and falling. Hitler shouts something, but we can't make out what. Martin Bormann comes out looking agitated and hands Fräulein Krüger some sheets to be typed out immediately. For a moment we see uniformed backs bent over the street map of Berlin. The meeting looks baffled. Distraught, we move back into the anteroom, where we smoke, wait, whisper . . .

At last the heavy iron door opens. Linge calls Frau Christian and me in to the Führer. With an expression on his face that tells us nothing he goes on to fetch Fräulein Manziarly too. Only a few steps separate us from the life-and-death decision. Now we shall hear the truth.

All the officers who have been discussing the situation are standing outside the open door of the conference room with white, stony faces. Hitler stands motionless in the little anteroom outside his study. All the expression has vanished from his face; his eyes are blank. He looks like his own death mask. His gaze sees nothing. Impersonally, in commanding tones such as I've never heard him use to a woman before, he says, 'Get changed at once. A plane is leaving in an hour and will take you south. All is lost, hopelessly lost.'

I am frozen rigid. The picture on the wall is hanging crooked, and there's a mark on the lapel of Hitler's jacket. Everything feels far away, as if it were packed in cotton wool.

Eva Braun is the first to rouse herself. She goes towards Hitler, who has already placed his hand on the handle of his door, takes both his hands and says, smiling and in the comforting tones you might use to a sad child, 'But you know I shall stay with you.

I'm not letting you send me away.' Then Hitler's eyes begin to shine from within, and he does something none of us, not even his closest friends and servants, have ever seen him do before: he kisses Eva Braun on the mouth, while the officers stand outside waiting to be dismissed. I don't want to say it, but it comes out of its own accord; I don't want to stay here and I don't want to die, but I can't help it. 'I'm staying too,' I say.

I had to pack a crate with the most important files, the paperwork and documents given to me by Schaub. Mechanically I put them together one by one. Should I send my own things home too? Perhaps there wouldn't be any room left for luggage in the last few planes going south tomorrow? But perhaps we'd have to hold out here for weeks? I didn't send anything. The plane that took off with its important cargo and two of Hitler's orderlies was never seen again.

Hitler shook hands with everyone in turn, saying goodbye. Only the most important liaison officers stayed behind. And Bormann too, of course, always the channel for any news that had to reach Hitler.

That afternoon there was another long military briefing. The Russians were now right outside the gates of the city. Hitler gave orders for one final attack, with all the troops and planes to be found in Berlin. Every single tank, every gun must go to the front. The bunker echoed with the explosions of the small bombs that the Russians kept dropping over the city, and with Hitler's imperative voice too. The generals left the small, stuffy conference room red-faced. Frau Christian and I sat timidly outside in the corridor. Fräulein Krüger, Bormann's secretary, had joined us in these last few days. She too could say only that her boss expected either to leave Berlin in the next few days, or ... We had no clear idea of the other alternative.

Once again we had to wait. Even Hitler could do nothing more now. He retreated to be with his dogs, which were now being kept in a cubicle near the lavatories. Then he sat in silence on the little bench in the corridor with the puppy on his lap, watching people coming and going. The staff unwaveringly went about their duties. The servants functioned calmly and reliably as ever, carrying out Hitler's wishes. Theo Morell, who had heart trouble, sat in his room in the bunker worrying. The tension was unbearable.

Eva Braun came out of her room. It was quiet outside now. We had no idea what the weather was like. There was no window to show us where the sun stood in the sky. We wanted to go out in the park, to give the dogs and ourselves a little fresh air and daylight. A hazy cloud of dust and smoke hung over Berlin. The air was mild and you could feel the spring. Eva Braun, Frau Christian and I walked through the park of the Reich Chancellery in silence. There were deep holes everywhere in the well-tended turf, with empty metal containers and broken branches lying around. We saw dugouts and heaps of bazookas at regular intervals along the perimeter wall. Was this to be the final line of defence? We didn't believe it. Tomorrow, or maybe in the next few days, German troops would drive out the enemy.

We passed through a gap in the ruined, fallen wall and went into the grounds of the Foreign Office. The trees were in blossom, quiet and peaceful. Only a few days ago we women had practised with pistols here. Hitler had finally given his permission. Back in East Prussia, when the Russians were coming closer and closer, Frau Christian and I had already asked if it wouldn't be a good idea for us to learn how to handle a pistol. At the time Hitler had replied, smiling, 'No, ladies! I don't want to die by the hand of a secretary. Aim darts with your eyes, that will do!' But now he suddenly had no more objections. We had shot at huntsman's practice targets under Rattenhuber's supervision. Hitler sent us into the abandoned grounds of the Foreign Office so that we couldn't do any harm, and here we still saw the tattered paper targets recording our hits. We had no chance to practise any more – the Russian artillery was doing all the shooting around here. But today, briefly, all was quiet. Hidden behind some shrubs in a small round flowerbed we found a beautiful bronze statue. A young naiad with a charming figure stood here in the garden under the blossoming trees. She suddenly seemed to us incredibly beautiful in all this bleakness. All at once we heard the birds still twittering, we saw the daffodils flowering in the grass, and nature waking to new life. We were almost glad to see that all this still existed. That dreadful bunker was surely to blame for the terrible, oppressive atmosphere. Up here in the open air you could breathe more easily, your head was clearer. The dogs romped about on the grass, and we sat on a rock and smoked. Even Eva Braun lit a cigarette. Seeing our surprised looks, she said, 'Oh, children, I just have to start smoking again. With extraordinary worries like mine, surely I can do something out of the ordinary too.' But she had a box of menthol pastilles in her bag and took the precaution of popping one in her mouth when we heard the first siren sound and clambered down again.

Down in the bunker Hitler was sitting in the corridor with Goebbels, Bormann and Burgdorf. They were discussing the coming attack. Hitler seemed physically rather more erect and stronger again. We came in from outside, feeling better and full of fresh air, to be received by a surge of hope and confidence. At least a decision would finally be made now. Tomorrow we would find out whether Hitler was going to Berchtesgaden or meant to stay in Berlin for ever. Hitler told us to sit down with him. Everything was very unconventional now that there were so few of us. Eva Braun sat beside Hitler, and taking no notice of the other men she immediately began wheedling him into what she wanted. 'I say, do you know that statue in the Foreign Office? A lovely sculpture! It would look really good by the pool in my garden. Do please buy it for me if everything turns out all right and we get out of Berlin!' She looked hopefully at him. Hitler took her hand. 'But I don't know whose it is. It's probably state property, in which case I can't buy it and put it in a private garden.' 'Oh,' she said, 'if you succeed in beating the Russians back and liberating Berlin you can make an exception for once!' Hitler laughed at this feminine logic, but he didn't discuss the matter any more. Eva, who was painfully clean and tidy, discovered some red and blue specks of colour on Hitler's field-grey uniform tunic. 'Oh look, you're all dirty! You can't wear that jacket any more. You don't have to imitate "Old Fritz" in every-thing and go around looking as scruffy as he did.' Hitler pro-tested. He was no longer a commander, a politician, a dictator. 'But this is my working suit, after all. I can't put on an apron when I'm holding a conference and I have to use coloured pens.' In fact she wasn't being fair, since he was meticulous about cleanliness himself. He never shook hands with anyone if he had just touched his dog, however lightly.

The conversation was interrupted by bombs and anti-aircraft fire. Another raid had started, as it did at this time every evening. The bunker filled up, the heavy iron door to the first part of the corridor was closed. Hitler had the radio switched on. He never listened to music, only to the news reports of the approach of enemy aircraft, with the regular ticking of the clock on the wall breaking into them. He listened to those reports. Berlin was suffering badly again. And suddenly the ghost of hopelessness came back to haunt us.

[. . .][93] Now all the self-delusion is over. Finally, at last, that desperate, seductive voice in me is silenced, the part of me that wouldn't see and know reality, that *wanted* to believe. At the same time I suddenly feel very sorry for Hitler. A hopelessly disappointed man, toppled from the greatest heights, broken, lonely. [. . .] I feel guilty all of a sudden. I think of all the dreadful things going on up there, a few metres above us, the things that have been going on for years, caused by my employer. Should I leave now? Go back to people who will look at me reproachfully, and tell them, 'I'm back. I was wrong, but when my own life was at stake I saw where I'd gone wrong.' Pity and a guilty conscience kept me here, and Frau Christian may have had similar feelings. We said, almost at the same moment, 'We're staying too!' Hitler looked at us for a moment. 'I'm ordering you to go.' But we shook our heads. Then he shook hands with us. 'I wish my generals had your courage,' he said. Fräulein Manziarly, that quiet little woman who had really wanted to be a teacher, and was not bound in any way to stay here, said she wouldn't leave Berlin either.

Footsteps dragging, Hitler went out to the officers. 'Gentlemen, it's over. I shall stay here in Berlin and shoot myself when the moment comes. Anyone who wants to go can go now. Everyone is free to do so.'

One by one they left the bunker, silently saluting the Führer. Most of them left Berlin for ever, only a few returned to their staff and departmental offices.

In his room, Hitler looked out the documents and paperwork to be destroyed from all the drawers and cupboards. This confidential task was entrusted to Julius Schaub. Looking miserably unhappy, he limped through the bunker, up the stairs to the park, and there, with his heart bleeding, burned his Führer's treasures. He was told to go and do the same in Munich and Berchtesgaden. Eyes wet with tears, he said goodbye to us, since he would have to leave that same day. Now the liaison officers had left too, and the only people left were Hewel, Reichsleiter Bormann, General Krebs,[94] General Burgdorf, Hermann Fegelein, Admiral Voss,[95] Adjutants von Below and Günsche and Heinz Lorenz. Of the servants, only Heinz Linge and three orderlies had stayed. Apart from that almost all the domestic staff had stayed too, the people who worked in the kitchen and ran the house and the switchboard, the chauffeurs, and so on. They all had makeshift accommodation on camp beds and temporary sleeping places in the upper rooms of the Führer's bunker. The kitchen too was underground now, and the front part of the corridor served as a dining room. We secretaries were sharing our bunker bedroom in the New Reich Chancellery with several other women, most of them secretaries and telephonists from the Führer's adjutancy office. We could get straight to the Führer bunker down a long underground corridor.

The hours crept by. I felt completely empty, hollowed out and numb. I really thought I ought to sleep for a couple of hours, but restlessness kept me in the Führer bunker. Perhaps some decisive news would come within the next hour? It must be late afternoon by now. Had Hitler eaten any lunch? There probably hadn't been time. Now he was sitting in his room talking to Goebbels. How would the great Propaganda Minister take Hitler's decision to die in Berlin? What would he tell the German people? The door opened and Goebbels went to the telephone. When he came back he looked enquiringly around. There was no one there except for the orderlies and me. The Minister came over to me. 'My wife will soon be arriving with the children. At the Führer's wish they will be staying in his bunker from now on. Please be kind enough to receive my family when they arrive.' My God, I thought, where are we going to put so many people? Six small children in all this turmoil! I went a few steps up to the upper part of the bunker and looked for Günsche. He cleared a room that was full of cases, crates, furniture and provisions, and put beds in.

By now Hitler had summoned Keitel and Jodl. The two generals had one last brief discussion with Hitler. I heard them talking to Bormann and Hewel afterwards. Yet again they had tried in vain to make it clear to Hitler that there was nothing he could do in Berlin now. The OKW offices were going south. He couldn't command his generals any more from Berlin. [. . .] Hitler emphasized his firm resolve to stay in Berlin and die there. He was going to shoot himself, he said, he didn't want to fall into enemy hands alive or dead. He couldn't fight any more, physically he was a broken man. So saying, he dismissed his generals, and now they finally left the bunker.

Meanwhile the Goebbels family had come over from the bunker underneath the Propaganda Ministry to the Führer bunker. I went to meet them and welcome the children. Frau Goebbels was taken straight to Hitler. The five little girls and the boy were happy and cheerful. They were pleased to be staying with 'Uncle Hitler', and soon filled the bunker with their games. They were charming, well brought-up, natural-mannered children. They knew nothing of the fate awaiting them, and the adults did all they could to keep them unaware of it. I took them over to the storeroom where Hitler's birthday presents were kept. There were children's toys and clothes among them, and the children chose what they liked.

When we came back there was another air-raid warning. The raids were coming thick and fast now, concentrating on the area round the Reich Chancellery. We had almost got used to the artillery fire. We noticed only when the roaring noise stopped. Once again we were sitting with Hitler. He was getting more oddly behaved and difficult to understand all the time. Just as yesterday he hadn't said a word to suggest that he didn't think victory certain, today he said with equal conviction that there was no longer any hope for a change in the situation. We pointed to the picture of Frederick the Great looking down from the wall, and now we all quoted the words Hitler had used so often. 'My Führer, where's the last battalion? Don't you believe in the lessons of history any more?' He shook his head wearily. 'The army has betrayed me, the generals are no good for anything. My orders haven't been carried out. It's finally over. National Socialism is dead and will never rise again!' How upset we were to hear these words! The change had been too sudden. Perhaps we hadn't really and truly meant it when we said we wanted to stay in Berlin? Perhaps we had hoped to get away with our lives after all. Now Hitler himself was depriving us of that hope.

Eva Braun developed a kind of loyalty complex. 'You know,' she told Hitler, 'I can't understand the way they've all left you. Where's Himmler, where are Speer, Ribbentrop, Göring? Why didn't they stay with you where they belong? And why isn't Brandt here?' And Hitler, who may well have been thinking how readily and light-heartedly many whom he had raised to great heights had now abandoned him, spoke up for his men. 'You don't understand, child. They can serve me better if they're out of here. Himmler has his divisions to lead, Speer has important work to do, they all have their official duties which are more important than my life.' 'Yes,' said Eva Braun, 'I can understand that. But take Speer, for example. I mean, he was your friend. I know him, I'm sure he will come.'

During this conversation Himmler rang. Hitler left the room

and went to the telephone. He came back looking pale, his face rigid. The Reichsführer had been trying once again, by phone, to get Hitler to leave the city. Once again the Führer had firmly refused. He spoke quite impersonally of his intended suicide, as if it were something to be taken for granted. And we kept seeing our own deaths before our eyes as well as his. We were getting used to the idea. But I hardly slept that night.

Next day the artillery fire comes closer again. The Russians have moved into the suburbs of the city. There is desperate fighting against a huge number of mighty tanks. The situation in the bunker is still the same. We sit and wait. Hitler has become dull and listless after his outburst of fury yesterday, when he shouted about betrayal. It's as if he has abdicated his office. There are no official military briefings now, the day has no set timetable. In the bright light reflected from the white concrete walls we don't notice day giving way to night. We secretaries keep close to Hitler, always uneasily expecting him to put an end to his life. But for the time being he goes on with this half-life. Goebbels has brought his state secretary Dr Naumann[96] and his adjutant Schwägermann[97] with him. They are discussing a final propaganda campaign with Hitler. The population must know that the Führer is in the besieged city and has undertaken its defence. That, they say, will give people strength to resist and make the impossible possible. But while the desperate and homeless flee from the ruined buildings and seek refuge in the U-Bahn tunnels, while every man and every boy is supposed to fight and risk his life using some kind of makeshift weapon, Hitler has already buried all hope.

The six children play in the corridors, happy and contented. They read their fairy-tales at the round table on a landing on the stairs, halfway down to the deepest part of the bunker. They don't hear the explosions getting louder and louder, they feel safe with 'Uncle Führer'. In the afternoon they drink chocolate with their 'uncle' and tell him what they have been doing at school. Helmut, the only boy, reads aloud the composition he wrote for Hitler's birthday. 'You stole that from Daddy,' says his sister Helga. And the adults laugh when the boy replies, 'Or Daddy stole it from me.' But in her handbag their mother is carrying the poison that means the end of six little lives.

I suddenly wonder where Professor Morell is. His room is being used by Goebbels and his wife now; the physician has left. Linge, who goes about his work in as calm and friendly a way as ever, tells me that after a dramatic scene with the Führer, Morell left Berlin by plane early in the morning. The previous evening Morell went to the Führer as usual to give him his daily injection before bed. And suddenly Hitler was overcome by a feeling of fear and distrust, suspecting betrayal and plots. 'Morell, leave my room at once! You want to anaesthetize me so that they can take me out of Berlin by force. That's what they all want, but I'm not going,' he shouted. And when the trembling Morell almost had a heart attack with the shock of it, he ordered him to leave Berlin on the next plane. Never before had Hitler gone for so much as a day without the support of his physician, who had to accompany him on every flight and every drive. Now he was sending him away. He didn't need a doctor any more, or medication or a special diet. Nothing mattered.

New faces suddenly appeared in the Führer bunker. There was Artur Axmann[98] the Reich youth leader. One of the devoted believers, a blind idealist! He had only one arm, but eyes full of warlike zeal shone in his calm, composed face. He too had come to be with his Führer at the last. Then there was an inconspicuous little man, greying at the temples. He wore the field-grey SS uniform and was to be found anywhere you saw a couple of officers standing together discussing the situation. This was Obergruppenführer Müller,[99] Kaltenbrunner's deputy.

Suddenly Speer appeared again. Eva Braun went to meet him, hand outstretched. 'I knew you'd come. You won't leave the Führer on his own.' But Speer smiled quietly. 'I'm leaving Berlin again this evening,' he replied after a pause. Then he went to see Hitler. We learned nothing of this long, serious conversation between them.

Another event was the subject of excited discussion: Göring's 'treachery'. Goebbels, Hewel, Voss, Axmann and Burgdorf were standing together in the corridor outside the conference room. Out in the anteroom I heard muted voices saying that Göring had betrayed the Führer, now, at the vital moment. What exactly had happened? On my way to the upper part of the bunker I met Frau Christian. She had heard about it from Colonel von Below, a colleague of her husband. Göring had sent a telegram to say that he was about to take over as Hitler's successor, since he assumed that the Führer no longer had complete freedom of action, and if he received no reply from the Führer by 22.00 hours he would consider that his succession had come into effect.

This telegram fell into Bormann's hands. He showed it to Hitler, putting his own interpretation on it. No wonder that Hitler saw treachery in Göring's proposition, fell into a furious rage against the Reich Marshal and removed him from all his offices. Bormann may have smiled with self-satisfaction to think that now, at five minutes to midnight, he had succeeded yet again in strengthening his own power. At his orders, Göring and his whole staff were arrested on the Obersalzberg.

Göring's telegram is the sole subject of conversation in the bunker all day. We hardly notice that, after a long conversation with Hitler, Speer has disappeared again and has finally left Berlin. Hitler has withdrawn into his room and won't see anyone. Meanwhile the officers are putting their heads together over the street map of Berlin in the conference room, discussing salvage operations. The Führer takes no further interest in that. But the general staff isn't giving up yet. Some kind of army under General Wenck[100] is supposed to be on its way to the West somewhere. So if Wenck is told to come back and storms Berlin, we could be saved! And Obergruppenführer Steiner[101] is to lead an attack from the north in support of Wenck! I don't understand the military details of this plan, but it does give me back a tiny spark of hope, and the officers take it to the Supreme Commander. They manage to get the Führer to look at the map table. Once more he rouses himself from his lethargy and gives the order for the attack! Wenck will change course and relieve Berlin.

None of us can sleep. We wander round the rooms like shadows, waiting. Sometimes we slip upstairs, wait for a pause in the artillery fire, and are horrified to see the devastation spreading further and further. We are surrounded by ruins and the remains of buildings. A dead horse lies in the middle of the white paving of the Wilhelmsplatz. But my feelings are deadened, I feel quite hollow. There is nothing real or natural left about us. We are indifferent and composed, we laugh because we can't cry, and we talk in order to silence the frightened voices of our despairing hearts, voices reminding us of home, our mothers, our families. Sometimes I think fleetingly of people living by a Bavarian lake, people who are waiting for me, who love me and are worried about me. People who don't have to make decisions. Where women don't have to fear the occupying power. Where life goes on. But the tense, oppressive atmosphere of the bunker has me in its grip. The Führer, now a broken old man, still holds the invisible strings. His presence is enough to stifle any real emotion, any natural feeling.

We women usually stick together. Eva Braun joins us too. We play with the children and the dogs. All the rooms are open to us, no work is officially being done any more. When a report comes in, when a dusty, perspiring officer arrives from the nearby front to announce that the Russian tanks are coming closer, Hitler receives the news in silence, with little interest. The Reich Chancellery has a defence commander now: Gruppenführer Mohnke.[102] I feel really faint and desperate to think of us still sitting here in a trap when the Russians begin storming the Reich Chancellery building. But the watchword is 'Chin up, while there's life there's hope', and we live by it, dulled and rigid as puppets. We don't know what the date is any more. Sometimes we snatch an hour of sleep, but our nervousness soon wakes us again. We want to be there when news that General Wenck is attacking arrives. We keep venturing out into the hell above us and listening, hoping to hear the thunder of German guns at last.

There is fighting right inside the city now. The heavy Russian tanks are taking street after street. What's the use of the Hitler Youth boys defending all the bridges and blowing them up? They get decorated by the Führer in person, a few Russian tanks are shot down, hundreds more replace them. And not a trace of Wenck. No news of Steiner's attack.[103] The reconnaissance patrols that set out from the Reich Chancellery come back without anything to report. [... *Manuscript illegible* ...] Hanna Reitsch[104] lands in a Fieseler Storch on the East-West axis just outside the Brandenburg Gate, bringing General Greim,[105] an excellent Luftwaffe officer. Today is the first time I've seen either of them. Hanna Reitsch is a small, delicate, very feminine person, you'd never have thought she had such masculine courage. She wears the Iron Cross on her smooth black rollneck sweater. Greim limps into the bunker on one leg, leaning on her shoulder. He was wounded on their adventurous flight here, shot in the leg by Russian fighter pilots. Now he has come to succeed Göring and take over command of the Luftwaffe. But first he disappears into the operating theatre to be treated by Dr Stumpfegger, the silent, pale, reserved doctor. Hanna Reitsch hurries to see the Führer. She must have been one of those women who adored Hitler unconditionally, without reservations. Today that seems to me amazing, because she was the only woman who knew Hitler not just privately, as a man, but as a soldier and a military commander too. She sparkled with her fanatical, obsessive readiness to die for the Führer and his ideals. [...]

In the evening she put the Goebbels children to bed. Eva Braun kept her company. Their mother hardly had the strength to face her children with composure now. Every meeting with them made her feel so terrible that she burst into tears afterwards. She and her husband were nothing but shadows, already doomed to die.

When I passed the door of the children's room I heard their six clear childish voices singing. I went in. They were sitting in three bunk beds, with their hands over their ears so as not to spoil the three-part round they were singing. Then they wished each other good night cheerfully, and finally fell asleep. Only the oldest, Helga, sometimes had a sad, knowing expression in her big brown eyes. She was the quietest, and sometimes I think, with horror, that in her heart that child saw through the pretence of the grown-ups.

I left the children's room wondering how anyone could allow these innocent creatures to die for him. Frau Goebbels talked to me about it. There were no differences of class or rank any more, we were all bound together by fate. Frau Goebbels was in greater torment than any of us. She was facing six deaths, while the rest of us had only to face one. 'I would rather have my children die than live in disgrace, jeered at. Our children have no place in Germany as it will be after the war.'

We still kept Hitler company at mealtimes. Only Eva Braun, Frau Christian, Fräulein Manziarly and me. There was no subject of conversation interesting enough for us to discuss it now. I heard my own voice like a stranger's. 'My Führer, do you think National Socialism will be revived?' I asked. 'No. National Socialism is dead. Perhaps a similar idea will arise in a hundred years' time, with the force of a religion sweeping through the whole world. But Germany is lost. It was probably never mature and strong enough for the task I intended it to perform,' said the Führer, as if talking to himself. I didn't understand him any more.

Everything was in hopeless confusion in the rooms of the New Reich Chancellery bunker. The officers there were von Below, Fegelein, Burgdorf, Krebs, Hewel, Captain Baur the pilot and Oberführer Rattenhuber, who were both homesick for Bavaria. Apart from me these two were the only ones who came from Munich. Then there was Admiral Voss, with several staff officers I didn't know, and Heinz Lorenz from the press office. Bormann and his colleague had their quarters somewhere too. Exhausted Volkssturm and Wehrmacht soldiers haunted the long corridor. A field kitchen was supplying them with hot drinks and soup. Sleeping figures lay on the floor everywhere, with women running around to render aid – refugees, girls, nurses, employees of the Reich Chancellery, all lending a hand where necessary. An emergency operating theatre had been set up in one of the big rooms. Chief Surgeon Haase,[106] who had been bombed out of the Charité hospital, was working day and night, amputating, operating, applying dressings, doing whatever he could. There were no longer enough of the beds that had been put up wherever possible. Soon there were no more shirts or underclothes for the wounded.

The long corridor running underground from this part of the Reich Chancellery and over to the Führer bunker had already taken hits in many places, and its thin ceiling had fallen in. Hitler wanted Frau Christian and me to be near him by night too. A couple of mattresses were put on the floor of the little conference room, where we slept in our clothes for an hour or so, and outside the door, which was left ajar, lay the officers Krebs, Burgdorf, Bormann, etc., in armchairs, snoring and waiting for Wenck's army! Instead, all hell was let loose above us. The firing reached its height on 25 and 26 April. Shots crashed out without a pause, and each one seemed to be aimed directly at our bunker. Suddenly a guard ran in and told us, 'The Russians have turned their machine-gun fire on the entrance.' In panic he hurried through the rooms, but the listless people waiting there did not react. Finally it turned out that there had been a mistake. Only a single artillery shot had landed quite close. Another reprieve! I don't know now how I spent those hours. We smoked a great deal, everywhere, whether the Führer was with us or not. The thick cigarette smoke no longer bothered him, and Eva Braun stopped concealing her 'vice'. Sometimes a man who had made his way back from the front arrived with a report. The main fighting line was getting closer and closer to Anhalt Station. Now it was the cries of the women and children of Berlin that we thought we heard when we climbed up and looked out at the flames and smoke. We heard that German women were being used as human shields by Russian tanks, and once again we saw death as the only way of escape.

When I remember how we all talked, in depressing detail, of nothing but the best way to die, I can't understand how it is that I'm still alive. Hitler had heard of Mussolini's shameful death.[107] I think someone had even shown him the photos of the naked bodies hanging head downwards in the main square of Milan. 'I will not fall into the enemy's hands either dead or alive. When I'm dead, my body is to be burned so that no one can ever find it,' Hitler decreed. And as we mechanically took our meals without noticing what we were eating we discussed ways to make sure of dying. 'The best way is to shoot yourself in the mouth. Your skull is shattered and you don't notice anything. Death is instantaneous,' Hitler told us. But we women were horrified at the idea. 'I want to be a beautiful corpse,' said Eva Braun, 'I shall take poison.' And she took a little brass capsule containing a phial of cyanide from the pocket of her elegant dress. 'I wonder if it hurts very much? I'm so frightened of suffering for a long time,' she confessed. 'I'm ready to die heroically, but at least I want it to be painless.' Hitler told us that death by this poison was completely painless. Your nervous and respiratory systems were paralysed, and you died within a few seconds. And this 'comforting' thought made Frau Christian and me ask the Führer for poison capsules too. Himmler had given him ten, and when we left him after the meal he personally gave each of us one, saying, 'I am very sorry that I can't give you a better farewell present.'

26 April. We are cut off from the outside world, with nothing but a wireless telephone connection to Keitel. Not a sign of Wenck's army and Steiner's attack. It's becoming certain that no army capable of saving us exists any more. The Russians have already reached the Tiergarten. They are meeting with less resistance on their way into the city centre, and are coming close to Anhalt Station. Nothing can stop them now.

The Führer is still leading his shadowy life in the bunker. He wanders restlessly around the rooms. Sometimes I wonder what he's waiting for, why he doesn't finally put an end to it all, because there's nothing to be saved now. But the idea of his suicide disillusions me. To think of the 'first soldier in the Reich' committing suicide while children defend the capital! Once I talk to him about it. I ask, 'My Führer, don't you think the German people will expect you to fall in battle at the head of your troops?' You can talk to him about anything now. His answer sounds weary. 'I'm no longer in any physical shape to fight. My trembling hands can hardly hold a pistol. If I am wounded I won't find any of my men to shoot me. And I don't want to fall into the hands of the Russians.' He is right. His hand shakes as he lifts a spoon or fork to his mouth, he has difficulty getting out of his chair, and when he walks his feet drag over the floor.

Eva Braun is writing farewell letters. All her beloved dresses, her jewellery and anything valuable that she liked has been sent to Munich. She too is waiting and suffering. Outwardly she seems as calm and almost cheerful as ever. But once she comes to me, takes my hands and says in a husky, trembling voice, 'Frau Junge, I'm so dreadfully frightened. If only it was all over!' Her eyes show all the torment hidden in her heart. She is surprised that Hermann Fegelein doesn't seem at all concerned about her. She hasn't seen him for two days. And even before that he seemed to be avoiding her. She asks me if I have seen him. No, Fegelein wasn't in the bunker at all today. No one knows where he is. People are looking for him on some kind of SS business, but he can't be found. Perhaps he's gone to the front to see what's going on? The officers who share a room with him in the Reich Chancellery don't know. On 27 April Hitler wants to see Fegelein too. There's no trace of him. Now the security service follows up his trail. That night SS General Fegelein is back in the Reich Chancellery but without his orders and decorations, dressed as a civilian and hopelessly drunk. I have never set eyes on him since. But Eva Braun, disappointed and shocked, tells me that last night Hermann called her from his private apartment. 'Eva, you have to leave the Führer if you can't persuade him to get out of Berlin. Don't be stupid – it's a matter of life and death now!'

She replies: 'Where are you, Hermann? Come here at once, the Führer is asking for you, he wants to speak to you!' But the connection has been cut.[108]

No more newspapers are being published in Berlin. Only the radio keeps broadcasting information that the Führer is still in the unhappy city, sharing its fate and conducting its defence personally. But the few of us in the Führer bunker know that Hitler withdrew from the battle long ago and is waiting to die. Over in the Reich Chancellery bunker the soldiers of the company on guard are gambling and singing old battle songs, while nurses and women auxiliaries work frantically. Refugees and auxiliaries from all over the city are gathering in the Reich Chancellery. There are living people here who are still hoping, fighting, working. But the Führer bunker is a waxworks museum. Yet human nature is still here too. There's a birthday. Old Rattenhuber is sixty. We sit in the upper corridor of the bunker, where there are tables and benches and the staff of the Führer bunker have their meals, and drink schnapps with the birthday boy. Eva Braun on one side, me on the other. We talk about Munich and Bavaria, and how sad it is to have to die so far from home. 'Among Prussians, of all things,' says Rattenhuber, and his merry eyes are damp. We laugh once again, and try to forget everything for a few minutes.

Suddenly a great many people arrive in the bunker, some of them strangers, some of them faces I know from the other parts of the bunker complex. A long line forms, going all the way down to the Führer bunker. And then we see the Führer slowly coming closer. Stooping, left hand behind his back, he shakes hands with everyone, looking into all those faces but seeing none of them. Their eyes light up, they are glad to hear the Führer thanking them, and go back to their work feeling proud and refreshed. But we know better. This is not a way of saying thank you for their courage and industry, this is goodbye. We have fallen silent. I ask Eva Braun, 'Has the time come, then?' But she says, 'No, you'll hear about it first. The Führer will say goodbye to all of you too.'

That night there is even a wedding. A kitchenmaid is marrying one of the drivers of the column of heavy vehicles. One brave driver has even fetched the bride's mother and family from the inferno of the city. We go up through dark corridors into the ruins of the Führer's apartment. Somewhere there's a high-ceilinged room dimly lit by candles. It is strange and uncanny. There are rows of chairs, and a podium. State Secretary Dr Naumann makes a speech, the couple join hands, and the guns known as Stalin organs make terrible music outside. Then we congratulate the young couple and go back to the bunker of death. The wedding guests celebrate, one of them has an accordion, another a fiddle. The newly-weds dance – on top of the volcano.

I play with the Goebbels children, read them fairy-tales, play forfeits with them and try to shield them from all the horrors. Their mother hardly has the strength to talk to them any more. At night they sleep peacefully in their six little beds, while the waiting in the bunker goes on and our doom comes closer and closer.

The last crushing blow falls on Hitler on 28 April. He still hasn't decided what is to be done with Hermann Fegelein, who he feels has let him down and betrayed him, when Heinz Lorenz of the press office brings him alarming news: according to a Reuter's report, SS Reichsführer Heinrich Himmler has been conducting negotiations with the Allies through Count Bernadotte.[109]

I don't know just where I was when the news reached Hitler. He may have ranted and raged one last time, but when I saw him again he was as calm as before. Only Eva Braun's eyes were red with weeping, because her brother-in-law was condemned to death. He had been shot like a dog in the park of the Foreign Office, under the blossoming trees and near the sweet bronze statue of the girl. She had tried to explain to Hitler that it was only human nature for Fegelein to think of his wife and their child, and try to help them get through to a new life. But Hitler was implacable. All he saw was deceit and treachery. His 'faithful Heinrich', whom he had taken for a rock of loyalty in the middle of the sea of weakness and deceit, had gone behind his back too. Suddenly Fegelein's actions took on another aspect: he had been part of a conspiracy. Hitler imagined terrible things about Himmler's intentions. Perhaps Himmler meant to assassinate him? Hand him over to the enemy alive? By now he not only distrusted everyone from Himmler's entourage still here with him, he even distrusted the poison that Himmler had given him. Dr Stumpfegger, who was with us in the bunker looking pale and thin, was more silent than ever. Hitler suspected him too.

So Professor Haase was brought over from the operating bunker in the New Reich Chancellery. We saw the Führer speak to him, give him one of the poison capsules, and then go with him to the little place at the entrance to the lavatories where Blondi and her puppies were kept. The doctor bent over the dog, a little waft of the bitter-almond scent reached us, and Blondi didn't move again. Hitler came back. His face looked like his own death mask. Without a word he shut himself in his room. Himmler's poison could be relied on!

Hanna Reitsch and General Greim prepared to fly out. [. . .] After a long conversation with Hitler, they left the bunker.

We women took refuge in Eva Braun's room with the children and the dogs. Decision was in the air now. Our nerves were stretched to breaking point. Eva told Frau Christian and me, 'I bet you'll be shedding tears this evening.' We looked at her in alarm. 'Has the time come?' No, she said, we would see something else, something really touching, but she couldn't tell us any more yet.

I don't know now how we passed all those hours. It was like a nightmare. I don't remember any more conversations or other details. What was there to talk about? Only the hellish noise made by the bombs, grenades, artillery and tanks spoke now. Soon the Russians would have reached the Potsdamer Platz, perhaps in a few hours' time, and then they would be nearly at our door. Nothing happened in the bunker. The nation's leaders sat there inactive, waiting for the decision, the last that Hitler would make. Even for the ever-zealous Bormann and the industrious Goebbels there was nothing more to do. Axmann, Hewel, Voss, the servants and adjutants, the orderlies and staff, they were all waiting for a decision. No one expected victory now. We all just wanted to be out of this bunker at last.

It seems to me almost incredible that we could still eat and drink, sleep and talk. We did it mechanically, and I have no memory of such things.

Goebbels made long speeches about the disloyalty of his colleagues. He was particularly indignant over Göring's behaviour. 'That man was never a National Socialist,' he claimed. 'He just basked in the Führer's glory, he never lived by idealistic, National Socialist principles. It's his fault that the German Luftwaffe failed, we have him to thank for it that we're sitting here now about to lose the war.' You suddenly realized that these two great figures had been bitter enemies and rivals. Frau Goebbels joined her husband in accusing the Reich Marshal.

We had become perfectly indifferent in those hours. We'd given up waiting. Time dragged wearily by while bedlam raged outside. We sat about talking, smoking, vegetating. You get tired doing that. The tension of the last few days now relaxes. There is only a great emptiness in me. I find a camp bed somewhere and sleep for an hour. It must be the middle of the night when I wake up. Servants and orderlies are busily coming and going in the corridor and in the Führer's rooms. I wash, change my clothes, it must be time to drink tea with the Führer. We still drink tea with him. And death is always an invisible guest at the tea-party. But today something unexpected awaits me when I open the door to Hitler's study. The Führer comes towards me, shakes hands and asks, 'Have you had a nice little rest, child?' When, surprised, I say yes, he adds, 'There's something I'd like you to take down from dictation later.' I had entirely forgotten that this weary, weak voice sometimes used to race through dictation so energetically that I could hardly keep up. What was there to be written now? My glance passes Hitler and is attracted to the festively laid table. It is laid for eight tonight, with champagne glasses. And the guests are already arriving, Goebbels and his wife, Axmann, Frau Christian, Fräulein Manziarly, General Burgdorf and General Krebs. I can't wait to know why they have all been summoned. Is Hitler going to make a big occasion of his farewell? Then he beckons me over. 'Perhaps we could do it now. Come along,' he says, leaving the room. Side by side we go to his conference room. I am about to remove the cover from the typewriter, but the Führer says, 'Take it down on the shorthand pad.' I sit down alone at the big table and wait. Hitler stands in his usual place by the broad side of the table, leans both hands on it, and stares at the empty table top, no longer covered today with maps or street plans. For several seconds, if the concrete didn't act like a drumskin, mercilessly amplifying the reverberations of every bomb blast and every shot, you could have heard only the breathing of two human beings. Then, suddenly, the Führer utters the first words. 'My political testament.' For a moment my hand trembles. Now, at last, I shall hear what we've been waiting for for days: an explanation of what has happened, a confession, even a confession of guilt, or perhaps a justification. This final document of the 'Thousand-Year Reich' should contain the real truth, told by a man with nothing more to lose.

But my expectations are not fulfilled. In tones of indifference, almost mechanically, the Führer comes out with the explanations, accusations and demands that I, the German people and the whole world know already. I look up in surprise as Hitler names the members of the new government. I really don't understand what's going on. If all is lost, if Germany is destroyed, if National Socialism is dead for ever, and the Führer himself can see no way out but suicide, what are the men he is appointing to government posts supposed to do? I can hardly grasp it. Hitler goes on speaking, scarcely looking up. He pauses for a brief moment, and then begins dictating his private will. And now I discover that he is going to marry Eva Braun before they are united in death. I fleetingly remember what Eva said, about the tears we'd shed today. But I can't summon up any tears. The Führer lists his legacies, but here, suddenly, he does mention the possibility that there may be no German state left after his death. Then the dictation is over. He moves away from the table on which he has been leaning all this time, as if for support, and suddenly there is an exhausted, hunted expression in his eyes. 'Type that out for me at once in triplicate and then bring it in to me.' There is something urgent in his voice, and I realize, to my surprise, that this last, most important, most crucial document written by Hitler is to go out into the world without any corrections or thorough revision. Every letter of birthday wishes to some Gauleiter, artist, etc., was polished up, improved, revised – but now Hitler has no time for any of that.

The Führer returns to his party, which will soon be a wedding party. As for me, I sit in the waiting-room outside Goebbels' room and type out the last page in the history of the Third Reich. Meanwhile the conference room has been turned into a registry office, a registrar fetched from the nearby front has married the Hitlers, Eva has begun to write her surname with a B when signing the register, and has had to have it pointed out that her new name begins with H. And now the wedding party is sitting in Hitler's room. What will they raise their champagne glasses to? Happiness for the newly married couple?

The Führer is impatient to see what I have typed. He keeps coming back into my room, looking to see how far I've got, he says nothing but just casts restless glances at what remains of my shorthand, and then goes out again.

Suddenly Goebbels bursts in. I look at his agitated face, which is white as chalk. Tears are running down his cheeks. He speaks to me because there's no one else around to whom he can pour out his heart. His usually clear voice is stifled by tears and shaking. 'The Führer wants me to leave Berlin, Frau Junge! I am to take up a leading post in the new government. But I can't leave Berlin, I cannot leave the Führer's side! I am Gauleiter of Berlin, and my place is here. If the Führer is dead my life is pointless. And he says to me, "Goebbels, I didn't expect you to disobey my last order too ..." The Führer has made so many decisions too late – why make this last one too early?' he asks despairingly.

Then he too dictates me his testament, to be added as an appendix to the Führer's. For the first time in his life, it says, he is not going to carry out an order by the Führer because he cannot leave his place in Berlin at the Führer's side. In later times, an example of loyalty will be more valuable than a life preserved ... And he too tells the world that he and his whole family prefer death to life in a Germany without National Socialism.

I type both documents as fast as I can. My fingers work mechanically, and I am amazed to see that they make hardly any typing errors. Bormann, Goebbels and the Führer himself keep coming in to see if I've finished yet. They make me nervous and delay the work. Finally they almost tear the last sheet out of my typewriter, go back into the conference room, sign the three copies, and that very night they are sent off by courier in different directions. Colonel von Below, Heinz Lorenz and Bormann's colleague Zander take Hitler's last will and testament out of Berlin.[110]

With that, Hitler's life is really over. Now he just wants to wait for confirmation that at least one of the documents has reached its destination. Any moment now we expect the Russians to storm our bunker, so close do the sounds of war seem to be. All our dogs are dead. The dog-walker has done his duty and shot our beloved pets before they can be torn to pieces up in the park by an enemy grenade or bomb.

Any of the guards or soldiers who have to go out in the open now are gambling with their lives. Some of our people have already been wounded. The leader of the escort commando has been shot in the leg and can't move for pain.

Almost no one stops to think of the five blonde little girls and the dark-haired boy still playing in their room, enjoying life. Their mother has now told them it's possible they may all have to be inoculated. When there are so many people living together in a small space you have to take precautions against disease. They understand that, and they're not afraid.

29 April. We're trapped here, we just sit waiting.

30 April begins like the days that went before it. The hours drag slowly by. No one knows just how to address Eva Braun now. The adjutants and orderlies stammer in embarrassment when they have to speak to the 'gnädiges Fräulein'. 'You may safely call me Frau Hitler,' she says, smiling.

She asks me into her room because she can't spend the whole time alone with her thoughts. We talk about something, anything, to distract ourselves. Suddenly she opens her wardrobe. There hangs the beautiful silver fox fur she loved so much. 'Frau Junge, I'd like to give you this coat as a goodbye present,' she says. 'I always liked to have well-dressed ladies around me – I want you to have it now and enjoy wearing it.' I thank her with all my heart, much moved. I am even glad to have it although I've no idea how, where and when I can wear it. Then we eat lunch with Hitler. The same conversation as yesterday, the day before yesterday, for many days past: a banquet of death under the mask of cheerful calm and composure. We rise from the table, Eva Braun goes to her room, and Frau Christian and I look for somewhere to smoke a cigarette in peace. I find a vacant armchair in the servants' room, next to the open door to Hitler's corridor. Hitler is probably in his room. I don't know who is with him. Then Günsche comes up to me. 'Come on, the Führer wants to say goodbye.' I rise and go out into the corridor. Linge fetches the others. Fräulein Manziarly, Frau Christian, I vaguely realize there are other people there too. But all I really see is the figure of the Führer. He comes very slowly out of his room, stooping more than ever, stands in the open doorway and shakes hands with everyone. I feel his right hand warm in mine, he looks at me but he isn't seeing me. He seems to be far away. He says something to me, but I don't hear it. I didn't take in his last words. The moment we've been waiting for has come now, and I am frozen and scarcely notice what's going on around me. Only when Eva Braun comes over to me is the spell broken a little. She smiles and embraces me. 'Please do try to get out. You may yet make your way through. And give Bavaria my love,' she says, smiling but with a sob in her voice. She is wearing the Führer's favourite dress, the black one with the roses at the neckline, and her hair is washed and beautifully done. Like that, she follows the Führer into his room – and to her death. The heavy iron door closes.

I am suddenly seized by a wild urge to get as far away from here as possible. I almost race up the stairs leading to the upper part of the bunker. But the Goebbels children are sitting halfway up, looking lost. They felt they'd been forgotten in their room. No one gave them any lunch today. Now they want to go and find their parents, and Auntie Eva and Uncle Hitler. I lead them to the round table. 'Come along, children, I'll get you something to eat. The grown-ups have so much to do today that they don't have any spare time for you,' I say as lightly and calmly as I can. I find a jar of cherries, butter some bread and feed the little ones. I talk to them to distract them. They say something about being safe in the bunker, and how it's almost fun to hear the explosions when they know the bangs can't hurt them. Suddenly there is the sound of a shot, so loud, so close that we all fall silent. It echoes on through all the rooms. 'That was a direct hit,' cried Helmut, with no idea how right he is. The Führer is dead now.[111]

I want to be on my own. The children, satisfied, go back to their room. I stay sitting by myself on the narrow bench at the round table on the landing. There is a bottle of Steinhäger standing there, with an empty glass beside it. Automatically, I pour myself a drink and swallow the strong liquor. My watch says a few minutes after three in the afternoon. So now it's over.

I don't know how long I sit like that. Men's boots have passed me by, but I didn't notice. Then the tall, broad figure of Otto Günsche comes up the stairs, and with him a strong smell of petrol. His face is ashen, his young, fresh features look gaunt.

He drops heavily to sit beside me, reaches for the bottle too, and his large, heavy hand is shaking. 'I've carried out the Führer's last order . . . his body is burned,' he says softly. I don't answer, I don't ask any questions.

He goes down again to make sure that the bodies are burned without trace. I stay sitting there for a while motionless, trying to imagine what will happen now. Then, after all, I suddenly feel an urge to go down to those two empty rooms. The door to Hitler's room is still open at the end of the corridor. The men carrying the bodies had no hands free to close it. Eva's little revolver is lying on the table with a pink chiffon scarf beside it, and I see the brass case of the poison capsule glinting on the floor next to Frau Hitler's chair. It looks like an empty lipstick. There is blood on the blue-and-white upholstery of the bench where Hitler was sitting: Hitler's blood. I suddenly feel sick. The heavy smell of bitter almonds is nauseating. I instinctively reach for my own capsule. I'd like to throw it as far away as I can and leave this terrible bunker. One ought to be able to breathe clear, fresh air now, feel the wind and hear the trees rustling. But freedom, peace and calm are out of reach.

Suddenly I feel something like hatred and helpless anger rise in me. I'm angry with the dead Führer. I'm surprised by that myself, because after all, I knew he was going to leave us. But he's left us in such a state of emptiness and helplessness! He's simply gone away, and with him the hypnotic compulsion under which we were living has gone too.

Footsteps are approaching the entrance door now. The last men to prop up the Reich have been present at the pyre and are now coming back. Goebbels, Bormann, Axmann, Hewel, Günsche, Kempka. I don't want to see anyone now, and once again I go over to my bunker room in the New Reich Chancellery, down the damaged corridor. Other women have taken up their quarters here now. Secretaries from the adjutancy office; I know them too. They don't yet know what has happened over there, they're talking about holding out and showing courage, they're laughing and still working. As if there were any point in that!

My cases are all there, neatly packed with my possessions, my books and wedding presents. I wanted to keep them safe and have them near me. Now they don't belong to me any more. I can't take anything with me.

There's nowhere to be alone in this terrible, huge building. I throw myself on my camp bed and try to think sensibly. It's hopeless, and finally I fall asleep.

I wake up late at night. My companions in the bunker room are just going to bed to get a few hours' sleep. They still don't know that the Führer is dead. There's no one to talk to. I go over to the Führer bunker again. All the others who were left behind have assembled there. Suddenly they are human beings thinking and acting independently again. They are all sitting together and talking. Frau Christian and Fräulein Krüger are there too. Young Fräulein Manziarly is sitting in a corner, eyes red with weeping. She had to cook supper for the Führer as usual today, 30 April, so that his death could be kept secret. But no one ate the fried eggs and creamed potatoes.

They are discussing what to do next. General Krebs is to go to Russian headquarters as a peace negotiator and offer our total surrender on condition that everyone in the bunkers can have safe conduct. He sets out with one companion late at night. The rest of us wait over coffee, schnapps, pointless conversation. I would like to get out of this bunker, I don't want to wait for the Russians to come and find my corpse in this mousetrap! I hear Otto Günsche talking to General Mohnke. They want to lead a group of fighting men and break out of the Reich Chancellery. There's no hope of surviving such a venture, but it's better than committing suicide in this trap. Almost without knowing we're saying, Frau Christian and I say, with one voice, 'Take us too!' A brief sympathetic and understanding look is bent on us, then the two men nod. But for the time being we'll wait and see what news Krebs brings.[112]

It is a long time before he comes back. It's the First of May now. A great festival! Hitler couldn't wait for it, he had thought this was the day that the Russians wanted to celebrate by storming the Reich Chancellery. But in fact the gunfire isn't as fierce today as on the days before.

I take Otto Günsche aside and look for a quiet corner where we can talk undisturbed. I want to know how the Führer died. And Günsche is glad to be able to talk about it. 'We saluted the Führer once more, then he went into his room with Eva and closed the door. Goebbels, Bormann, Axmann, Hewel, Kempka and I stood out in the corridor waiting. It may have been ten minutes, but it seemed an eternity to us, before the shot broke the silence. After a few seconds Goebbels opened the door and we went in. The Führer had shot himself in the mouth and bitten on a poison capsule too. His skull was shattered and looked dreadful. Eva Braun hadn't used her pistol, she just took the poison. We wrapped the Führer's head in a blanket, and Goebbels, Axmann and Kempka carried the corpse up all those stairs and into the park. It was heavier than I'd thought it could possibly be, with his slim figure. Up in the park we put the two bodies down side by side, a few steps from the entrance to the bunker. We couldn't go far because the firing was so fierce, so we picked a bomb crater quite close. Then Kempka and I poured petrol over the bodies, and I stood in the entrance and threw a burning rag on them. Both bodies went up in flames at once . . .' Günsche stops, and I think how quickly human beings pass away. The most powerful man in the Reich a few days ago, and now a little heap of ashes blowing in the wind. I didn't doubt what Günsche said for a moment. No one can pretend to be as shaken as he was – and certainly not Günsche, an uncomplicated, muscular young man. Where else could the Führer be now, anyway? There was no car, no plane, nothing within reach, no secret underground passage leading out of this bunker to freedom. And Hitler couldn't even walk properly any more, his body didn't obey him . . .

Finally Krebs comes back. He looks worn out, exhausted, and we don't even need to ask what news he brings. His offer was rejected. So now we prepare to set out. At this point Goebbels announces on the radio that the Führer is dead, 'fallen at the head of his troops'. The other inmates of the bunkers under the whole building know too, now. [. . .] The big storerooms stocked with provisions by the household manager are emptied. There are scarcely enough takers for all the canned food, bottles of wine, champagne and schnapps, chocolate. These things have lost their value. But everyone gets weapons from the leader of the escort commando. We women are each given a pistol too. We are not to fire it, we are told, except in the utmost need. Then we get practical clothing. We have to go over to the camp at the very back of the bunker, on Vossstrasse. It means passing through the operating theatre. I've never seen a dead body before, and I've always run away from the sight of blood. Now, empty-eyed, I see two dead soldiers in a terrible condition lying on stretchers. Professor Haase doesn't even look up as we come in. Sweating and concentrating hard, he is working on a leg amputation. There are buckets full of blood and human limbs everywhere. The saw grates as it works its way through bone. I see and hear nothing, the pictures don't penetrate my conscious mind. Automatically, I let someone hand me a steel helmet, long trousers and a short jacket in the room next door, try on boots and go back to the other bunker.

The new clothes feel odd hanging on my body. Now the men are in full marching gear too. Many of them have removed their epaulettes and decorations. Captain Baur has taken the oil painting of Frederick the Great out of its frame and rolled it up. He wants it as a souvenir. Hewel can't make up his mind what to do. He always was an indecisive character. Now he doesn't know where to die – should he take his poison or join our fighting group? He decides on the latter, and so does Admiral Voss. And so do Bormann, Naumann, Kempka, Baur, Schwägermann, Stumpfegger, they all want to get out.

I suddenly remember the children. There's no sign of Frau Goebbels. She has shut herself in her room. Are the children still with her? Some girl from the kitchen, or maybe it was a chambermaid, had offered to take the six children out with her.

The Russians might not harm them. But I don't know if Frau Goebbels accepted this offer.

We sit around and wait for evening. Only Schädle,[113] the wounded leader of the escort commando, has shot himself. Suddenly the door of the room occupied by the Goebbels family opens. A nurse and a man in a white coat are carrying out a huge, heavy crate. A second crate follows. My heart stands still for a moment. I can't help thinking of the children. The size of the crate would be about right. So my dulled heart can still feel something after all, and there's a huge lump in my throat.

Krebs and Burgdorf stand up, smooth down their uniform tunics, and shake hands with everyone in farewell. They are not leaving, they're going to shoot themselves here. Then they go out, parting from those who mean to wait longer. We must wait for darkness to fall. Goebbels walks restlessly up and down, smoking, like a hotel proprietor waiting discreetly and in silence for the last guests to leave the bar. He has stopped complaining and ranting. So the time has come. We all shake hands with him in farewell. He wishes me good luck, with a twisted smile. 'You may get through,' he says softly, in heartfelt tones. But I shake my head doubtfully. We are completely surrounded by the enemy, and there are Russian tanks in the Potsdamer Platz . . .

One by one we leave these scenes of horror. I pass Hitler's door for the last time. His plain grey overcoat is hanging from the iron coat-stand as usual, and above it I see his big cap with the golden national emblem on it and his pale suede gloves. The dog's leash is dangling beside them. It looks like a gallows. I'd like to take the gloves as a memento, or at least one of them. But my outstretched hand falls again, I don't know why. My silver fox coat is hanging in the wardrobe in Eva's room. Its lining bears the golden monogram E.B. I don't need it now, I don't need anything but the pistol and the poison.

So we go over to the big coal-cellar of the New Reich Chancellery. Otto Günsche leads us through the crowds; his broad shoulders forcing a way for us four women (Frau Christian, Fräulein Krüger, Fräulein Manziarly and me) through the soldiers waiting here ready to march. Among them I see the familiar faces of Bormann, Baur, Stumpfegger, Kempka, Rattenhuber and Linge, all now wearing steel helmets. We nod to each other. Most of them I've never seen again.

Then we wait in our bunker room to be fetched. We have all destroyed our papers. I take no money with me, no provisions, no clothes, just a great many cigarettes and a few pictures I can't part with. The other women pack small bags. They are going to try to find their way out through this hell too. Only the nurses stay behind.

It could be about eight-thirty in the evening. We are to be the first group leaving the bunker. A few soldiers I don't know from the guards battalion, we four women, Günsche, Mohnke, Hewel and Admiral Voss make our way through the many waiting people and go down underground passages. We clamber over half-wrecked staircases, through holes in walls and rubble, always going further up and out. At last the Wilhelmsplatz stretches ahead, shining in the moonlight. The dead horse still lies there on the paving stones, but only the remains of it now. Hungry people have come out of the U-Bahn tunnels to slice off pieces of meat . . .

Soundlessly, we cross the square. Sporadic shots are fired, but the gunfire is stronger further away. Then we have reached the U-Bahn tunnel outside the ruins of the Kaiserhof. We climb down and work our way on in the darkness, over the wounded and the homeless, past soldiers resting, until we reach Friedrichstrasse Station. Here the tunnel ends and hell begins. We have to get through, and we succeed. The whole fighting group gets across the S-Bahn bend uninjured. But an inferno breaks out behind us. Hundreds of snipers are shooting at those who follow us.

For hours we crawl through cavernous cellars, burning buildings, strange, dark streets! Somewhere in an abandoned cellar we rest and sleep for a couple of hours. Then we go on, until Russian tanks bar our way. None of us has a heavy weapon. We are carrying nothing but pistols. So the night passes, and in the morning it is quiet. The gunfire has stopped. We still haven't seen any Russian soldiers. Finally we end up in the old beer cellar of a brewery now being used as a bunker. This is our last stop. There are Russian tanks out here, and it's full daylight. We still get into the bunker unseen. Down there Mohnke and Günsche sit in a corner and begin to write. Hewel lies on one of the plank beds, stares at the ceiling and says nothing. He doesn't want to go on. Two soldiers bring in the wounded Rattenhuber. He has taken a shot in the leg, he is feverish and hallucinating. A doctor treats him and puts him on a camp bed. Rattenhuber gets out his pistol, takes off the safety catch and puts it down beside him.

A general comes into the bunker, finds the defending commander Mohnke and speaks to him. We discover that we are in the last bastion of resistance in the capital of the Reich. The Russians have now surrounded the brewery and are calling on everyone to surrender. Mohnke writes a last report. There is still an hour to go. The rest of us sit there smoking. Suddenly he raises his head, looks at us women and says, 'You must help us now. We're all wearing uniform, none of us will get out of here. But you can try to get through, make your way to Dönitz and give him this last report.'

I don't want to go on any more, but Frau Christian and the other two urge me to; they shake me until I finally follow them. We leave our steel helmets and pistols there. We take our military jackets off too. Then we shake hands with the men and go.

An SS company is standing by its vehicles in the brewery yard, stony-faced and motionless, waiting for the order for the last attack. The Volkssturm, the OT men and the soldiers are throwing their weapons down in a heap and going out to the Russians. At the far end of the yard Russian soldiers are already handing out schnapps and cigarettes to German soldiers, telling them to surrender, celebrating fraternization. We pass through them as if we were invisible. Then we are outside the encircling ring, among wild hordes of Russian victors, and at last I can weep.

Where were we to turn? If I'd never seen dead people before,

I saw them now everywhere. No one was taking any notice of them. A little sporadic firing was still going on. Sometimes the Russians set buildings on fire and searched for soldiers in hiding. We were threatened on every corner. I lost track of my colleagues that same day. I went on alone for a long time, hopelessly, until at last I ended up in a Russian prison. When the cell door closed behind me I didn't even have my poison any more, it had all happened so fast.[114] Yet I was still alive. And now began a dreadful, terrible time, but I didn't want to die any more; I was curious to find out what else a human being can experience. And fate was kind to me. As if by a miracle, I escaped being transported to the East. The unselfish human kindness of one man preserved me from that. After many long months, I was at last able to go home and back to a new life.

NOTES

1. State control of jobs as practised by the National Socialists in order to realize the ideas and plans of the 'New Order of German Living Space'. Job allocation and changes of workplace were supervised and regulated by 'obligatory services'.

2. Albert Bormann, *b* Halberstadt 2 September 1902, *d* Berlin May 1945 (probably committed suicide by taking cyanide); profession: bank clerk; from 1931 employed in the Führer's private chancellery office; 1933 head of the Führer's private chancellery office; 1938 member of the Reichstag; 1943 NSKK Gruppenführer and personal adjutant to Adolf Hitler.

3. Martin Bormann, *b* Halberstadt 17 June 1900, *d* probably Berlin 2 May 1945 (suicide by cyanide); profession: agriculturalist; 1924 joins the NSDAP; 1933–1941 head of staff in the Deputy Führer's office; 1933 appointed Reichsleiter of the NSDAP; from 1938 on Hitler's personal staff; 12 May 1941 appointed head of the Party Chancellery; 1946 condemned to death *in absentia* as a war criminal at Nuremberg.

4. Gerda Christian, née Daranowski ('Dara'), *b* Berlin 13 December 1913, office clerk at Elizabeth Arden in Berlin; 1937 secretary in Hitler's personal adjutancy office; from 1939 works with Hitler in his various Führer headquarters; 2 February 1943 marries Eckhard Christian, a major in the Luftwaffe and adjutant to the Wehrmacht head of staff at Führer headquarters, stops working for Hitler until mid-1943; then until 1945 works at Führer headquarters; 1 May 1945 succeeds in fleeing to West Germany from the Reich Chancellery.

5. Johanna Wolf, *b* Munich 1 June 1900, *d* Munich 4 June 1985; from 1929 clerical assistant in Hitler's private chancellery and member of the Nazi Party; after 1933, when Hitler comes to power, secretary in his chancellery and later in his personal adjutancy office in Berlin; is with Hitler during the war at his various Führer headquarters. Hitler says goodbye to her and Christa Schroeder on the night of 21 April

Until the Final Hour

1945, and advises her to leave Berlin. Interned until 14 January 1948.
6. Christa Schroeder, *b* Münden, Hanover 19 March 1908, *d* Munich 28 June 1984; 1930–1933 secretary to the Reich leadership of the NSDAP in Munich; 1933–1939 secretary in the Führer's personal adjutancy office. Until 22 April 1945 accompanies Hitler as his secretary during the war, on all his journeys and at all the Führer headquarters. Interned until 12 May 1948.
7. Heinz Linge, *b* Bremen 23 March 1913, *d* Bremen 1980; profession: mason; 1933 joins the Leibstandarte-SS Adolf Hitler (LSSAH, Hitler's bodyguard); 1935–1945 Hitler's valet; 2 May 1945 taken prisoner by the Red Army and interned in Russia; 1950 condemned to 25 years' penal labour; 1955 released.
8. Walther Hewel, *b* Cologne 2 January 1904, *d* Berlin 2 May 1945 (probably suicide); 1923 standard-bearer of the 'Hitler Stormtroop' in the attempted putsch in Munich and imprisoned, works as a businessman abroad after his release until 1936; 1933 joins the NSDAP; 1938 enters the Foreign Office as Legation Councillor First Class, head of the Reich Foreign Minister's personal staff; 1940 appointed Envoy First Class and Head of Section in the Foreign Office as the Foreign Minister's permanent liaison officer with Adolf Hitler. He leaves the Reich Chancellery with Martin Bormann on 2 May 1945.
9. Joachim von Ribbentrop, *b* Wesel 30 April 1893, *d* Nuremberg 16 October 1946 (executed); trained in banking in Montreal; 1915 a lieutenant in the First World War; 1920 marries Annelies Henkel and becomes a representative of the Henkel sparkling wine firm in Berlin; 1930 joins the NSDAP; from 1933 works on foreign policy with Hitler; 1934 responsible for questions of disarmament; 1936 ambassador in London; from 1938 Reich Foreign Minister; May 1945 arrested by the British Army; 1946 condemned to death at Nuremberg.
10. Hans Hermann Junge, *b* Wilster in Holstein 11 February 1914, *d* Dreux, Normandy, 13 August 1944. Profession: white-collar worker; 1933 joins the SS; 1934 volunteers for the LSSAH; 1936 joins the SS Führer's escort commando; 1940 becomes valet and orderly to Adolf Hitler; 19 June 1943 marries Traudl Humps; 14 July 1943 joins the Waffen-SS; from June 1944 at the front with the 12th SS HitlerYouth Armoured Division. The organization for the care of German war graves, based in Kassel, gives the date of death as 18 August 1944. The same date is given on Junge's gravestone in the German Military

197

Cemetery at Champigny St.-André in Normandy (block 6, grave no. 1816).

11. Julius Gregor Schaub, *b* Munich 20 August 1898, *d* Munich 27 December 1967; profession: pharmacist, member of the SS, membership number 7, Nazi Party membership number 81, SS-Obergruppenführer and personal adjutant to Hitler; 1936 member of the Reichstag, Hitler's chauffeur; 1945 destroys Hitler's confidential files in Munich and Berchtesgaden. Interned in various camps until 1949.

12. Christian Weber, *b* Polsingen 25 August 1883, *d* Munich 1945; innkeeper, bookie and politician, one of the first members of the 'Hitler shock troops'; 1926–1934 Nazi city councillor in Munich; 1935 city councillor, inspector of the SS riding schools and many other offices; killed by Bavarian rebels in 1945.

13. The cook Otto Günther was originally an employee of Mitropa, and in 1937 was employed in Hitler's special train and then in Führer headquarters at the Wolf's Lair.

14. Alfred Jodl, *b* Würzburg 10 May 1890, *d* Nuremberg 16 October 1946 (executed); 1912 lieutenant in artillery regiment; 1918 captain and adjutant to the artillery commander; 1933 lieutenant colonel and commander with the Turkish army; 1935 colonel in chief with leadership function at Wehrmacht operations office of High Command; 1939 major general and until the end of the war chief of staff of the Wehrmacht office of High Command, Hitler's military adviser with responsibility for operations; 1940 promoted to artillery general; 1944 to colonel general; 7 May 1945 signs Germany's unconditional surrender; 22 May 1945 arrested by British soldiers in Flensburg; 1 October 1946 condemned to death by the military tribunal at Nuremberg. Holder of the 865th award of the Knight's Cross of the Iron Cross with oakleaves.

15. Hitler had originally been an enthusiastic fan of films and the theatre. However, he had given up such entertainments since the beginning of the war.

16. Theodor Morell, *b* Trais-Münzenburg 22 June 1886, *d* Tegernsee 26 May 1948; 1913 qualifies as a doctor; 1914 naval doctor, war volunteer; 1918 goes into practice in Berlin; 1933 joins the NSDAP; 1936–1945 Hitler's personal physician; 23 April 1945 leaves Berlin for the Berghof, is in various camps and hospitals from 1945 to his death.

17. Karl Brandt, *b* Mühlhausen, Alsace 8 January 1904, *d* Landsberg 2

June 1948 (executed); 1932 joins the NSDAP; 1934 Hitler's attendant doctor; 1937 medical director of the Berlin Surgical Hospital; on the staff of the Reich Chancellery until 1944 and thus close to Hitler both at Führer headquarters and in his close private entourage at the Berghof. After the assassination attempt on Hitler of 20 July 1944 relieved of all his medical posts with Hitler. Arrested by the SS on Hitler's personal orders on 16 April 1945, accused of insufficient belief in the final victory. 1947 condemned to death by an American military tribunal.

18. Otto Dietrich, *b* Essen 31 August 1897, *d* Düsseldorf 22 November 1952; studied philosophy and political sciences, newspaper editor; 1929 joins the NSDAP; 1932 joins the SS; 1930/31 deputy chief editor of the *Nationalzeitung*; 1931 head of the Party press office; 1933 head of the Reich press office; 1949 condemned to seven years' imprisonment, released 1950.

19. Heinz Lorenz, *b* Schwerin 7 August 1913; studies law and national sciences; 1932 press shorthand writer for the German Telegraph Office; 1936 responsible for foreign news to Reich press chief Dietrich; end of 1942 chief editor of the German News Bureau and in Führer headquarters until 29 April 1945. A prisoner of the British until 1947.

20. Johann Rattenhuber, *b* Oberhaching, Munich, 30 April 1897, *d* Munich 30 June 1957; 1920 joins the Bayreuth police; 1933 adjutant to Police President Himmler; 1933 appointed to set up the 'Special Purposes Commando' for Hitler in Berlin; 1935 head of the independent Reich Security Service (RSD), builds up various RSD departments, head of the RSD until 1945; 2 May 1945 captured by the Red Army, prisoner of war in Russia until 16 November 1951.

21. Peter Högl, *b* Poxau, Dingolfing, 19 August 1897, *d* Berlin 2 May 1945 (shot through the head); profession: miller; 1919 attends police college in Munich; 1920 joins the police; 1932 joins the criminal police; 1933 in the Führer's security department; 1934 SS-Obersturmführer; 1935 head of Department 1 in the Reich Security Service; 1944 criminal director of the Reich Security Service; 1945 witnesses Hitler's suicide.

22. Traudl Junge's tasks included typing itineraries and reports of losses, and taking down Hitler's public speeches and letters from dictation. Military orders were typed by the secretaries of the various departments concerned with them.

23. Wilhelm Keitel, *b* Helmscherode in the Harz Mountains 22 September

1882, *d* Nuremberg 16 October 1946 (executed); 1901 begins military career; 1914–1918 fights in the First World War, as captain and general staff officer; 1923 major; 1929 lieutenant colonel at the Reich Defence Ministry; 1931 colonel; 1934 major general and infantry commander VI in Bremen; 1935 head of Wehrmacht office in the Reich Defence Ministry; 1936 lieutenant general; 1937 general of artillery; 1938 colonel general and appointment to head of the OKW, thereafter Hitler's closest military adviser; 1940 field marshal; 8 May 1945 signs the unconditional surrender of the German Wehrmacht in Berlin Karlshorst; 1 October 1946 condemned to death by the military tribunal in Nuremberg. Holder of the Knight's Cross of the Iron Cross.

24. Friedrich 'Fritz' Darges, *b* Dülseberg 8 February 1913; 1933 joins the SS; 1934 trains at Bad Tölz Junkerschule; from 1935 SS Untersturmführer on active service and as staff officer; 1940 SS Hauptsturmführer, assigned to the adjutancy office at Führer headquarters; 1942 company commander in SS Panzer division Viking, wounded; 1943 SS Sturmbannführer and personal adjutant to Hitler at Führer headquarters; 1944–1945 SS Obersturmbannführer, divisional commander and regimental commander in SS Panzer division Viking on the Eastern Front; 8 May 1945 interned by the US Army; released in 1948. Holder of the Knight's Cross of the Iron Cross.

25. Otto Günsche, *b* Jena 24 September 1917; 1934 joins the Leibstandarte-SS Adolf Hitler (LSSAH); 1941/1942 trains at Bad Tölz Junkerschule, sees active service; January to August 1943 personal adjutant to Adolf Hitler at the Wolf's Lair, followed by service at the front; from February 1944 Hitler's personal adjutant again; 1944 SS Sturmbannführer; 2 May 1945 captured by the Russians; labour camp in Russia; May 1956 released from the East German penitentiary of Bautzen.

26. In these comments Traudl Junge was referring to the regular passenger trains on German railways of the time. Modern readers might get the impression that she meant the deportation trains taking Jewish prisoners east in inhuman conditions, but she did not intend any such association when writing this manuscript in 1947.

27. Willi and Gretl Mittlstrasser, husband and wife, looked after the Berghof household until the collapse of the Third Reich.

28. This was Paula Hitler, *b* Hafeld, Austria 26 January 1896, *d* Schönau, Berchtesgaden 1 June 1960; takes a commercial studies course, works

in the Chancellery in Vienna, sacked in 1930 apparently because Hitler is her brother; receives a monthly pension from Adolf Hitler from 1933 to 1945; 26 May 1945 tracked down by the British army at the Dietrich Eckart hut in Berchtesgaden and interrogated; campaigns until her death for her share of the legacy from Hitler's estate.

29. Rudolf Schmundt, *b* Metz 13 August 1896, *d* Rastenburg, East Prussia, 1 October 1944; 1938 appointed chief Wehrmacht adjutant to the Führer, promoted to lieutenant general; 20 July 1944 severely injured in the plot to assassinate Hitler. Dies a few weeks later in Rastenburg military hospital.

30. Karl-Jesko von Puttkamer, *b* Frankfurt an der Oder 2 April 1900, *d* Neuried 4 March 1981; 1917 enters the Reich navy; 1930 lieutenant captain; 1933 to 1935 naval liaison officer to High Command of the army in Berlin; 1935 2nd adjutant and naval liaison officer to Führer headquarters; 21 April 1945 reaches the Berghof by way of Salzburg; 10 May 1945 arrested by the US Army; 1947 released.

31. Walter Frentz, *b* Heilbronn 21 August 1907; studies electrotechnology in Munich and Berlin, cameraman with the UFA film studios, camera director for Leni Riefenstahl; 1939 film reporter at Führer headquarters; 1942 lieutenant in the Luftwaffe, accompanies Hitler on all his journeys and is also with him in the various Führer headquarters to film and photograph events; 24 April 1945 flees from Berlin; May 1945 taken prisoner by the US army, released at the end of 1946.

32. Hugo Blaschke, *b* Neustadt 14 November 1881, *d* Nuremberg 6 December 1959; studies dentistry in Philadelphia and London; 1911 opens a dental practice in Berlin, is Hermann Göring's dentist; 1931 joins the NSDAP, is Hitler's dentist from the end of 1933 to 1945; 1946 interned; 1948 released, practises dentistry in Nuremberg until his retirement.

33. Traudl Junge means the Zum Türken inn, which is still standing.

34. The Platterhof was a restaurant or café with a hairdressing salon attached; its clients included Eva Braun and Traudl Junge. The building was demolished in 2000.

35. Hans-Karl von Hasselbach, *b* Berlin 2 November 1903; studies medicine; 1936 surgical training at Munich University Hospital; 1933 joins the NSDAP; 1934 joins the SS; 1936 attendant doctor to the Führer's staff as deputy to Dr Brandt; 1942–1944 appointed attend-

ant doctor to Hitler at Führer headquarters; October 1944 dismissed on account of a dispute about Professor Morell, medical director of a field hospital on the Western Front until the end of the war, interned by the US army; 1948 released from internment.

36. Herta Schneider, née Ostermeier, *b* Nuremberg 4 April 1913; schoolmate and closest friend of Eva Braun. She met Hitler through Eva Braun in 1933, and was a frequent guest at the Berghof until April 1945.

37. Fritz Todt, *b* Pforzheim 4 September 1891, *d* Rastenburg 8 February 1942; 1923 joins the NSDAP, inspector general of the German roads network, is in charge of the building of the Reich autobahn and the West Wall, founds the 'Organisation Todt' (OT); 1940 appointed Reich Minister of Armaments and Ammunition. His successor was Albert Speer.

38. Heinrich Hoffmann, *b* Fürth 12 September 1885, *d* Munich 16 December 1957; works in his father's photography business; 1908 sets up independently in Munich; 1920 joins the NSDAP, membership number 425; 1933 becomes a member of the German Reichstag; 1938 given the title of Professor by Hitler; 1945 interned by the US Army, released May 1950.

39. Traudl Junge means Margarete, known as 'Gretel' or 'Margret' Speer, Albert Speer's wife since 1928.

40. Nicolaus von Below, *b* Jargelin 20 September 1907, *d* Detmold 24 July 1983; air cadet at the German School of Commercial Aviation until 1929; 1933 commissioned as lieutenant; 1933–1936 in the Reich Air Ministry; 1936–1945 Luftwaffe adjutant to Hitler. With his wife is a member of Hitler's close entourage at the Berghof. 1946–1948, interned by the British Army.

41. Wilhelm Brückner, *b* Baden-Baden 11 December 1884, *d* Herbstdorf, Chiemgau 18 August 1954; member of the civil defence (Freikorps Epp) until 1919; 1923 joins the NSDAP, regimental leader of the SA in Munich at the time of Hitler's putsch; 1930 adjutant to Adolf Hitler, SA Obergruppenführer; 1936 member of the Reichstag; 1940 dismissed as chief adjutant; 1941 appointed to the Wehrmacht as lieutenant colonel; 1945–1948 interned by the US Army.

42. The dancer and actress Inga Ley, who committed suicide in 1942. She was the wife of Robert Ley, *b* Niederbreidenbach in the Rheinland 15 February 1890, *d* Nuremberg 25 October 1945 (suicide); studies chemistry in Münster; 1914 to 1918 fights in the First World War;

1923 gains a doctorate, first post with I.G. Farben; 1925 Gauleiter of the Rhineland; 1930 member of the Prussian Landtag; 1932 organization leader of the NSDAP; 10 May 1945 arrested in Salzburg. Hangs himself in his cell at Nuremberg.

43. Hermann Esser, *b* Röhrmoos 29 July 1900, *d* Dietramszell 7 February 1981; 1919 joined the DAP; 1920 leader-writer of the *Völkischer Beobachter*; 1923 propaganda chief of the NSDAP, notorious for his inflammatory anti-Semitic speeches; 1932 member of the Bavarian Landtag, sidelined for his political intrigues; 1935 writes the anti-Semitic *Die jüdische Weltpest*; 1945–1947 prisoner of the US Army; 1949 condemned to five years in a labour camp, released 1952.

44. Baldur von Schirach, *b* Berlin 9 May 1907, *d* Kröv, Mosel 8 August 1974; 1924 joins the NSDAP and SA; 1927 leader of the Nazi Student League; 1931 'Reich Youth Leader'; 1933–1940 'Youth Leader of the German Reich'; 1940–1945 Gauleiter and Reich governor of Vienna; 1946 condemned to 20 years' imprisonment by the international military tribunal in Nuremberg for crimes against humanity.

45. Marion Schönmann, née Petzl, *b* Vienna 19 December 1899, *d* Munich 17 March 1981; met Hitler through Heinrich Hoffmann's future wife Erna, a frequent guest at the Berghof in 1935–1944.

46. Albert Speer, *b* Mannheim 19 March 1905, *d* London 1 September 1981; studies architecture in Karlsruhe; 1927–1932 assistant to Heinrich Tessnow in Berlin; 1931 joins the NSDAP; 1933 organizes the May Party Rally; 1936 commissioned by Hitler to redesign Berlin; 1937 appointed to the Führer's staff with responsibility for buildings and made Inspector General of Buildings for Berlin; 1942 Reich Minister for Armaments and Ammunition; 23 May 1945 arrested in Flensburg with the Dönitz government; 1946 condemned to 20 years' imprisonment at Nuremberg; 1966 released.

47. Henriette von Schirach, née Hoffmann, *b* Munich 3 February 1913; 1930 joins the NSDAP, 1932 marries Baldur von Schirach; 1945 interned; 1980 publishes her book *Anekdoten um Hitler. Geschichten aus einem halben Jahrhundert* [*Anecdotes of Hitler. Stories from Half a Century*].

48. Although Frau von Schirach was born in Munich, at this time she was indeed living with her husband, the Gauleiter and Reich Governor of Vienna, in the capital of Austria, then known in Germany as the 'Ostmark'.

49. Josef 'Sepp' Dietrich, *b* Hawangen 25 May 1892, *d* Ludwigsburg 21 April 1966; 1910 completes training in the hotel trade; 1911 begins

a military career, serves in the First World War, acting sergeant; 1919 sergeant with Wehrregiment 1 in Munich; 1920–1927 serves with Bavarian police and is a member of the Freikorps Oberland, takes part in Hitler's putsch in Munich; 1928 joins the newly formed SS as Sturmbannführer and joins the NSDAP; 1929 promoted to SS Standartenführer and leader of SS Brigade Bayern; 1930 SS Oberführer, leader of SS Group Süd, member of the Reichstag; 1931 SS Gruppenführer, leader of SS Group Nord; 1933 leader of SS Special Commando in Berlin, builds up the Leibstandarte SS Adolf Hitler; 1934 SS Obergruppenführer; 1935 Berlin city councillor; 1939 takes part in the Polish campaign; 1940–1943 takes part in the Western, Eastern and Balkan campaigns, commander of 1st SS Panzer division LSSAH, general in the Waffen SS; 1944–1945 SS Oberstgruppenführer and colonel general of the Waffen SS, commanding general of 1st SS Panzer corps and supreme commander of the 5th Panzer army, finally supreme commander of the 6th Panzer army, sees action at the Eastern Front, the Western Front and then the Eastern Front again; 8 May 1945 captured in Austria by the US Army; 1946 condemned to life imprisonment; 1955 released; 1957–1959 imprisoned for complicity in the killings during the Röhm putsch of 1934. Holder of the 16 brilliants to the Knight's Cross of the Iron Cross with oakleaves and swords.

50. Jakob Werlin, *b* Andritz near Graz 10 May 1886, *d* Salzburg 23 September 1945; profession: businessman; 1921 director of the Benz & Co branch in Munich, in this capacity meets Hitler, to whom he sells several cars, a personal friend of Hitler; 1932 joins the NSDAP and the SS; 1943 SS-Obergruppenführer, 'Inspector General of Motor Vehicles'; 1945–1949 interned by the US Army.

51. The actress Emmy Sonnemann, who married Hermann Göring on 10 April 1935. Hitler was a witness at their wedding.

52. Gerda Christian returned to Adolf Hitler's employment in the middle of 1943.

53. The Grosse Deutsche Kunstausstellung (GDK), the 'Great German Art Exhibition', an exhibition also selling works of art held annually in the House of German Art between 1937 and 1944, to promote 'new German art' – conservative works related to 19th-century realism.

54. Gerhardine 'Gerdy' Troost, née Andersen, *b* Stuttgart 3 March 1904, meets Paul Ludwig Troost when she is 19 in her father's woodworking studio; 1925 marries him; 1932 joins the NSDAP, continues to manage

her husband's architect's office after his death in 1934; 1935 on the committee running the House of German Art; 1935 awarded the title of Professor by Hitler; 1938 artistic adviser to Bavarian Film Art Ltd; after 1945 settles in Schützing by the Chiemsee. – Paul Ludwig Troost, *b* Elberfeld 17 August 1878, *d* Munich 21 January 1934; studies architecture in Darmstadt; 1902 gains his doctorate and sets up as an independent architect in Munich; 1912 to 1929 interior designer of North German Lloyd; 1929 meets Adolf Hitler; 1932 draws up plans for the House of German Art, designs the Königlicher Platz (now the Königsplatz) with Party buildings, etc.

55. Erich Kempka, *b* Oberhausen in the Rhineland 16 September 1910, *d* Freiburg-Heutingsheim 24 January 1975; profession: electrician; 1930 joins the NSDAP and SS, driver for the Gau Essen; 1932 driver for the SS escort commando in Munich; 1936 Hitler's permanent chauffeur and head of motor vehicles department; 1 May 1945 flees from the Führer bunker; 20 June 1945 arrested by the US Army, interned in various camps until 1947.

56. Traudl Junge was misinformed. In fact Hitler's niece Angela Maria Raubal, known as Geli, committed suicide on 18 September 1931 after a quarrel with Hitler.

57. In 1931 Adolf Hitler was on his way not to Nuremberg but to Hamburg for elections. However, he was near Nuremberg when news of his niece's death reached him.

58. SS-Obersturmführer Hans Pfeiffer was detailed for duty as Adolf Hitler's aide-de-camp on 10 October 1939.

59. Ernst 'Putzi' Hanfstaengl and his wife Erna were among Hitler's principal early companions at the beginning of the 1920s.

60. Helene Marie 'Marlene' von Exner, *b* Vienna 16 April 1917; trains as a dietician at Vienna University; Sept. 1942–July 1943 dietician cook to Marshal Antonescu in Bucharest; July 1943 dietician cook to Hitler until she leaves the post on 8 May 1944.

61. Traudl Junge is referring to Adolf Hitler's meeting with Benito Mussolini on 19 July 1943 in Feltre near Belluno.

62. Hans Baur, *b* Ampfing 19 June 1897, *d* Neuwiddersberg 17 February 1993; profession: businessman; 1916 pilot with the Bavarian Aviation Division I; 1920 joins Bavarian Air Mail Service; 1922 joins Bavarian Air Lloyd; 1926 joins Lufthansa, flies Adolf Hitler to his election campaigns in 1932; 1933 (as Hitler's pilot) becomes SS Standartenführer on Himmler's staff; 1944 appointed SS Brigadeführer,

Traudl Junge

finally becomes lieutenant general of police; 1 May 1945 breaks out of the Führer bunker; 2 May 1945 taken prisoner by the Russians, interned in various prisons and labour camps until 1955.

63. Mussolini was in fact removed from power on 25 July 1943, just a week after his talks with Hitler, and was arrested and stripped of his offices. German paratroopers freed him from imprisonment on the Campo Imperatore (Gran Sasso d'Italia) on 12 September 1943. Thereafter he led a shadowy existence in northern Italy as a dependent of Hitler.

64. As Traudl Junge herself says, she remembered only a few outstanding points of the eventful year 1943, and then not in chronological order. Stalingrad 'fell' before Hitler's meeting with Mussolini. The southern defences around Stalingrad surrendered on 31 January 1943, the northern defences on 2 February 1943. The High Command of the Wehrmacht officially announced: 'The battle for Stalingrad is over. True to their oath of allegiance to the last breath, the army, under the exemplary leadership of Field Marshal Paulus, has fallen to the superior power of the enemy and the unfavourable weather conditions. [...] They died that Germany might live.'

65. The SD – Sicherheitsdienst – was the security service of the Reichsleiter's SS, after 1936 officially the intelligence and counter-intelligence service of the German Reich, its main business being to provide the Secret State Police (the Gestapo) with information about opponents of National Socialism at home and abroad.

66. Here Traudl Junge is obviously anticipating an event in the spring of 1945. On 6 April Soviet troops entered Vienna, and by 13 April the city was in the hands of the Red Army. The following text, however, returns to the spring of 1944.

67. The SS 'mist department' had over 270 smoke mortars, each of which could hold about 200 litres of mist-generating acid. If an enemy attack threatened, the Berchtesgadener Land could be covered with artificial mist within thirty minutes.

68. Eduard Dietl, *b* Bad Aibling 21 July 1890, *d* Semmering, Austria 23 June 1944 (in a plane crash); was not, as Traudl Junge says, a field marshal, but a colonel general (from 1 June 1942), and was finally commanding officer of the 20th Mountain Army (the Lapland Army). On his last visit to Hitler on the Obersalzberg on 22 June 1944, a day before his death, it was agreed that he would negotiate with the leading Finnish politicians and military men in Helsinki because

Finland looked like breaking away from the confederacy of states allied to Germany, and that Joachim von Ribbentrop, the Foreign Minister, would take part in these negotiations. From 1 October 1909 a professional soldier, fights in the First World War (as captain); 1918 joins the Freikorps Epp; 1920 joins the German Workers' party; 1 February 1930 major; 1 February 1933 lieutenant colonel; 1 January 1935 colonel and on 15 October 1935 commander of Mountain Regiment 99; 1 April 1938 major general; 1 September 1939 commander of 3rd Mountain Army division in Graz; 1 April 1940 lieutenant general; 19 July 1940 general of infantry, position later renamed general of Mountain Army, leader of Mountain Corps Norway; 15 January 1942 commander of the 20th Mountain Army (Lapland Army); 1 June 1942 colonel general; 1 July 1944 is given a state funeral attended by Hitler at Schloss Klesheim near Salzburg, buried in Munich North Cemetery on 2 July 1944. Holder of the 72nd award of swords to the Knight's Cross of the Iron Cross with oakleaves.

69. Traudl Junge is confusing Colonel General Dietl's visit with that of General Hans-Valentin Hube of the Panzer troops on 20 June 1944 (for Hube, see also under note 70). The award to General Hube of the brilliants to the Knight's Cross of the Iron Cross with oakleaves and swords was the fourth level of award of the Knight's Cross, and was made 27 times in all. The order of the Iron Cross was revived on 1 September 1939 and comprised the Iron Cross first and second class, the Knight's Cross of the Iron Cross (7,318 awards) as well as the Grand Cross of the Iron Cross (1 award). Further variations were as follows: instituted on 3 June 1940, the Knight's Cross of the Iron Cross with oakleaves (882 awards); on 28 September 1941, the Knight's Cross of the Iron Cross with oakleaves and swords (159 awards) and the Knight's Cross of the Iron Cross with oakleaves, swords and brilliants (27 awards); and on 29 December 1944, the Knight's Cross of the Iron Cross with golden oakleaves, swords and brilliants (1 award). The original order goes back to the Iron Cross instituted by King Friedrich Wilhelm III of Prussia on 10 March 1813.

70. The air accident in which Colonel General Hans-Valentin Hube was killed and Liaison Officer Hewel badly injured near Salzburg was not, as Traudl Junge writes, a few weeks later but a few weeks earlier, on 21 April 1944. Panzer General Hube was summoned to Hitler's 55th birthday celebrations on the Obersalzburg on 20 April 1944 to receive the (13th) award of brilliants to the Knight's Cross of the Iron Cross

with oakleaves and swords. At the same time Hube was promoted to colonel general. Hans-Valentin Hube, *b* Naumburg, Silesia 29 October 1890, *d* near Salzburg 21 April 1944 (in a plane crash); 1909 begins his military career, fights in the First World War, has his left arm amputated in 1914; 1918 captain; 1931 major; 1934 lieutenant colonel; 1 August 1936 colonel, later commander of Döbertiz infantry school and commander of Infantry Regiment 3; 1940 commander of the 16th Infantry division which became the 16th Armoured division, major general; 1942 general of Panzer troops; 1943 supreme commander of the 1st Panzer army; 20 April 1944 promoted to colonel general; 21 April 1944 dies in an air crash, state funeral in the presence of Hitler at the Invaliden cemetery in Berlin.

71. Hermann Fegelein, *b* Ansbach 30 October 1906, *d* Berlin 28 April 1945 (executed); 1925 takes school-leaving examinations, 2 years of service as temporary volunteer with the 17th (Bavarian) Cavalry regiment; 1927–1929 in the Munich police as an officer cadet; 1931 joins the NSDAP; 1933 joins the SS; 1935 founds the SS Principal Riding School in Munich; 1936 SS Sturmbannführer, one of the most successful show-jumpers of his time, on the outbreak of war becomes SS Obersturmbannführer in the Waffen SS, as commander of the SS Cavalry Brigade and SS Standartenführer is successful in 1941–1942 on the central section of the Eastern Front; 2 March 1942 awarded the Knight's Cross of the Iron Cross; 1 May 1942 inspector of riding and driving at SS head office, then promoted to SS Oberführer, returns to the Eastern Front; 22 December 1943 is the 157th soldier of the German Wehrmacht to be awarded oakleaves to the Knight's Cross of the Iron Cross for his achievements as commander of the Fegelein fighting group; until the end of 1943 commander of the 8th Cavalry division 'Florian Geyer'; on 30 July 1944 receives the 83rd award of swords to the Knight's Cross of the Iron Cross with oakleaves; from 1 January 1944 liaison officer of the Waffen SS to Hitler; 3 June 1944 marries Gretl Braun, sister of Eva Braun; 21 June 1944 promoted to SS Gruppenführer and lieutenant general of the Waffen SS; deserts from the bunker of the Reich Chancellery on 27 April 1945, is found in civilian clothing in Berlin and arrested, is interrogated by criminal police chief Peter Högl, condemned to death by a drumhead court martial and immediately shot in the garden of the Foreign Office by an execution squad of the Waffen SS.

72. Benno von Arent, *b* Görlitz, Saxony, 19 June 1898, *d* Bonn 14 October

1956; profession: interior designer and stage designer; 1916–1918
military service, then member of a Freikorps in the East; 1931 joins
the NSDAP, founder of the National Socialist League of Stage Artists,
member of the National Socialist Reich Chamber of Drama; 1945
interned by the Russian Army; 1953 released from Russian captivity.

73. Lieutenant Colonel Heinz Waizenegger was an adjutant to Field
Marshal Wilhelm Keitel.

74. OT – Organisation Todt, see Note 37.

75. This was Major Ernst John von Freyend, one of Wilhelm Keitel's
adjutants.

76. Claus Count Schenk von Stauffenberg, *b* Jettingen 15 November
1907, *d* Berlin 20 July 1944 (executed); professional officer with the
Reichswehr; 1927 lieutenant; 1934 captain; 1940 major on the Army
General Staff; 1943 badly wounded; 1 July 1944 chief of staff to the
commander of the reserve army. Stauffenberg planned the assassination attempt of 20 July 1944 on Hitler with Field Marshal Witz-
leben and Generals Olbricht, Beck and Wagner.

77. OKW = Oberkommando der Wehrmacht, Wehrmacht High
Command.

78. This was Major Otto Ernst Remer, loyal to Hitler and – Traudl
Junge's memory was inaccurate here – head of the guard battalion.
Hitler had told him by phone that his superior officer, Lieutenant
General Paul von Hase, commandant of Berlin, belonged to a 'small
clique of traitors' and was to be arrested at once. Meanwhile he,
Remer, was to take over command of all the Wehrmacht troops
in Berlin and follow the orders of Goebbels. Otto Ernst Remer, *b*
Neubrandenburg 18 August 1912, *d* Marbella, Spain, 4 October 1997.
Traudl Junge is incorrect in saying that as commander of the Führer's
escort brigade Remer received the Knight's Cross from Hitler in
Berlin next day. Indeed, this would have contravened the regulations
governing the order, since it would not have been won in action
against the enemy, but only in the course of restoring internal security in Berlin. Remer had already received the Knight's Cross of the
Iron Cross as a major on 18 May 1943, and the 325th award of oakleaves
to the Knight's Cross of the Iron Cross on 12 November of the same
year. He was promoted to colonel retrospectively with effect from 1
July 1944, skipping the rank of lieutenant colonel, and was promoted
to major general on 31 January 1945.

79. As Traudl Junge says today, there was no separate tea-house at the

Wolf's Lair such as there was at the Berghof. Here she means an annexe to the mess.

80. Erwin Giesing, *b* Oberhausen, Rhineland 7 December 1907, *d* Krefeld 22 May 1977; studies medicine in Marburg, Düsseldorf and Cologne; 1936 qualifies as specialist in ear, nose and throat medicine; 1932 joins the NSDAP; until 1929 a specialist at the Virchow Hospital in Berlin. Summoned to the Führer headquarters on 20 July 1944 to treat Hitler's ear injury, dismissed in September over disputes with Theodor Morell; 1945 interned by the American Army; 1947 released.

81. Erich von Manstein, *b* Berlin 24 November 1887, *d* Irschenhausen, Upper Bavaria after 10 June 1973, real name Fritz-Erich von Lewinski; 1896 adopted by Georg von Manstein, entered the Plön cadet corps; 1907 promoted to second lieutenant; 1914–1918 first lieutenant and captain in the First World War; 1921–1927 company commander in Angermünde; 1923–1927 trains as general staff officer; 1927 major; 1933 colonel; 1934 chief of staff of Wehrkreis Command III in Berlin; 1936 adjutant to chief of general staff Ludwig Beck; 1939 chief of general staff to supreme command in the East; 1940 infantry general and chief of the XXXVIII Army Corps; 1941 commander of the 11th Army; 1942 promoted to colonel general; 31 March 1944 Manstein falls out of favour with Hitler and is sacked from his command; 1945 interned by the British Army; 1946 found not guilty at the Nuremberg trials; 1949 condemned to eighteen years' imprisonment for war crimes by the British military tribunal in Hamburg, released early in 1953; 1953 to 1960 official adviser to the Federal government on the reconstruction of the army. Holder of the 59th award of swords to the Knight's Cross of the Iron Cross with oakleaves.

82. Hans Junge died on 13 August 1944 as an SS-Obersturmführer in a low-flying aircraft attack in Dreux, Normandy. (For Junge, see also note 10.)

83. Carl von Eicken, *b* Mühlheim, in the Ruhr 31 December 1873, *d* Heilbronn 1960; 1922 professor of ear, nose and throat medicine at the Charité hospital in Berlin; 1926 medical director of the ear, nose and throat hospital at the Charité, retired 1950.

84. Constanze Manziarly, *b* Innsbruck 14 April 1920, *d* Berlin 2 May 1945; trains as a dietician; 13 September 1943 takes up post as dietician cook at the Zabel sanatorium in Bischofswiesen; September 1944 became dietician cook to Adolf Hitler, probably commits suicide by taking prussic acid.

85. Wilhelm Burgdorf, *b* Fürstenwalde 15 February 1895, *d* Berlin 2 May 1945 (missing); 1914 ensign; 1915 lieutenant; 1930 captain; 1938 lieutenant colonel; 1940 major; 1942 major general and head of the 2nd department of the army personnel office; 1942 deputy chief of the same department; 1944 infantry general and head of the army personnel office and chief adjutant of the Wehrmacht; April 1945 present in the Führer bunker. Holder of the Knight's Cross of the Iron Cross.

86. Arthur and Freda Kannenberg worked from 1933 to 1945 as household managers of the Reich Chancellery. Arthur Kannenberg, *b* Berlin, Charlottenburg 23 February 1896, *d* Düsseldorf 26 January 1963; trained as a chef, waiter and bookkeeper; 1924 took over his father's business; 1930 went bankrupt, then business manager of Pfuhls Wein- und Bierstuben, hostelries patronized by Göring and Goebbels among others; 1931 catering manager in the 'Brown House' in Munich. May 1945 to July 1946 interned; 1957 landlord of the Schneider-Wibble-Stuben in Düsseldorf.

87. Ludwig Stumpfegger, *b* Munich 11 July 1910, *d* Berlin 2 May 1945 (suicide); 1930 begins studying medicine; 1933 joins the SS; 1935 joins the NSDAP; 1937 takes his doctoral degree; 1938–1944 makes his career in the SS and in medicine; 1944 appointed attendant doctor to Hitler at Führer headquarters in the Wolf's Lair at Himmler's suggestion; until 1 May 1945 in the Reich Chancellery in Berlin.

88. The wedding between Hermann Fegelein and Gretl Braun had in fact taken place only a few months earlier, on 3 June 1944.

89. Karl Rudolf Gerd von Rundstedt, *b* Aschersleben 12 December 1875, *d* Schloss Oppershausen near Celle 24 February 1954; professional soldier; 1893 officer with the Prussian infantry; 1914–1918 on the general staff; 1928 commander of the 2nd Cavalry Division; 1932–1938 commander of the Group Command I Berlin; 1939 colonel general, head of Army Group South on the march into Poland; 1940 Field Marshal; 1942–1945 supreme commander in the west. Holder of the 133rd award of swords to the Knight's Cross of the Iron Cross with oakleaves.

90. Karl Dönitz, *b* Grünau, Berlin 16 September 1891, *d* Aumühle near Hamburg 24 December 1980; 1910 joined the navy; 1913 naval lieutenant and professional officer; 1916 U-boat fleet; 1934 commander of the cruiser *Emden*; 1935 frigate captain; 1936 commander of the U-boat fleet; 1940 vice-admiral; 1942 admiral; 1943 grand admiral and commander of the navy; 1944 awarded the Golden Party emblem; 30

April 1945 appointed President of the Reich and supreme commander of the Wehrmacht by Hitler; 23 May 1945 arrested by the British Army, condemned to 10 years' imprisonment as a war criminal at Nuremberg, released from imprisonment in Berlin-Spandau in 1956. Holder of the 223rd award of oakleaves to the Knight's Cross of the Iron Cross.

91. In fact Johanna Wolf had worked for Adolf Hitler from 1929 to 1945, and thus for about 16 years.

92. Else Krüger, married name James, *b* Hamburg-Altona 9 February 1915; 1942 secretary to Martin Bormann; 1 May 1945 leaves the Führer bunker and flees to the West, interned by the British Army, moves to England.

93. The passage omitted here is one that occurs twice in the original manuscript, in almost identical wording, beginning '22 April. Feverish restlessness in the bunker.' However, the end of the passage does vary, and in the one that has been omitted runs: '[...] It sounds impersonal and commanding. It goes round and round in my head like a millwheel. The Führer, who has never before hinted at any lack of confidence, is giving up, giving up everything entirely!'

94. Hans Krebs, *b* Helmstedt 4 March 1898, *d* Berlin 1 May 1945 (suicide by shooting himself); 1914 volunteered for the army; 1915 lieutenant; 1925 first lieutenant; 1933–1944 career officer reaching the rank of head of general staff of various Army Groups, finally infantry general; 1 April 1945 head of army general staff in the Führer bunker. Holder of the 749th award of oakleaves to the Knight's Cross of the Iron Cross.

95. Hans-Erich Voss, *b* Angermünde 30 October 1897; 1915 naval cadet; 1917–1942 naval career officer from naval lieutenant to captain; 1943 rear-admiral and permanent representative of naval command at Führer headquarters; 1944 vice-admiral; 2 May 1945 arrested by the Red Army; 1955 released from internment.

96. Werner Naumann, *b* Guhrau 1 June 1909, *d* 25 October 1982; 1928 joins the NSDAP; 1933 SA brigade leader; 1937 head of the Reich propaganda department in Breslau; 1938 head of ministerial department in Berlin; 1944 state secretary in the Propaganda Ministry; April 1945 with Goebbels and Hitler in the Führer bunker, flees to the West; January 1953 arrested by the British occupying power; July 1953 released.

97. Günther Schwägermann, *b* Uelzen 24 July 1915; studies business;

1937 joins the Leibstandarte SS Adolf Hitler; 1938 attends SS Junker college; 1939 joins central Berlin police force, then adjutant to Joseph Goebbels; 1 May 1945 flees from the Führer bunker; 1947 released from American imprisonment.

98. Artur Axmann, *b* Hagen, Westphalia, 18 February 1913, *d* Berlin 24 October 1996; studies law; 1928 founds the first Hitler Youth group in Westphalia; 1933 head of the social department of the Reich youth leadership; 1 August 1940 Reich youth leader of the NSDAP; 1941 at the Eastern front; 15 December 1945 imprisoned by the American army; 1949 released from American POW camp.

99. Heinrich Müller, *b* Munich 28 April 1900, *d* 29 May 1945 (missing); aircraft mechanic; 1919 joins the Bavarian police; 1933 criminal police inspector; 1937 criminal police superintendent and SS Obersturmbannführer; 1939 joins the NSDAP, head of Department IV (the Gestapo) at the Reich Security head office in Berlin; 1941 SS Gruppenführer; 29 April 1945 last seen in the Führer bunker.

100. Walther Wenck, *b* Wittenberg 18 September 1900, *d* 1 May 1982 (in a car accident); professional soldier; 1942 teacher at the War Academy, chief of general staff of the LVII Armoured Division; November 1942 of the 3rd Romanian Army; 1943 major general, chief of general staff of the 1st Tank Army; 1944 lieutenant general, chief of operations department at the OKH; September 1944–February 1945 chief of leadership group at High Command; April 1945 general of Panzer troops and commander of the 12th Army which was intended to relieve Berlin, and for which Hitler was still hoping until the last. Holder of the Knight's Cross of the Iron Cross.

101. Felix Martin Steiner, *b* Ebenrode 23 May 1896, *d* Munich 12 May 1966; 1914 begins a military career; 1914–1918 fights in the First World War, first lieutenant and company commander; 1919 enters the East Prussian volunteer corps; 1922 studies at the Kireigskademie; 1927 captain in Königsberg and regimental adjutant; 1932 company commander; 1933 leaves the Reichswehr and becomes head of training of the Landespolizei Inspektion West, joins the NSDAP; 1935 joins the newly created SS combat troops as SS Sturmbannführer; 1936 commander of the SS Standarte (Regiment) Deutschland; 1940 promoted to SS brigade leader, major general in the Waffen SS and commander of the SS Panzer Grenadier division Viking; 1942 SS Gruppenführer and lieutenant general of the Waffen SS; 1943 commanding general of the 3rd SS Panzerkorps; 1944 SS

Obergruppenführer and general in the Waffen SS; October 1944 to January 1945 recuperates from a severe attack of jaundice; February 1945 commander of the 11th Panzer Army (the 'Steiner' army); 3 May 1945 taken prisoner by the Americans; 1948 released. Holder of the 86th award of the Knight's Cross of the Iron Cross with oakleaves.

102. Wilhelm Mohnke, *b* Lübeck 15 March 1911, *d* Hamburg 6 August 2001; salesman and storekeeper; 1931 joined the SS; 1933 SS Sonderkommando in Berlin, a member of the Leibstandarte SS Adolf Hitler; 1933 SS Sturmführer; 1943 SS Obersturmbannführer; January 1945 SS Brigadeführer; February 1945 Führerreserve of the Waffen SS in Berlin; 23 March 1945 entrusted by Hitler, and as second in line to him directly, with the defence of the 'citadel' (the Reich Chancellery and its surroundings); 2 May 1945 taken prisoner by the Russians; 1955 released from imprisonment. Holder of the Knight's Cross of the Iron Cross.

103. On 21 April 1945 Adolf Hitler ordered a counter-attack against the advancing Soviet Army in the north of Berlin. SS Obergruppenführer and Waffen SS General Felix Steiner, commander of the 'Steiner' army, was to carry out the attack.

104. Hanna Reitsch, *b* Hirschberg 29 March 1912, *d* Frankfurt 28 August 1979; studies medicine but does not qualify, trains as a glider pilot; 1932 breaks the women's world record for high-altitude aviation; 1937 flight captain; 1939 test pilot; 1942 awarded the Iron Cross II Class; 26 April 1945 flies to Berlin with Greim; 29 April 1945 flies from Berlin to Grand Admiral Dönitz and then on to Kitzbühel; imprisoned by the Americans until 1946.

105. Robert Ritter von Greim, *b* Bayreuth 22 June 1892, *d* Salzburg 24 May 1945 (suicide); 1913 second lieutenant; 1916 pilot and first lieutenant; 1918 squadron leader and captain; 1920–1922 studies law; 1924–1927 is in China; 1928–1934 runs the training school for airmen in Würzburg; 1934 major in the Reichswehr; 1938 major general; 1940 lieutenant general and commanding general of the V Flying Corps; 1943–25 April 1945 colonel general and commander of the 6th Air Fleet; 26 April 1945 appointed by Hitler field marshal and commander of the Luftwaffe in succession to Göring; May 1945 captured by the American army. Holder of the orders *Pour le Mérite* and the 92nd award of swords to the Knight's Cross of the Iron Cross with oakleaves.

106. Werner Haase, *b* Köthen, Anhalt 2 August 1900, *d* Moscow 1945; 1924 qualifies as a doctor, specialist surgical training; 1927 ship's doctor; 1934 joins the SS; 1935 attendant doctor on the Führer's staff; 1935 SS Sturmführer; 1943 SS Obersturmbannführer, medical director of the Charité hospital in Berlin; April 1945 runs the medical ward in the Reich Chancellery bunker; 3 May 1945 taken prisoner by the Red Army in the Führer bunker.

107. Benito Mussolini was shot by Italian resistance fighters, together with his mistress Clara Petacci, on 28 April 1945 in Giulino di Mezzegra near Dongo, in the province of Como. Their bodies were hung from scaffolding in the Piazza Loreto in Milan.

108. Adolf Hitler assumed that as Himmler's liaison officer, Hermann Fegelein had taken part in Himmler's negotiations with the Swedish diplomat and head of the Swedish Red Cross, Count Folke Bernadotte, or at least had knowledge of them.

109. Heinrich Himmler had allegedly met Count Folke Bernadotte four times to negotiate with him for surrender in the West.

110. Hitler's Luftwaffe adjutant Colonel von Below was to take one copy of the testament to Wilhelm Keitel, Heinz Lorenz was taking the second to the 'Brown House' in Munich, and Wilhelm Zander was taking the third to Karl Dönitz.

111. Traudl Junge thinks she heard the shot. Experts have tried to reconstruct the course of Hitler's suicide and have come to the following conclusion: '[. . .] At this point Frau Junge was far away, on the stairs from the lower to the upper part of the bunker. What she thinks she heard [. . .] was probably an illusion caused by the running diesel generator and the constant heavy firing on the Reich Chancellery.'

112. Infantry General Hans Krebs, acting on behalf of Joseph Goebbels, negotiated surrender to the Russian general Vassily I. Chuikov on the night of 30 April 1945. For Krebs, see also note 94.

113. Franz Schädle had been head of the escort commando of well over 100 men since 20 December 1944.

114. As she said in conversation with Melissa Müller, Traudl Junge's poison capsule was not taken from her until there was a cell inspection at Lichtenberg prison for women and young people.

CONFRONTING GUILT —
A CHRONOLOGICAL STUDY
WRITTEN IN 2001

by Melissa Müller

We have seen them published again and again since the 1950s —
the 'I was there' accounts of former functionaries of the Third
Reich, justifications by friends of Hitler, whitewash operations
carried out by his intellectual supporters. More or less frank
confessions which critics mock as trashy memoirs.

'Old Junge speaking.' Traudl Junge (whose surname means
'young') is on the phone. She is calling to tell me — yet again —
about her reservations. Why *another* book on National Socialism?
Why make a spectacle of the way she has come to terms with her
own past? And why now?

She is used to providing information about her impressions of
Adolf Hitler and Eva Braun. Ever since the 1950s she has been
giving interviews to historians and journalists. Until now,
however, she has avoided making her own life public. The prob-
able reason is that she has never before definitively faced and
understood the key experience of her life: those two and a half
years closely involved with Adolf Hitler.

Traudl Junge served a criminal regime, but she took no part
in the murders committed by the National Socialists. That does
not excuse her, but it should be borne in mind if we want to
understand what happened. Although she was so close to those
criminal actions, she does not fit the black-and-white ideological
pattern of those who see the situation as polarized between Nazi
villains and anti-Fascist heroes.

She has never, says Traudl Junge, felt sorry for herself, even in the chaotic days and hours of the collapse of the Third Reich. 'I should think not too', the reader may reflect. However, her lack of self-pity distinguishes her not only from many of her closest colleagues of that time but also from the great majority of her contemporaries, who saw themselves in retrospect as 'victims'. After 1945, such turns of phrase as 'Those were difficult times ...', or 'There was a war on ...' made it easier for many to repress, or at least play down in their minds, the truth about the persecution of the Jews, the death camps and many other Nazi atrocities. They had been through 'total war' and experienced its material and ideological destruction as 'total ruin', taking heart from the fiction of a new beginning at 'zero hour'. They spoke of 'eradicating the horrors' and 'breaking the spell'. They pinned their hopes on a new era beginning 'after the war', persecutors and persecuted alike, passive hangers-on and the complicit, among whom Traudl Junge may be classed.

After the war she never felt that she was innocent. However, painfully present in her mind as her shame and grief over the crimes of the Nazis are, until now it has been hard for her to define her share in the responsibility beyond a diffuse, abstract self-accusation. Her personal failure, she has finally realized, lay in accepting Albert Bormann's help. She desperately wanted to go to Berlin in 1941, she was furious about the obstacles put in her way by her Munich employer, she was defiant and obstinate. To get where she wanted to be – which was Berlin, not the Reich Chancellery, let alone Adolf Hitler – she silenced the warning voice in her that told her: Don't get involved with the Party – no good can come of it. When she finally and after a series of chance events found herself in Hitler's presence, she says, it was too late to resist. Today she knows that she let herself be dazzled by him – not by his ideological and political intentions, in which she never took any particular interest, but by Hitler's personality. She does not play down the fact that she provided him with female company while he and his accomplices were implementing the 'final solution'. She admits that she probably knew nothing of the full extent of the persecution of Jews simply because she didn't want to know. All the same, in her attempts at a later date to understand those murderous events, even to link them with herself, her immediate impressions of the time she spent with Hitler keep coming to the fore and, as we can gather from her manuscript, those impressions were over-whelmingly positive. That should not seem surprising, for here, after all, lies the source of the battle with herself that Traudl Junge still has not fought to the end: how to accept that this man made her feel he cared about her welfare while his unbounded instinct for destruction was simultaneously bringing suffering to millions of people.

'*Our total collapse, the refugees, the suffering — of course I held Hitler responsible for that. His testament, his suicide — that was when I began to hate him. At the same time I felt great pity, even for him. But when your love for someone, say your partner in marriage, turns to hate, you usually try to preserve the memories of the happy times you first knew. I suppose my relationship with Hitler was something like that . . . He didn't exert any erotic influence over me, but of course I wanted him to like me. He was a kindly paternal figure, he gave me a feeling of security, solicitude for me, safety. I felt protected there in the Führer headquarters in the middle of that forest, in that community, with that "father figure". I can still look back to that time with warm emotions. I never again felt that I belonged anywhere in just the same way.*'

In the turbulent months after Hitler's suicide and the end of the war, Traudl feels personally disappointed in 'her Führer'. In a letter to her mother and sister as late as January 1945 she says, parroting Hitler: '[. . .] I am well, and we must either win the victory or fall, there's no alternative.' And then, cravenly, he had given up. Her dominant feelings in the summer and autumn of 1945, it is true, are life-threatening in their nature: she is afraid of being at the mercy of the Russian occupying forces, and there are existential needs such as hunger. But although many of her colleagues chose suicide as a way out in the days around 1 May 1945, she never sees it as a solution for herself. She too treasures the poison capsule given to her by Hitler personally as a kind of goodbye present, but she wants to live.

'I wasn't one of those idealists who couldn't imagine how anything could go on without the Führer, or couldn't see it going on at all; people like Magda Goebbels, who obviously drew the logical conclusions from her own view of the world. To me, suicide was only ever a very vague safety net in case I was badly mistreated — tortured or raped. It was reassuring to have the poison with me.'

The surviving inmates of the bunkers in the catacombs under the Reich Chancellery began moving out on the night of 1 May 1945. Ten groups of about twenty people each set off to get away from the Russians. As she describes it in detail in her manuscript, Traudl Junge was among the first group, led by SS Brigadeführer Mohnke. On the second evening she became separated from her female companions – her secretarial colleague Gerda Christian, Martin Bormann's secretary Else Krüger, and Constanze Manziarly. Apparently Hitler's dietician cook looked the ideal image of Russian femininity, well-built and plump-cheeked, and she was, stupidly, wearing a Wehrmacht jacket. She said she was going to find some civilian clothing and asked Traudl Junge to wait for her, while the two other women waited by a water collection point and tried to organize a place to sleep next night. When Traudl Junge next saw Fräulein Manziarly, a little later, two Russian soldiers were taking her towards a U-Bahn tunnel. Constanze Manziarly just had time to call back to Traudl Junge, 'They want to see my papers', before she disappeared with the Russians. No one saw her again after that.

Traudl Junge lost sight of the other two women too, and went on alone. She wanted to go north, away from the Russians and into the English zone, where Hitler's designated successor Grand Admiral Dönitz and his men were thought to be. She had no money for her journey, no papers and no luggage, and was dressed only in trousers and a check blouse. Thousands and thousands of refugees were on the roads, some fleeing from the bombed city, others coming from the country areas already occupied by the Russians and seeking shelter in the city. Traudl Junge tried to strike up acquaintanceships; she did not know the region, had never before heard the names of the villages through which she passed, and forgot them again at once. For a while she walked beside a former concentration camp inmate. He was still wearing his striped camp uniform.

'At that moment this man and I were companions brought together by fate; we were both afraid of the Russians, and we went part of the way together. We didn't say anything about our immediate past. I didn't yet have any idea what conditions in the concentration camps had really been like. I could still hear Himmler's voice describing them as well-organized labour camps. From today's viewpoint it's hardly imaginable, but at the time I asked the man no questions. And what really matters is that I asked myself no questions either.'

She walks through the countryside for days on end. She hears nothing about the surrender of Germany and the official end of the war. The discrepancy between the exuberance of spring, with its pretty flowering meadows and blossoming trees, and all the human misery, the ruined buildings, the unmilked cows bellowing in pain, makes a deep impression on her. By night she seeks shelter with strangers, sleeps in barns, sometimes even in a bed, friendly people give her boiled potatoes, someone even makes her a present of an old coat. It is a nuisance to carry in the mild weather, but a welcome blanket by night. She meets German soldiers who deserted in the chaos of the closing stages of the war and are trying to make their way home in scruffy civilian clothing. At one farm she meets Erich Kempka, Hitler's personal chauffeur, who had been a witness at her wedding – he is wearing shabby clothes, and he too is on the run. He tells her that his aim is to swim the river Elbe and then give himself up to the Americans. He must finally have managed to reach southern

Germany, for in the middle of June he falls into American hands in Berchtesgaden.

The refugees form small groups, creating a sense of security for themselves. Traudl Junge soon makes friends with Katja, married to an SS officer and herself a 'Party comrade', who left Berlin in panic when the Russians marched in. Traudl Junge tells her that she herself was Hitler's secretary, but both women are more concerned with day-to-day events. What shall we eat this evening, where shall we sleep? Together, they try to cross the 'green frontier' and reach the British zone, and when that attempt fails they go on along the Elbe to Wittenberge, about halfway to Hamburg, looking for a way to get across the river. The American zone begins on the opposite bank. Traudl Junge is suffering from scabies; she hasn't seen a bar of soap, let alone used one, since the day she broke out of the bunker. The doctor she visits prescribes an ointment, baths, and a daily change of underwear. For this well-meant advice he charges five marks, which she has to owe him.

There are no ferries across the Elbe, and Traudl and Katja don't trust themselves to swim to the opposite bank. The river is too wide and too cold. Instead, they decide to go back to Berlin. Traudl Junge means to hide in her new friend's apartment until trains to Munich are running again. She is back in Berlin after about a month, having walked more than three hundred kilometres, and now goes under the name of Gerda Alt. She adopted this cover name on the road when she had a permit allowing her to draw food rations made out in one village – in the naive hope that anyone looking for her who may hear the name Gerda Alt ('old') will connect it with Traudl Junge.

She spends a week in Berlin. Katja has to go out in the daytime to clear rubble; she herself hardly leaves the building. There are small moments of pleasure: the first chance in many weeks to wash her hair, a packet of real coffee that Katja finds in the kitchen cupboard. The first glimmer of confidence: something like normality seems to be returning to her life. On 9 June, the day when the commander of the Soviet occupying forces, Marshal

Gyorgy Zhukov, sets up the Soviet Military Administration in Germany, two civilians, a young man and a girl, knock at the door of Katja's apartment and, speaking with an obvious Russian accent, say they are journalists.

'I realized at once that I was about to be arrested. To this day I don't know who informed on me. I didn't take my pass in my false name with me, because people said that anyone caught out lying would be condemned to a Russian hell. And it was normal enough to have no papers in those days. I left a message for Katja with the caretaker of the building and went with them. Of course I was dreadfully frightened, but I didn't feel it was wrongful arrest. The terrifying part was the unpredictability of the Russians.'

Traudl Junge's odyssey through various temporary prisons now begins. The first place where she is imprisoned is a Russian commandant's headquarters in Nussbaumallee, where she is held for a night. She is taken from there to Lichtenberg, formerly a prison for women and young people, where she is held for fourteen weeks in a cell meant for solitary confinement – at first really alone in it, later with seven other women. Only then does anyone show an interest in her and take her off for her first interrogation. They question her, in particular, about the circumstances of Hitler's death. She constantly keeps hearing tales of the personal tragedies suffered by the Russian soldiers on duty as warders: how their children were shot by German soldiers, their women dragged away, whole villages razed to the ground. For the first time, and with growing horror, Traudl Junge realizes that the massacres in East Prussia were the aftermath of an equally brutal prelude in Russia – and that she had let herself be deceived by Nazi propaganda.

One night she is fetched without warning and moved to the basement floor of the Rudolf Virchow Institute, where 'special cases' presumed to be spies are held in a large communal cell. They sleep on the floor. Someone takes Traudl Junge's wedding ring, her last remaining possession.

She has already lost the poison capsule in Lichtenberg. The woman commissar on duty in the Nussbaumallee cells had ordered a strip search, but Traudl Junge took the poison capsule of thin glass out of its protective brass case, slipped it into a handkerchief, and put it under her tongue while blowing her nose. Only then did she undress. After the search she managed to hide the capsule, now without the brass case, in her jacket pocket and take it safely with her to Lichtenberg prison.

'The woman who shared my cell there knew about the capsule. I had told her that I still had the poison for use in an emergency, and it kept my fear within bounds. I think she informed on me. Anyway, the capsule was taken away from me during a cell inspection. I felt desperate. Every night I could hear the screams of people being tortured, and the roll-call in the yard when transports set off for Russia. Suddenly I felt completely helpless, now that the power to make that final decision had been taken from me.'

Traudl Junge is not taken to Russia. Is she kept in Berlin as an important witness, or do the occupying force think her too harmless to be seriously punished? It is impossible to clear up these questions with any certainty after the event. But Fate is kind to her, particularly when it sends her an Armenian called Arkady. This man, who wears civilian clothing, works as an interpreter for the Russian occupiers. One night in October 1945 he fetches her from the basement of the Rudolf Virchow Institute and takes her to another basement cell at the Russian command post in Marienstrasse. On the way he says scarcely a word, but she notices his courteous manners and refined speech. Sinister as the man seems to her at first, in the end she has much to thank him for. Over the next few weeks he is her guardian angel, getting her clothes, a room, papers, and after that even work. The one condition is that she must stay in the Russian zone. One day, when he gives her a tomato, its poetic name of 'Paradise apple' strikes her suddenly as being literally true.

'Arkady interrogated me only once at the command post, while a uniformed

officer sat in the other corner of the room. I just had to say what had happened in the last days in the Führer bunker. After that I had to sign an agreement stating that I was prepared to give the Red Army the names of survivors from those who had been at Führer headquarters.'

She spends about a week in part of the Marienstrasse command-post basement, now converted to a cell, and then Arkady decides, 'We must have you out of here' – and commandeers a small room in a building which he chooses at random. From now on she lives here. Her landlady – at first unwilling, but later glad of Traudl's company – is Fräulein Koch, a piano teacher. When Arkady, in the course of 'occupying' the room, tries the bed to see if it is comfortable Traudl Junge has forebodings of worse to come. But Arkady does not molest her either then or later. Instead, he ensures that over the next few weeks she is listed as an assistant at the command post, because then he can get her fed at the canteen there. On 5 October she is issued with a 'work-book replacement card', stating that she is employed for ten to twelve hours a day as a worker at the command post. On 4 December 1945 she describes the way she is really spending her time in a long letter to her mother in Bavaria, for after almost a year of uncertainty they are finally in touch again. She does not go into detail about her flight from Berlin and her prison experiences in either this or subsequent letters, nor does she mention Arkady – she knows, after all, that mail is still censored, only this time by the occupying power.

'[. . .] You'll want to know how I'm living – well, I'm alive! I can't say much about that, but I have enough to eat and I'm getting quite fat. Most of the time I help with the housework, and I'm also knitting gloves and sweaters, and I make dolls and stuffed toy animals, and use my many amateurish talents. If I ever come home maybe I can find a job as attendant in a lavatory or cloakroom. My memories mostly take me back to the Munich years and don't cling to the recent past. Mankind's most precious gift is being able to forget.

I'm living with an elderly spinster, what you might call an old maid.

She's very kind and at least equally silly. Terribly prejudiced, but all the same she's taken me to her heart because I'm as good as quite a number of workmen to her, I can nail windows and doors in place, I chop wood, I make myself useful. [...] My life is hard but I've felt new-born now that I know you are waiting for me at home, however long it may take to get there. [...]'

She tries to present her situation in a humorous light, but all the same her nerves give way in the course of that November: she complains that she'd rather be shut up in the basement cell again than sit around here doing nothing, just waiting until they want her to denounce someone. She feels that she is at Arkady's mercy, and is still afraid of him. But once more he surprises her. 'You need work,' he says next. He has a photo of her taken and a pass made out in her name. On 10 December 1945 he arranges for her to begin working as an administrative assistant, later at the reception desk of the Charité hospital and finally at its cash desk.

'This man systematically rescued me, and he obviously had no personal advantage in mind. He said the most peculiar things, he talked about Providence. And when I asked why he was doing all this for me he just said, "I'm not your enemy. Perhaps you can help me too some day."'

For the first time since the fall of the Third Reich she can now earn a meagre living for herself; before that, what she earned from the home-made dolls scarcely paid her rent. Now she is earning 100 Reichsmarks a month and gets food ration coupons. As Hitler's secretary she was earning 450 Reichsmarks with free board and lodging. A loaf of bread costs about forty on the black market these days, a kilo of sugar about ninety, a carton of ten packets of Chesterfield cigarettes up to 1500 Reichsmarks. Traudl Junge is a smoker, but has no black-market connections; she has no money or goods to barter for that.

Lonely as she is, all her potential for love is concentrated on her mother. Their relationship is the one fixed point in these months of outward and inward uncertainty, and she clings to it with positively childlike force. On 11 December she writes one of her many letters of this period to Breitbrunn on the Ammersee, where her mother has been living since she was bombed out of her Munich apartment.

'Myself, I've always got out of my difficulties relatively well [. . .] and now I'm working again. [. . .] At least I'm glad to have occupation, so my thoughts don't have too much time to wander. They're mostly with you anyway [. . .] I'm really scared of the Christmas holidays. I shall probably stay in bed and sleep the time away, with all its memories. [. . .] One can't even afford a candle here, and a branch of fir costs so much that it's right beyond my means. [. . .] Dear Mother, have as nice a time as you possibly can, and be glad the two of you can spend the holiday together. That's the best thing of all, not having to be among strangers. It would be all right if I could shut myself up in my little room and be really alone with myself and my memories. I'd be able to fill my time then. But as it is, the cold weather means we all have to spend our free time together in a dark kitchen which is never cleared out and can never be got really warm. Even worse off are the people who have central heating [with no fuel] and no other means of heating. [. . .]'

In the following weeks Traudl Junge's thoughts and actions revolve around making a new start in Munich. It is with mixed feelings that she tries to approach her old world, her life before she made that wrong decision. *'My brain is constantly occupied with a single thought: going home,'* she writes on 30 December. A few lines further on comes an explanation for her strong sense of family affection: *'I just long for you and Inge; I'm afraid other people might pity me or take pleasure in my misfortunes.'* She spends the last day of 1945, New Year's Eve, with friends of her late husband in Wilmersdorf, a part of the city that is occupied by the British. She has already secretly entered that forbidden zone several times, and this time she stays for almost two months, for on New Year's Day of 1946 she falls ill with a temperature of 41 degrees and a sore throat. She is admitted to the Robert Koch

Hospital on the same day with diphtheria. The fact that her absence from the Russian zone has obviously not been noticed strengthens her resolve to flee to Bavaria as soon as possible. *'Most of the time I try to sleep, to take my mind off bitter memories of the past and anxiety about the future. Or I dream of lovely times at home with you and build the most beautiful castles in the air'* (15 January 1946). She makes concrete plans for flight with her neighbour in her hospital bed, who also wants to go to Munich.

'Since yesterday I have been working at the Charité again, but my job there won't keep me from setting out to go home when the time comes,' she writes on the last day of February 1946. *'But you can eat up those cabbages before they go mouldy, and then I'll be home to enjoy the first radishes.'* And on 1 March she writes to her sister: *'You ask if I'm perfectly free and have release papers. Unfortunately no to both questions. I'd have been well away from here long ago if it was as simple as that.'*

In Breitbrunn, meanwhile, her mother is trying to get Traudl a permit to stay in Bavaria and a certificate of entitlement to live in Breitbrunn. Both documents are the prerequisite for her flight from Berlin, because it depends on them whether she can get a work permit, a ration card, and so on at home. On 2 April the document she has been longing for reaches Traudl Junge. 'Hooray! My Bavarian permit has arrived!' She has already given a month's notice to the Charité on 15 March, the day before her twenty-sixth birthday. A brief last encounter with Arkady reinforces her determination to venture on flight. She meets him in the street and waves to him from a distance, but he does not respond. Only when he comes level with her does he tell her, briefly, that a new commandant has arrived and wants to see Traudl Junge's files. Then he hurries on.

15 April 1946 is marked as the 'day of termination of employment' in her 'work-book replacement card'. Immediately afterwards she sets out on another adventurous flight. She and Erika, her acquaintance from the hospital, take the S-Bahn to the zone border, where they board a tractor. It delivers them, whether deliberately or otherwise, straight into the hands of a Russian

border guard, but the women are in luck; he merely sends them back to the Russian zone. A second attempt is more successful. In a village they meet a farmer whose land lies on the border between the Russian and British zones. They spend the night at his farmhouse, and next morning he goes out with his tractor to spread manure. Traudl and Erika hide in the trailer, jump off at the border when the helpful farmer gives the word, and run into the bushes doubling back and forth like rabbits.

'It must have been near Göttingen and Hanoverian Münden. There in the early morning I heard a nightingale for the first time in my life. People were so helpful at that time. We came to a house where they gave us a big pan full of potatoes. With salt. That was my first step out of the Russian zone. We finally caught a train – the trains were still running at very irregular times – and reached Bavaria by way of Kassel. Neither the British nor the Americans checked up on us. I went straight on from Munich to Herrsching on the Ammersee, and from there I hitchhiked to Breitbrunn. I was home again on Easter Sunday.'

★

The joy of reunion. A time of forgetting? Traudl is safe home again – her mother and her sister Inge ask hardly any questions about her past in Berlin. For one thing they themselves have suffered a good deal: there was the air raid that destroyed almost all Traudl's mother's possessions; the end of Inge's career as a dancer after she had an inflamed tendon and her return to Munich; the general difficulty of finding provisions to live on. It also seems to Traudl that they want to spare her, and so they ask no questions.

'We never discussed what they thought might have happened to me after Hitler's death, either immediately after my return or later. They didn't guess that a suicide epidemic had broken out in the Führer bunker either. But I felt safe with my mother, because I knew she would always stand by me whatever I had done. And of course after those terrible experiences

228

I badly needed to talk. She listened without ever reproaching me.'

What the family and the population in general lived on just after the war is a mystery to Traudl Junge today. But she clearly remembers that it was a very warm, happy time, with everyone pulling together. Refugees kept passing, and the family took them in. When she was evacuated to Breitbrunn Traudl's mother Hildegard had rented a small patch of ground from the parish, and she made it into a vegetable garden. *'[. . .] The thought of our little piece of land soothes me enormously. I shall husband my strength to cultivate it myself,'* writes Traudl Junge in one of her letters (4 December 1945). *'If it's possible for me to come home some time, I always hoped you'd be living in the country and not the ruins of a big city. Out in the woods and fields you forget the horrors and misery of the war and peace.'*

She still has to search her memory for details of her wartime past. A few days after her return she goes to Munich to visit old friends. She also meets one of those friends of Greek descent she knew in her youth; his partner is working as a secretary to an officer in the American military government. The Greek tells this partner that Traudl had been in the Führer bunker. Immediately afterwards he realizes what his indiscretion might mean for her, and warns her.

Sure enough, a policeman turns up in Breitbrunn while Traudl Junge is still in Munich. Her mother sends him away, telling him that her daughter is staying in the city. However, he returns to Breitbrunn a few days later, on Whit Sunday, and this time Traudl is at home and gives herself up immediately. Her mother gives her a piece of Camembert and an apple for the journey, and then the armed policeman takes her to Inning on the pillion of his motorbike. She spends a night there in the cell of the fire station, and on Whit Monday morning she is shut up in a large communal cell in Starnberg prison. After a weekend raid by the American authorities it is full of prostitutes. They are all to be medically examined next day, and Traudl Junge with them. But after lengthy argument the warders agree that she is a political prisoner, and she escapes the procedure.

The Americans keep her there in a double cell for about three weeks. Her fellow prisoner introduces herself as the niece of Grand Admiral Erich Raeder, here under suspicion of spying. The two young women pass the time while they wait by sewing bras, which are rare and desirable items of clothing at this time. A US officer of German-Jewish descent conducts a single interrogation of Traudl Junge, which lasts several hours, and then tells her to write down her memories of the last days in the Führer bunker. She fills three sheets of paper with them, and the officer is so fascinated by her account that he offers her 5000 dollars for publication rights. However, Traudl declines in alarm, fearing that the attention of the Russian occupying forces whose territory she left illegally might be drawn to her. Contrary to her expectation, the officer is discreet. Prisoners like Traudl Junge reap the benefit of the fact that the separate occupying powers are already pursuing very different ends.

'With the Americans I was never afraid for a moment of being taken away or tortured. They behaved properly, you didn't feel any hatred or hostility. I was surprised to find how uninhibited they were – politically they didn't know a thing, but they were curious and liked sensationalism. I couldn't tell them much anyway; in 1946 I had no idea what had become of people like Bormann, Göring and Goebbels. No one was interested in the fate of the adjutants, servants, chauffeurs and secretaries, that didn't come until much later. When I was finally released the American officers invited me to go sailing to Starnberg with them . . . I was a young woman, after all, and tanned by the spring sun . . . but I didn't accept. Then I stayed for a while in Breitbrunn under a kind of local house arrest.'

★

Munich 1947. Everyday life in the ruined city. Inge, who has now trained as an actress, is a member of a cabaret group run by Ralph Maria Siegel, performing under her professional name of

Ingeborg Zomann. Traudl too tries to start out again in her home city this year. The sisters share an attic room in the house of Walter Oberholzer, the sculptor for whom Traudl had modelled when she was fifteen; since then the whole family have been friends with him. He finds Traudl her first job with an electrical firm making items known as fireless cookers: zinc-plated containers which can be electrically heated and will then hold the heat, so that with their aid hot meals can be served even during power cuts. There is also a good market for 'warming rolls', items in the shape of a small rolling pin that you connect to the electricity supply for a minute; you can then carry one about with you to warm your hands. Traudl Junge finds them very useful when she gets a new job as secretary at Helge Peters-Pawlinin's studio theatre, where her sister is part of the original ensemble. It is so cold there that she cannot type without thawing out her fingers first on the warming-roll.

'It was wonderful to be living under American democracy. I hadn't realized before that I wasn't hearing music by any Polish or Russian composers, couldn't read Jewish literature ... that so much was banned or taboo. All of a sudden the intellectual world opened up again.

In Munich at this time the world of theatre and cabaret was starting up again ... In fact there was a new sense of life in the air. Hitler's prophecy that Germany would be finished and become an agrarian country again was not realized ... Of course the Americans brought their modern music with them ... and their authors. Hemingway, for example. We had to scrape and save, but we lived a fulfilling life.'

Traudl Junge is not short of work, although it is badly paid. In 1947 to 1950 she does secretarial work for the Meto Medical and Technical Marketing Company, for the Iranian journalist Davoud Monchi-Zadeh who also lectures at Munich University, for the firm of Munich Publishing and for the printing works of Majer & Finckh, usually working half-days and for several employers in parallel. Obviously none of them shuns contact with her. The fact that she once worked for the head of state vouches for her good qualifications, '[...] *which enabled her to work part-time, to our complete satisfaction, in the post for which a full-time employee always used to be necessary,*' say Majer & Finckh in writing her a reference. '*Frau Junge was an extremely valuable member of staff, and we were sorry to see her go,*' says Munich Publishing enthusiastically. '*Both management and her colleagues felt particular respect for her abilities. Her pleasant manner to everyone made her universally popular.*'

For some time she also types for Hans Raff. He is a lawyer, and has married her close friend Ulla, whom she has not seen since 1942. Hans accepted Traudl immediately, says Ulla Raff, something that could not be taken for granted because, being half Jewish, he had suffered persecution during the Third Reich. In 1933 Raff, a qualified mechanical engineer then training as a lawyer, was expelled from the university eight weeks before his finals, in 1941 he was dismissed from the army as 'unworthy to fight', until 1944 he managed a Munich factory making artists' canvases that he had taken over from Jewish relatives, and then he was put in a labour camp and forced to work in a salt-mine. He finally took his examinations in 1946, changed his original plan to make a career in patent law and decided to specialize in compensation cases instead, and was soon one of the country's most respected lawyers working in the field of compensation and reimbursement.

They avoided talking to Traudl about her time with Hitler, says Ulla Raff. From today's viewpoint, their reason seems surprising: 'We wanted to spare her. We always felt sorry for her because we saw how much she was suffering in her heart.' Instead of confronting her with her past, Hans Raff gives her financial support, and several times provides money for her mother, knowing how poor Hildegard is.

'When I came back from Berlin I felt very small and wretched and was grateful for any kind of human affection. I never heard personal accusations from the people around me. They all said: but you were so young. You couldn't know what was going on ... No one discussed it with me at more length. And when I'd written my memoirs no one wanted to read

them. For many years I was glad of that, because their encouragement meant I could quieten my conscience. In the end, though, there's no deceiving your own subconscious mind.'

A particularly important event for Traudl Junge is her working relationship with Karl Ude, which soon becomes a close friendship with him and his family. She meets the writer when she, her mother and her sister come to live in Bauerstrasse in the Schwabing district of Munich. Number 10, into which they move (illegally), was so badly bombed during the war that it has been struck from the records of the housing department as a total write-off. But a Catholic priest called Berghofer, who originally lived on the fourth floor, has done some makeshift repairs to the ground floor and lets the three women have two rooms. They have to cover them with roofing felt before they actually have the proverbial roof over their heads. 'From Berghof to Berghofer. You're going up in the world!' joke Traudl's friends. Karl Ude has made himself a rough-and-ready office among remnants of walls on the first floor; one of his activities is to edit the literary journal *Welt und Wort*. His son Christian, now Mayor of Munich, describes him as an impeccably democratic but otherwise non-political man, who waited quietly during the Third Reich for the terrible times to be over. He did show a great interest in contemporary history all his life, says his son, but basically he adopted no particular stance towards it. He was too diplomatic for that, and anyway he had chosen the role of the artist. Traudl Junge acts as Karl Ude's secretary in the afternoons, while in the mornings she works as editorial assistant in the publishing firm of Rolf Kauka and edits a crime magazine.

'Karl Ude was very liberal and democratic, and as a writer and a cultured man he had a great influence on my mind. Of course he knew I had been Hitler's secretary — I always told that to anyone I was closely involved with at once, because I didn't want my past to spoil our relationship. But Ude never asked me about details or my motivation. We didn't dwell on the recent past. Our thoughts, feelings and activities were bent on the

future. We were working to build a normal life again, bit by bit ... I also came into contact with the SPD Cultural Forum through the Udes. I'm still a member.'

Christian Ude is only a year old when Traudl Junge enters the life of the family – he, his parents and his sister Karin live in the building opposite, Number 9 Bauerstrasse. Even at primary school he is beginning to take an interest in history and politics, and asks her questions about her job with Hitler. In many conversations with her, he says looking back, he developed an awareness that 'Adolf Hitler and the Second World War were not just huge historical events of the past, but that political activities were going on in my immediate vicinity, almost close enough for me to touch.' When he joined in conversations at mealtimes with his parents and their friends later, as a boy old enough to be taken seriously, he found that Traudl Junge had a 'lively, critical mind', and said she was 'better at discussion and more committed than many other people we knew'.

'A life of conscious thought began for me only after the war, when I started thinking about important things, asking questions. Wondering about the meaning of human relationships. Until then I'd just accepted everything as it happened to me. I moved from one place to another without consciously wanting to leave my mark on them. Wherever I was, I just tried to take an interest in what I was doing, and give of my best.'

Absolution – absolution in duplicate – is officially granted to Traudl Junge in 1947. Like all Germans over eighteen she has to fill in the questionnaire issued by the Military Government of Germany, a form eighty-six centimetres long and printed on both sides, with 131 questions about people's personal attitudes to the Nazi past. She fills in the form twice, once as Traudl Junge and then again as Traudl Humps – she doesn't now remember why. She truthfully describes her profession at the time as 'secretary in the Reich Chancellery', which was indeed where she was employed before being delegated to the Führer. She thus receives two notices of denazification; as a 'youthful fellow-traveller' she falls under the amnesty granted at the end of August 1946 to all who were born after 1914, and in the matter of other charges she – like 94 per cent of all Bavarians – is 'exonerated'. Traudl Junge does not realize that denazification, a unique attempt to subject the political attitudes of almost an entire population to national cleansing, is a farce performed for purposes of rehabilitation. To her, filling in the questionnaire is little more than a formality, and she wasn't expecting to be condemned anyway – after all, she was never a member of the NSDAP.

Most Germans regard this process as the end of the affair, and from then on preserve a collective silence about the Nazi period. This is also in the interests of the Allies themselves; Germans are needed as partners in the Cold War in both East and West. Furthermore, German politicians of the Adenauer era are courting the voters – and those politicians who are willing to go along with the demand to draw a final line under the past are more likely to win their favour. 'When we look back to those years, then,' writes Ralph Giordano, 'a suspicion that refuses to be suppressed emerges, to the effect that the Adenauer era, right into the 1960s, was in the nature of a gigantic bribe offered by the conservative leadership to the majority of voters who were unwilling to face facts. It was a kind of moratorium, the result partly of tacit agreement in the generally conspiratorial atmosphere, but partly of forceful organization.' Giordano describes this as the 'great peace' made with the killers. Only the second post-war generation, towards the end of the sixties, try to get their grandparents to make it clear where they stood – and at this point the period when Traudl Junge was apparently at peace with herself also comes to a sudden end. However, there are some twenty years to go before that, and she calls them the best years of her life.

Traudl Junge owes her increasing confidence in particular to Heinz Bald. He is 'factotum' or in modern parlance manager of Ralph Maria Siegel's cabaret group, which Traudl also frequents.

She describes him as an 'all-rounder' who can turn his hand to anything, and he cares for her devotedly. He was in the resistance movement during the Third Reich, and he accepts her despite her past, which gives her something to lean on. When he emigrates to America he is determined that she will follow him as soon as he has made a new start there. He wants to marry her.

★

The fifties: years of hope. The rest of the world's prejudices against Germany are gradually fading, the economic miracle is in full swing. Many Germans begin to feel that they count for something again. Traudl Junge's life has its highs and its lows, like anyone else's. In 1951 Inge leaves Germany for Australia, where she marries her Polish fiancé; he has emigrated a year earlier. Traudl was often jealous of Inge in their youth because she had managed to realize the dream of an artistic career. Now she misses her sister. She herself has applied for a visa for the USA, and Heinz Bald's American employer is prepared to sign the affidavit. When the ruins in Bauerstrasse are to be demolished in 1954, and everyone has to move out, Traudl's mother takes this as the chance to visit her daughter in Australia. She stays for almost two years. Since Traudl Junge has no official right to go on living where they previously did, she must be grateful to be allocated a simple council apartment in Munich-Moosach – 'a terrible slum dwelling', she calls it. She moves in, all the same, since her only alternative is the Frauenholz Camp, a hostel for the homeless.

So far as work is concerned, her prospects are very good at the moment. Although at the age of thirty she still has no definite professional aim in view, she keeps finding mentors who value and encourage her. Willi Brust, an acquaintance who works as a graphic artist on *Quick*, recommends her to the journal – at the time an illustrated news magazine that was well thought of and noted for its extensive research and critical reporting, which frequently focused on people with Nazi pasts. Although the reporters and editors of *Quick* know about their colleague's past history, she is never once questioned about her experiences under the Third Reich.

'I remember that one Shrove Tuesday the editorial office was working on a big story about several war crimes trials and executions in Landsberg. Only then did I find out, for the first time, details of what went on behind the scenes in the Third Reich. Above all, I discovered what lay behind the façades of people I had known as pleasant, cultivated companions. For instance there was Dr Karl Brandt, one of Hitler's attendant doctors, whom I had thought an educated, humane man, but he was hanged in 1948 for taking part in medical experiments on concentration camp prisoners and practising euthanasia. I could hardly grasp it.'

For three years Traudl Junge is the editor-in-chief's right-hand woman, but then, to his regret, she is tempted away to work as assistant to a freelance contributor to the science section of the magazine. The two come closer privately, too, on a two-week research trip to Italy – it is the beginning of a relationship that will last thirteen years.

'It was my first visit to Italy – Lake Garda, the cypresses, the orange and lemon trees . . . my heart was overflowing with gratitude and joy, and we began a serious flirtation. When he asked if I'd like to work for him I waved goodbye to Quick *magazine . . .'*

But her decision is not made as easily as she presents it in retrospect. She is engaged to be married, after all, and is soon to emigrate to America. *'[. . .] if you are not just feeling the pain of our parting today, but still doubt whether you have made the right decision, then dismiss both ideas [. . .] take a drink and wash them down. But don't forget the most important and quiet sip, as you drink to the time that begins next Monday,'* writes her future employer at the end of September 1953.

For a while she is still able to postpone making a final decision about her fiancé Heinz Bald. *'Heinz writes lovely letters, kind and affectionate. I am so glad I have his letters,'* she writes in her diary for 16 October 1954. And just two months later: *'[...] Heinz has written a reproachful letter, but it makes me happy all the same, I can always feel how he loves me.'* Her heart now belongs to the journalist, but he has a wife and children – the letters from America are a vague support to Traudl Junge. *'All the same [...] doubts and night-time anxieties keep coming back, like gloomy shadows that make me wonder whether everything is all right as it is. My inner commitment, indeed my exclusive devotion to someone who is out of my reach makes me outwardly lonely, and sometimes that's oppressive and almost unbearable. There are times when I long for an ordinary, down-to-earth love – but next day, as I go to the office, my great happiness drives such thoughts away,'* runs a diary entry of November 1954, one of many that are similarly ambivalent in tone.

During the year 1955 she gets her visa, but she has already decided against going to America – her ties to Germany, her career and her new love are too strong, and so is her sense of responsibility for her mother, who has announced that she is coming back from Australia. And Heinz Bald's attractions have paled over the years. The fact that he soon finds consolation makes Traudl Junge thoughtful: *'At Christmas [1956] he [Heinz Bald] will be coming over to get engaged to Manuela and perhaps marry her at once. It hurts just a little, less because I feel it as a personal loss, and must bury any hopes of my own, than because I myself am not lucky enough to have the courage to be part of a couple, although I take the longing for it around with me. However, it's some small satisfaction to me that Heinz himself now has that "funny feeling in the pit of the stomach" which I consider indispensable for love and always missed. How I would like to have such a happy sense of belonging with someone,'* she says in her diary. But by this time she herself doubts whether she was ever really ready for such a relationship after the Second World War.

'I obviously had a great fear of being tied down, having rushed so unthinkingly into my first marriage. Hans Junge and I had no opportunity at all of coming intellectually close. I never had deep, probing conversations

238

with him, and I didn't know nearly enough about his interests. We never even made plans for the future. His death did shake me badly at the time, but I came to terms with it quite quickly. I hadn't yet shared any kind of life with him. After his death in August 1944, events followed each other so thick and fast that my loss retreated into the background. And when the war was over that chapter was closed, so to speak ... I never again met a man of whom I could say, with conviction: that's the man I want to share my life with.'

No other entry in her diaries shows her at odds with herself so clearly as one at the beginning of January 1956: *'[...] In the files today I found a cutting about graphotherapy. It says that since your handwriting changes with your nature, it should be the same the other way round: if you deliberately made yourself change your handwriting, your nature would change too. I shall have a go. Perhaps I shall be greater in spirit and more energetic if my writing is large and energetic too.'* In fact from then on she does alter her handwriting, at least in the diary. To the outside world she is a cheerful woman who enjoys life, but she continues to be well aware of the ups and downs of her feelings. She cannot break free of her employer emotionally, although she has no illusions about her position as his mistress. One reason is that, despite occasional frustrations, she finds the professional side of their partnership fulfilling. She works independently, writes articles, although seldom under her own name, and in 1959 publishes a book: *Tiere mit Familienanschluss [Animals Who Are Part of the Family]*. It is published by the Munich firm of Franz Ehrenwirth, and is not a commercial success, but it shows that she has talent as a writer and a good sense of humour.

'For the first time in my life I felt that I was not just doing a job but was really interested in the subject of my work. I should have studied biology! I'd probably have been a good healing practitioner or physiotherapist too, but I didn't have the financial means for the three-year training.'

In the 1950s Traudl Junge focuses on the present – she is seldom reminded of her days as Hitler's private secretary, and avoids contact with her surviving colleagues from Führer headquarters rather than seeking them out.

'The other secretaries wouldn't or couldn't abandon their loyalty to the Führer. I didn't understand that. Christa Schroeder, for example, looked critically at all the literature written about Adolf Hitler, but she didn't really distance herself. The only one I was still friendly with was Hitler's dietician Frau von Exner: I met her now and then after the war when I went on holiday to Pörtschach on the Wörther See. And I still saw Hans-Bernd Lanze. He was on Press Chief Dietrich's staff, and stayed with us for a while in Breitbrunn after the war. Otto Günsche got in touch in 1955 after he was released from imprisonment in Russia. But I haven't seen him often over the last few years.'

However, several historians and journalists writing books on Hitler are interested in Traudl Junge's memories, and they do get in touch. In 1954 she has several meetings with the American naval captain Michael A. Musmanno. He was present as a lawyer at the Nuremberg trials, and between 1945 and 1948 questioned some two hundred witnesses to Hitler's end in the Führer bunker, including Traudl Junge. He published his book *Ten Days to Die* in 1950. Musmanno gets in touch again in the autumn of 1954, when Georg Wilhelm Pabst wants to film the material. The idea is for Traudl Junge, as an eyewitness who was there at the time, to advise the Austrian director. She meets Pabst and Musmanno in Munich several times, and agrees to spend two weeks as assistant director to Pabst while he is shooting in Vienna, although she hesitates a good deal at first. Austria, after all, is still occupied by the Allies, and she is afraid of attracting the attention of the Russian military, since she fled illegally from the Russian-occupied zone of Berlin. The 1500 marks she is paid as a fee are by far the largest sum of money she has ever yet earned all at once, and enable her to move from the council dwelling in Moosach to an attractive one-room apartment in her familiar Schwabing.

In April 1955 *Der letzte Akt* [*The Last Act*] has its première, with Albin Skoda and Oskar Werner in the lead roles, and is panned by the critics, one reason being that G. W. Pabst's conduct under the Third Reich is a source of controversy. During the twenties, when he made *Die freudlose Gasse* and the film version of the *Dreigroschenoper*, he rose to fame as the most socially critical of German directors. In 1933 he emigrated for the sake of his convictions and tried his luck first in Paris and then in Hollywood, but for lack of success returned to Germany, and by the end of the war had made two films in the contemporary National Socialist spirit, *Komödianten* and *Paracelsus*.

'At the time Pabst and I didn't discuss our own experiences during the Third Reich at all. Shooting a movie is such hectic work, and you have so many things to think of, that there was no question of a quiet conversation that might have probed rather deeper. Today, of course, I regret it.'

Another encounter with her past comes at the end of the 1950s, when she is reunited with Erika Klopfer, now Stone, who is living in New York and working as a photographer. Erika learns from Traudl's mother – who returned to Munich from Australia in 1956 – that her old friend 'was Hitler's private secretary until the end'. At first she couldn't believe it, says Erika, who did not emigrate voluntarily, and she did not want to get in touch again. In the end she feels curious after all, and visits Traudl without 'feeling the slightest prejudice', as she says in her book *Heimat wider Willen. Emigranten in New York* [*A Homeland Against One's Will. Emigrants in New York*] (Berg am See, 1991). She got on well with her, says Erika, and adds that she is convinced there wasn't a young girl at the time who would have turned down such a job offer. She even says, 'It could have happened to me.' So Traudl Junge is exonerated once more – although she does not now remember this occasion. Traudl Junge, Erika Stone concludes, is not a happy woman. 'Her time with Hitler really messed up her life.'

The sixties – years of loss.

Traudl Junge's father dies in 1962. His death is not a very painful blow, for even in his last years of life she has had little contact with him. Such was the impression left on her by the events in the Führer bunker that she even assumed, directly after the end of the war, that he too had committed suicide. *'[. . .] Although death may be easier for many than the life that lies ahead – for instance for my father, whose birthday it would have been today,'* she wrote on 4 December 1945. Max Humps, as a member of the NSDAP and the SS, and during the war working as a security director 'otherwise engaged' (i.e. exempt from armed service), was one of the more than 300,000 Nazi activists who were arrested and provisionally interned by the Allied occupying powers. Like many of his companions who shared that fate, he saw himself as the victim of a misconceived and unjust policy of occupation rather than a criminal figure of the Nazi regime.

'After the war I scarcely thought about my father's fate until his wife got in touch with us. "So aren't you girls worried about your father? The poor man's in a concentration camp. The French arrested him and treated him very badly." She sounded as if he had been unjustly held in a concentration camp. This kind of repression was typical of the time. My father was very soon released, but the experience left its mark on him. His wife had to earn a living for both of them. First she opened a small Lotto shop in Friedrichshafen, and over the years she made it into an elegant emporium in Bahnhofstrasse selling cigarettes, magazines and alcohol. My father was her best customer. After he died my sister and I built up a warm relationship with his wife, our Aunt Miezl. She was the ideal wife for my father.'

Her mother's death in 1969 hits Traudl Junge much harder, although it is a release for the old lady, who by now is suffering from Parkinson's disease and lives in a care home.

'*She sat there for years looking at the door, waiting for me to come through it. She managed to make me feel constantly guilty in her own gentle way. Once, when I was going away for the weekend, she said sadly, "Yes, you go, I'm used to being on my own." I did go, but I couldn't really enjoy myself. But I was terribly sorry for her, because she never had a good life. The first money she ever earned for herself was as a seamstress when she was sixty-five. She did sewing for my girlfriends too. It gave her great satisfaction.*'

But the real break in her life comes three years earlier, when her lover dies of a heart attack. His sudden death deprives her of the central figure in both her private and her professional life. '*I've always come to terms with grief well,*' she says. '*Although I've always needed to talk about my pain.*'

The main people to whom she turns as a substitute family in these and the following years, and not only at difficult times, are the Lanzenstiels. Luise Lanzenstiel is a sister of Heinz Bald and – quite apart from Traudl Junge's affectionate relationship with her former fiancé – a very understanding friend, Traudl's best friend for many years.

'*Luise was married to a pastor and had had six children. She was amazingly cheerful and steadfast. The family got through the Nazi period very bravely, without sacrificing their ideals. Luise told me she never once said "Heil Hitler" in all that time. The whole family were securely anchored in their faith, in an open-minded way – not at all bigoted. They always said grace before meals, which made me feel very awkward at first, but then I got to feel more and more like part of the family. I owe it to Heinz Bald that I have a substitute family today, because I am friends with those six children and thirteen grandchildren too. I'm their Auntie Traudl.*

With the Lanzenstiels, I saw for the first time what it's like for people to have the strength of faith. I envied them very much for their ability to believe – it's not a gift given to me. But they weren't missionaries, they accepted me as I am. I've gone to Luise when I wanted to hide from the rest of the world. I felt safe with her, I knew I was with someone who understood me.'

Traudl Junge is speaking of those bouts of depression that have afflicted her from around the middle of the sixties to the present day. At first she has a generalized sense of failure. 'No one's life story is so clear-cut that there was only ever one possible choice,' writes the political scientist Claus Leggewie. Traudl Junge reproaches herself for having chosen the wrong path through life, and even worse for simply having let life sway her without going her own way at crucial moments.

Only later does she link her depression with the atrocities of the Nazi regime, which are in such painful contrast to what she felt was her innocuous role in the Third Reich. Guilt feelings of an increasingly concrete nature weigh down on her – suddenly even the excuse 'You were so young at the time', which has comforted her for so long, seems hollow.

'At that time I must often have walked past the commemorative plaque to Sophie Scholl in Franz-Joseph-Strasse without noticing it. One day I did, and I was terribly shocked when I realized that she was executed in 1943, just when I was beginning my own job with Hitler. Sophie Scholl had originally been a BDM member herself, a year younger than me, and she saw clearly that she was dealing with a criminal regime. All of a sudden I had no excuse any more.'

Years of developing her own awareness. Long periods of depression, hospitalization, unsuccessful psychotherapy, lack of enthusiasm for her career. Between 1967 and 1971 Traudl Junge is responsible for the consumer magazine *Drogerie Journal* published by Wort und Bild.

'Suddenly I couldn't write any more. Even the simplest sentence was difficult. The idea of being unable to work at my profession made my condition even worse. Then I thought of flight – I would go to Australia, to seek refuge with my sister. I gave notice from my job and sublet my apartment . . .'

The Australian authorities refuse Traudl Junge a permanent

residence permit, giving as their reason her role in the Third Reich. For the first time, after more than twenty-five years, she meets with rejection because of her past. Finally she goes to Sydney as a tourist, stays for several months, and tells herself that she would rather live permanently in Germany anyway. In 1974 she is diagnosed with abdominal cancer, which is successfully treated. In 1981, after several other jobs in journalism, she retires at the age of sixty-one.

She cannot find peace. The public 'reappraisal of the past' is gradually getting under way in Germany. As one of the last eyewitnesses to have been present at the final scenes in the Führer bunker in Berlin, Traudl Junge is invited to appear before the cameras several times. An unfortunate side effect is that Nazi fanatics and autograph hunters also keep seeking her out, wanting to shake the hand that was once shaken by 'the Führer'. Traudl Junge does not want to be a public figure. She lives quietly, befriends and looks after a blind old lady, makes pottery and records audiocassettes for the blind. She reads whole books into the microphone.

Paradoxical as it may sound, Traudl Junge has radically distanced herself from National Socialism. She never felt she belonged to its system, and yet she shared part of the responsibility for it. She has not built up a façade, but has tried to be honest with her fellow human beings. The years of painful confrontation with herself did have a purpose: they matured her.

'I withdrew and let the guilt feelings, the grief and sorrow eat into me. Suddenly I had become interesting as an eyewitness — which brought me into severe conflict with my guilt complexes. Because the conversations were never about the question of guilt, only about the historical facts. So I could describe them without having to justify myself. That was something that weighed on me even more — and gave me even more to think about. Today I mourn for two things: for the fate of those millions of people who were murdered by the National Socialists. And for the girl Traudl Humps who lacked the self-confidence and good sense to speak out against them at the right moment.'

ACKNOWLEDGEMENTS

The authors would like to thank their editor Ilka Heinemann, and also Jochen and Maria Maas. Without those three people this project would never have got off the ground.

Melissa Müller would like to thank André Heller for his wise advice, Christian Ude and Ursula Raff for their revealing memories of Traudl Junge, and Christian Brandstätter, Barbara Bierach, Rüdiger Salat and Heinz-Werner Sondermann, the critical first readers, for their valuable suggestions and for asking the right questions.

Traudl Junge would like to thank the friends who are her substitute family wholeheartedly. They all know who they are.

INDEX

Erika (TJ's post-war acquaintance),
227–8

Esser, Hermann, 82, 94, 203n43

Exner, Helene Marie 'Marlene' von,
110–11, 112, 115, 117–18,
205n60, 240

Exner family, 118

'Faith and Beauty' organization, 18,
21

Fasbender, Lola: School of Dance, 16,
22

Fascists/Fascism, 89, 114

Fegelein, Hermann
at the Berghof, 123–4
appearance and personality, 123
engaged to Gretl Braun, 124
investigates assassination attempt
on Hitler, 136
tells TJ about her husband's death,
141
marries Gretl Braun, 152, 211n88
in Berlin, 167, 175, 178–9
death, 180–81
biographical information, 208n71
Hitler's suspicions about, 215n108

Fellgiebel, Erich, 132

Feuerbach, Anselm, 79

First World War, 9, 40

Fischer von Erlach, Johann Bernard,
88

Foreign Office, Berlin, 164–5, 180

France, 138

Franz Ehrenwirth publishing firm,
239

Franz-Joseph-Strasse, Munich, 244

Frauenholz Camp, 236

Frederick II the Great, 92, 159, 169,
191

Freikorps Oberland, 9–10

Frentz, Walter, 58, 80, 151, 201n31

Freudlose Gasse, Die (film), 241

Friedrichstrasse Station, Berlin,
193

Führer Building, Munich, 102

Furtwängler, Wilhelm, 80

Garda, Lake, 237

German Dance Company, 22

German Dance Theatre, 28

German Labour Front, 127

Gieseking, Walter, 80

Giesing, Erwin, 136, 210n80

Giesler, Hermann, 127, 128, 138

Giordano, Ralph, 235

Goebbels, Helga, 171, 175 *see also*
Goebbels children

Goebbels, Helmut, 170–71, 187 *see
also* Goebbels children

Goebbels, Joseph
at the Berghof, 94, 95–6
attractive to women, 95
wit, 95
relationship with Himmler, 95–6
informed of assassination attempt
on Hitler, 133
in Berlin, 159, 165, 168, 170, 171,
172, 182, 183, 184–5, 188, 190–
91, 192
attacks Göring's behavious, 182
disobeys Hitler's order to leave
Berlin, 184–5
announces Hitler's death on
radio,190–91
brief mentions, 41, 74, 130,
215n112, 230

Goebbels, Magda
brings family to bunker in Berlin,
168
carries poison, 171

251